POLITICS OF IDEOCRACY

POLITICS OF IDEOCRACY

JAROSLAW PIEKALKIEWICZ
AND ALFRED WAYNE PENN

STATE UNIVERSITY OF NEW YORK PRESS

Published by
State University of New York Press, Albany

For information, address State University of New York Press,
State University Plaza, Albany, N.Y. 12246

Production by M. R. Mulholland
Marketing by Dana E. Yanulavich

Library of Congress Cataloging-in-Publication Data

Piekalkiewicz, Jaroslaw.
    Politics of ideocracy / Jaroslaw Piekalkiewicz and Alfred Wayne
Penn.
        p.   cm.
    Includes bibliographical references and index.
    ISBN 0-7914-2297-6 (hard). — ISBN 0-7914-2298-4 (pbk.)
    1. Totalitarianism. 2. Authoritarianism. 3. Comparative
government. I. Penn, Alfred Wayne, 1937-   . II. Title.
JC481.P463 1995
320.5′3—dc20   94-8841
                                                              CIP
                                                              Rev

10 9 8 7 6 5 4 3 2 1

*We dedicate this work
to our children and grandchildren:
Jonathan, Ellen, Andrew, Andrew Michael II,
Natalie, and to the memory of Luke.*

CONTENTS

ACKNOWLEDGMENTS

Books are like children. Their parents hope that they will be ones to have the most influence on them. Over time, however, they are influenced by many others whose views form an integral part of what they become. As books grow, they change and assume their own distinct personalities, often very different from their original ones.

In the case of our book, it would be impossible to recognize all those who contributed to it over the years. Yet, we would like to acknowledge those whose impact has been most notable. First of all, there were our students who in class and seminar discussions tested our original assumptions and forced us to reassess many ideas. Jarek Piekalkiewicz is grateful for those who, during some thirty years, stimulated his perception of ideocracy in his courses and graduate seminars, entitled at first "Totalitarian Politics," and subsequently renamed "The Politics of Ideocracy." Special contributors were those graduate students who wrote master's theses and doctoral dissertations on different aspects of ideocracy, especially Peter Feuerle, Joseph Goldman, Randall Oestreicher, Chris Hamilton, Dae–Kyu Lee, and Saleh Al–Kathllan. Wayne Penn appreciates the contribution of the many students who took his courses on political theory and public administration. Of these, Ramesh Aurora stands out as one who persistently questioned prior formulations of political and social thought and pressed for new ways to conceptualize complex social phenomena. We are also grateful to

Anna Cienciala, professor of history at the University of
Kansas, and to Fred M. Woodward, director of the
University Press of Kansas. Both read the early version of this work, found it worthy of publication and
made many suggestions for its improvement. Fred
directed us to the State University of New York Press.

The four final reviewers deserve our special grati-
tude. Their perceptive evaluations of the book made us
see it in a slightly different light, and final revisions of
the text benefitted from their insightful comments.
Their bibliographical references proved to be of immea-
surable value. Above all, we would like to thank our
wives, Maura and Susan, for their help as readers,
critics, and friends.

We would also like to thank those who provided
essential technical support and would like to recognize
the help of the Political Science Department of the
University of Kansas, and especially its secretarial staff:
Gayle Vannicola, Gwen Jansen, and Virginia Postoak.
The unselfish dedication of Virginia Postoak, who typed
and retyped so many versions of this work can never be
sufficiently recognized. Earlier versions of the work were
supported by staff of the School of Public Affairs and
Administration at Sangamon State University. Without
the hard work of all these people, the book would still be
years away from completion. Our final thanks must go
to Clay Morgan, the editor at the State University of
New York Press, who first recognized the potential of
this study and made many valuable suggestions for its
improvement, and to the production editor, Megeen
Mulholland, who guided the book through its many
final stages. Naturally, we must absolve all the above
from any scholarly and literary sins that this book may
contain. We hope they may be found to be minimal and
that the reader will enjoy the subject as we have.

INTRODUCTION

Viewed by an outsider, most extreme human actions, warfare, for example, seem rooted in irrationality. Self-interested motives, to be sure, abound; yet, it seems unlikely that enlightened self-interest would often lead to such violence and its fruits. Max Weber has cautioned that the understanding of human action must take into account the meaning of that action for the participants. Since Freud, we have come to recognize that complex webs of meaning, only partially understood, stir people to action. Therefore perceptive studies of human behavior must uncover the broad patterns of symbolic meaning that make reasonable the actions of the participants. Further yet, these studies should reveal social and psychological factors that encourage such symbolic action. Factors that move human groups to *invest* common meaning to their collective efforts.

It is increasingly clear that such factors underlie the broad collective actions of politics, as well. However, many studies of comparative politics tend to separate the dynamics of political action from those of collective symbolizing. At the same time, works concerned with systems of political thought tend to abstract these from the political dynamics that give their concepts meaning for the participants. It is the contention of this book that systems of political thought have a real impact on the actions of political leaders and followers; that these systems of thought differ systematically from each other in regard to certain critical dimensions; and that political systems, in fact, may be categorized in relation to these differing belief systems. We also assert that evolving political activities may be fruitfully analyzed in regard to their relative conformance with, or divergence from, the fundamental tenets of these systems of thought.

At the extreme, some systems of thought demand complete submission to their tenets by their followers in all realms of life. The political dominance of such a totalistic belief system of thought results in what we choose to call *ideocracy*—a political system animated by a "monistic ideology" and that derives its legitimacy from this ideology. The goal of this book is to explain the key factors leading to the inception of ideocracy and the major political, social, and economic mechanisms characteristic of such a polity. We also examine the causes for, and fundamental ways in which, such a system could evolve: including disintegration, metamorphosis into another form of governance, or regeneration as an ideocracy.

This work of comparative political analysis is essentially rooted in empirically oriented theory. That is to say, we draw upon, and extend, social and political theory to enhance the empirical analysis of political life. One of us has studied for decades the evolution of ideocratic and other political systems; the other has a background as a political and social theorist. In the intersection of our overlapping areas of expertise, we have sought to fashion a work that usefully extends comparative political analysis in a way that is theoretically valid and empirically grounded. Drawing selectively upon the histories of a sample of governments considered by us to be ideocratic, we have induced a theoretical framework of analysis, which extends upon the work of others in the field and which is related in Chapter I to a taxonomy of political systems.[1]

Historically, most folk societies had ideocratic characteristics. Generally, tribal societies function in accordance with a comprehensive belief system, relating to all facets of tribal life, explaining the past, present, and future and prescribing all social organization and the norms of daily existence. At the same time, many folk societies lack a highly integrated political system that would serve as a vehicle for enforcing an ideological order. Often, social control is fragmented, with mutual adjustments among different authorities. Informal norms frequently override formal controls. Yet a strong distinction between those within the community and those who are outsiders predominates, as does the view that a settled social order should be maintained.[2] In early empires, powerful political centers emerged. The ancient empires of Egypt and Babylon, the empires of Aztecs and Incas,[3] Sparta, the Mohammedan empire, prerevolutionary and communist China and Russia, to name only few, all had strong ideocratic characteristics. The twentieth century has experienced various forms of communism and fascism. Today, a half century after the defeat of the Axis Powers in World War II, communism seems to have collapsed in Central Europe and the Soviet Union, thus ending the cold war. However, communism still survives in its original form in North Korea and, with some modifications, in China, Vietnam, and Cuba. It is still to be reckoned with as a powerful force for revolution in Latin America. In the meantime, neofascistic ideas have swept through portions of the Moslem World, either in the form of Islamic fundamentalism—already victorious in Iran and Sudan—or as Ba'thism, dominant in Syria and Iraq. Thus, since the beginnings of recorded history, ideocracy has been one of the typical forms of political organization.

The political analysis of what we term *ideocracy* has centered for the last half a century on a specifically modern form—totalitarianism. What this term means was ably defined by Benito Mussolini, the founder of Italian Fascism and the dictator of the Italian state between the two world wars and during World War II. We use his definition because Italian Fascism was explicitly based on a comprehensive social, economic, and political theory: "The fascist conception of the state is all-embracing; outside of it no human or spiritual value may exist, much less have any value. Thus understood Fascism is totalitarian and the Fascist State, as a synthesis and a unit which includes all values, interprets, develops and lends additional power to the whole life of a people."[4]

Mussolini's definition and Italian Fascism in general were not given proper attention by political scientists until the system was imitated in the 1930s in other parts of Europe, either as the dominant state ideology or as the foundation of a particular political party. By that time, Mussolini was already upstaged by Adolf Hitler, who came to dominate not only our thinking about totalitarianism, but world politics in general.[5]

World War II was the watershed in the study of what Mussolini called *totalitarianism.* There was a sudden and painful realization that Hitler was not a typical German leader who was seeking his country's escape from the world depression and who, further, demanded for it what it had unjustly lost in World War I. Neither was he a complete and somewhat comical lunatic whom nobody, much less the cultured Germans, would have taken seriously. As the war progressed, it was becoming obvious that one was witnessing a political phenomenon of a different order, capable of an incredible mobilization of human and material resources and a highly unified purpose. During World War II, for obvious military reasons, a number of more or less descriptive studies materialized.[6]

The postwar period witnessed a boom in works on totalitarianism. Political scientists were shocked by the brutality of the Nazi regime, through which between 12 and 20 million Europeans perished in mass executions, and especially by the almost total extermination of European Jewry, of which 6 million died in the holocaust. They searched for painful answers as to why such appalling crimes against humanity were committed by a nation that previously occupied one of the most distinguished positions in Western civilization. Why would Germany, a nation that throughout its illustrious history had produced so many classics of humanistic and ethical endeavor, suddenly descend to the lowest form of barbarism? Could something in the German national character provide an answer, or could some specific factors in the development of German history explain the emergence of Nazism? Was it an aberration, or was it a more normal form of political behavior previously overlooked and likely to be repeated in other places at other times? Many noted the similarity between Italian Fascism and German Nazism and the inspiration the two provided to the fascist movements in Hungary, Romania, Portugal, and Spain. They also noted the appeal of Nazism to some in the so-called Aryan nations,[7] the Dutch, Danish, and Norwegians. What made these people, as well as French and Spaniards, join the Nazi S.S. units in a crusade against communism for the "New Europe"? Even the "cradles" of democracy, Great Britain and the United States were not free from groups sympathetic to fascism or even Nazism, and both countries had their own equivalent of the boys in black or brown shirts. A flood of postwar information on the Soviet Union provided further food for thought. Those who fled the "Workers' Paradise" during the war's turmoil furnished additional evidence. Also, Western scholars gained access to Soviet government and party documents, originally captured by the Germans and subsequently recovered by the Western Allies. Soon this information led to the obvious realization that this wartime ally was of the same totalitarian mold as the defeated regimes in Italy and Germany.[8] By this time, totalitarianism had become closely identified with extreme and encompassing social violence.

Hannah Arendt had the most profound influence on the postwar study of totalitarianism.[9] Generations of American political scientists were influenced by her perceptive scholarship. Arendt, herself a German Jew who had to flee the Nazis, sought to understand the reasons for German atrocities against the Jews. In the effort, she probed deeply into the consciousness of Western civilization. According to her, totalitarianism was the result of the crisis of values produced by the industrialization of Europe, especially by rapid economic development of some countries, such as Germany. The industrial revolution produced "a mob" by transforming classes into masses and by creating "superfluous" people without social bonds and moral obligations. Some of those superfluous people accumulated "superfluous" wealth, which they possessed without simultaneously holding political power. They lacked the restraints that come from living with the immediate political consequences of one's actions. This superfluous capital, unattached to any social group or even nation, led to the expansion of the European colonial empires in Asia and Africa. This led to the spread of racism—the idea that the white race was superior to all others. Anti-Semitism was the internal European equivalent of this racism.[10] The European Pan-movements, and especially the German one and the Russian-sponsored Pan-Slavic movement, subordinated the concept of the brotherhood of humanity to the exclusive tribal affinity of Germans, Slavs, French, or English.[11] Individuals caught up in these movements became alienated from their Creator and viewed themselves to be in a hostile environment of competing tribal units.[12] The leaders of the victorious mob themselves came from the masses, but rose above the "Volk" or "Narod" (the tribal unit) by liberating their souls from the "shackles" of Judeo-Christian moral constraints. They created for themselves and for their "tribes" a new morality of the "superman"[13] and coupled with it a set of revolutionary political ideals.

Contrary to the logic of her own arguments, Arendt could not acknowledge the willing and enthusiastic support given by the Germans to Hitler and to the Nazi ideology, hence her insistence on the centrality of terror through which individuals are forced to subject themselves to prescriptions of totalitarianism. Totalitarianism is "unnatural" to "civilized people," who must obviously have been terrorized if they consented to it. In Arendt's model, terror becomes the most essential characteristic of the totalitarian system. Thus, only states with a relatively large population can be totalitarian, because only they can afford the necessary bloodletting. Arendt denied that Italy was totalitarian because, by comparison with Hitler's

Germany and Stalin's Soviet Union, Italian fascism exercised terror with considerable moderation. Thus, mass terror is seen to facilitate the total control of all aspects of society in the name of "the absolute logic of an idea."[14]

Such absolute control is possible for the first time in human history because of the development of technologically advanced means of communication and transportation. Science and technology free individuals from traditional moral restrains, which are considered the opium of the masses. A new spirit supersedes the rule of law, overcoming natural human timidity and subsuming human loneliness in a tribal paradise of eternal unity. Arendt establishes the model of totalitarianism as a uniquely modern phenomenon of total control through total mobilization and total terror. Because she considers its origins to be deeply historical and spiritual, Arendt pays less attention to the immediate social, economic, and political factors that contributed to the totalitarian victory in Russia and Germany or to the inner workings of totalitarian systems themselves. Despite the obvious weaknesses of Arendt's model—its European ethnocentrism, its historicism, its obsession with anti-Semitism, its reliance upon a "superfluous" category of actors, and its uncritical acceptance of Lenin's "Theory of Imperialism"—she had a tremendous impact on succeeding generations of political theorists. Her book on the origins of totalitarianism, because of its breadth of facts and ideas, is still a classic on the subject.

The second landmark in the development of what may be called the *totalitarian school*, was the publication of Carl J. Friedrich and Zbigniew Brzezinski's *Totalitarian Dictatorship and Autocracy*.[15] Combining their knowledge of Nazi Germany with that of the

Soviet Union and East-Central European communist states[16] and relying upon a growing body of literature on the subject,[17] the authors systematized the existing knowledge of totalitarianism within a comprehensive framework.[18] Although often criticized and sometimes adapted by others, it has stood the test of time and remains, even today, the foundation of all discussion of the subject. As much as others have tried, nobody has surpassed their construct in regard to its clarity and logical cohesion. Agreeing with Arendt and others, that totalitarianism is historically unique in its dependence on advanced technology and its connection with mass society, they argued that fascism and communism are basically the same. What is more, like John Hazard,[19] they asserted that totalitarianism is a gross perversion of democracy. But they were less interested in an explanation of the "origins" and "spirit" of totalitarianism, than in the inner workings of its integral parts. And herein lies their major contribution. Influenced by the recently published *General System Theory* of Bertalanffy,[20] they established a construct of totalitarianism containing six interrelated and interdependent components or "syndromes": "an ideology, a single party typically led by one man, a terroristic police, a communication monopoly, a weapons monopoly, and a centrally directed economy."[21] These syndromes cannot be viewed in isolation anymore than one can be considered superior to any other. The "system" has to operate as an "organic" whole, suggesting that the existence of one or more of the syndromes short of the total does not establish a totalitarian system.

Not long after the publication of the work by Friedrich and Brzezinski, the whole concept of totalitarianism came under sharp attack. The contenders

were those who rode the new wave of "behaviorism."
Many of them were the Soviet-area specialists, who,
with the relaxation of the cold war, were eager to
engage in empirical field work in the communist countries. They also wanted to bring "area studies" into
the mainstream of their disciplines. They argued for "a
method of analysis that would separate the actual consequences of political patterns and practices from the
ideological justification given to them."[22] Furthermore,
the behaviorists wanted to apply the new modes of
analysis—systems theory, organization theory, and
particular quantitative methods—to their studies of
communist states so as to make them truly comparative. And finally, they wanted to examine human activities and not the participant's professed intentions or
beliefs. People, for many of them, were logical and
practical beings, engaged in the struggle for power or
for the control over the authoritative allocation of values. Like Marx, they considered ideology to be a
screen, masking the true meaning of actions of those
striving for power. Therefore ideology was always false
and deceptive.

More specifically, they rejected formal institutions
as major variables to be studied and selected, instead,
the individual as the basic unit of analysis. Political
science became in their eyes a behavioral science in
unity with behavioral movements in other social sciences (such as psychology, sociology, and social
anthropology). The totalitarian "model" was criticized
for its extensive emphasis on the "totality" of political
control, based on an "irrational" ideology and perme-
ated by pervasive terror. They argued that this obsession with terror, and with other forms of political suppression and control, obscured the investigation of
other, and more important, "behavior" in these sys-

tems. The pursuit of more behavioral forms of inquiry could make the study of these political systems truly comparable to the study of Western democracies. Ideologies, even if of some symbolic importance, should be disregarded, because they could not be measured by any reasonable and objective scientific standards.

The totalitarian "model" was also a static framework, and this impeded the investigation of change over time. Its highly abstract and "ideal" nature prevented the application of the recent findings of social science. Finally, the totalitarian model had become a weapon in the cold war by which a distinction could be clearly drawn between the openness of Western democracies and the oppression of Nazi-like communism. After the cold war receded, many felt that a strict conceptual distinction between democracy and communism was untenable as an integral part of scientific inquiry, even if the totalitarian model had some initial validity in application to Nazi Germany and Stalinist Russia. According to this argument, with the destruction of Nazi Germany in 1945 and the death of Stalin in 1953, no totalitarian system was left in existence. Science could not tolerate the presentation of reality in such stark, exaggerated terms. For the behavioral school the defects of the totalitarian model were so damaging as to make the whole model completely useless. It had to be abandoned, even if no new model or "paradigm" could be immediately found to replace it.[23]

The departure from totalitarian model left political scientists, and other social scientists concerned with this phenomenon, without any generally agreed upon theoretical framework. The prescriptions of the behavioral school were too disparate and narrowly focused on particular social topics to provide even a minimal unifying concept for the study of what was previously called *totalitarianism*. Some social scientists engaged in what were basically case studies, but broke away from the prior configurative orientation of some area specialists.[24] They attempted to apply theories and approaches derived from the studies of Western democracies, most often from the United States.[25] Others were for "pure" comparison, which disregarded specific characteristics of any system and studied political behavior in complete abstraction from its environment. Individuals, stripped naked of any cultural or social clothing, were assumed to act predominately as human animals directed by their senses and logic, true to their universal human nature. Indeed, the comparison of the "most different systems" would make most sense because this would prove best the dominance of universal human characteristics over cultural or systemic variations.[26] Yet another group supported the convergence theory according to which all industrialized countries must eventually become similar to one another. They drew their inspiration from the theory of Walt Rostow that all societies progress through the same process of economic development from a primitive to highly advanced state, the final product to be not unlike the industrialized and democratic United States. Also influential was A. F. K. Organski, who extended Rostow's economic analysis to an investigation of stages of political development.[27]

In Soviet studies, the parallel argument was that, with industrialization and modernization, the Soviet Union was becoming more like the other industrialized societies, more rational and pragmatic and less committed to the orthodoxy of Marxism-Leninism. Eventually the two leading societies, the United States and the Soviet Union, would converge, through the dynamics of the "postindustrial" society, to resemble one another, or rather the Soviet Union would become more like the "end result of this process"—the United States. Even one of the founders of the totalitarian model, Zbigniew Brzezinski, for a period of time seemed to give some credence to this theory.[28]

Another variation of "convergence theory" can be traced to the writings of nineteenth century French social philosopher Claude Saint-Simon and later an American, Thorstein Veblen, who foresaw the emerging dominance of engineers in all industrial societies. More recently, another American, James Burnham, and another Frenchman, Jacques Ellul, proposed a theory of managerial revolution according to which all highly technologically developed countries, including the communist states, would fall under the control of "technocrats"—people skilled in technology and management—who would take over from the ideologically inclined politicians and who would make decisions on the basis of technical imperatives and efficiency.[29] Again, the Soviet Union would become more and more like the United States. According to all these theories, economic development and industrialization would cause ideology to give way to "rationality and pragmatism."

With the Soviet invasion of Czechoslovakia in 1968 and the overall decline in detente between the Soviet Union and the West at that time came the realization among Soviet specialists that communist societies were not yet converging toward "postindustrialism" and the democratic West. A general reevaluation developed among political scientists of the behavioral school. Some began to question the emphasis on the individual as the unit of inquiry and the general dis-

regard for norms, values, and beliefs and the institutions of a particular political system. They ridiculed
the behavioral approach, pointing to some conclusions
that violated the basic principles of logic. Some critics
of behaviorism returned to a modified version of the
"old" totalitarian model.[30] Others vehemently argued
against it for reasons similar to those offered by the
behavioral school, but unlike the latter approach, they
attempted generalization by equating totalitarianism
with modern authoritarianism. For this group, authoritarianism itself was divided into traditional and modern, and what was called *totalitarianism* by some was
in fact nothing more than a modern version of old-
time authoritarianism. Members of yet another group
focused specifically on one single aspect of totalitarianism, such as totalist ideology,[31] total revolution,[32]
one-party dominance,[33] or movement regimes[34] and
attempted to generalize from it, while avoiding as
much as possible the term *totalitarianism* itself. One
can consider those partial theories as attempts to create a theoretical framework that would avoid the pitfalls and the limitations of the totalitarian model.

The original totalitarian framework obviously suffered from serious limitations. Its emphasis on the
coercive aspects of the system disregarded evidence
of the success of propaganda and political mobilization
and the existence of mass support for the regime. The
system is not simply a perversion of democracy, a
humanity gone berserk, but a expression of human
political, social, and economic aspirations in certain
historical circumstances. It engages the human yearn-
ing for perfection, often at great costs. It may also be
asserted that the systematized framework of Friedrich
and Brzezinski identified the essential characteristics
of totalitarianism but failed to provide a framework

for analyzing dynamic change over time. Finally, the very concept of total control implicit in the term *totalitarianism* did not withstand the test of time. More specific research on Nazi Germany, Fascist Italy, or Stalinist Russia has shown the control by the leader of his lieutenants, and the system's control of its various structures and of the population, to be far from total.[35] Ideology, although a pivotal instrument in the system, was not absolute in the Arendt's sense and not completely inflexible. Instead, it was capable of being adjusted to changing circumstances, especially in its action-oriented portion.

On the other hand, the "behavioral" dismissal of ideology overlooked the fact that the "rationality" of action, as perceived by the actors, is defined by a set of references—assumptions made by the individual on the basis of a system of beliefs or "ideology." Humans are "rational," but "rational" within the parameters of their perception of reality. The fact that ideology cannot be "calculated," and hence submitted to "objective" analysis, does not negate its existence or its vital importance. Even if one uses the individual as the primary unit of analysis (as in the behavioral school), one cannot disregard the fact that a human being is "a thinking animal" capable of not only "pragmatically" evaluating reality, but also of imagining and striving for dreams of perfection. Present day actions are motivated by a vision of the future.[36] Neither can institutions be disregarded; they are rooted in historical developments, and participants typically act within their constraints. Moreover, institutions are to some degree the creatures of ideology, which justifies their major characteristics and provides them with legitimacy.

It is useless to engage in a debate as to whether ideology is the source of decisions or the "post facto"

justification for them. In both cases, ideology is important. Either it is the source or it is asserted to be the
source by the participants in the action. In the second
case, the decision maker must justify the decision
through ideology. Thus, the consideration of ideology
must still be part of the decision-making process, for
all decisions must be in some conformity with the ideology. Furthermore, ideology serves as a symbolic
means of internal communication. Words rooted in
ideology, or ideological symbols, used in communication between individuals, are abbreviations for complex concepts. Those symbols are keys to understanding how the broader concepts affect individuals
trained in that particular ideology. What may seem
pointless and transparent propaganda to the outsider
is full of meaning to the initiated. This linguistic
importance of ideology cannot be overlooked in our
analysis of human political behavior.

The outright rejection of the totalitarian model in
favor of the broader conception of authoritarianism
throws the baby out with the bathwater. In our dissatisfaction with the totalitarian model, we should not
disregard fundamental differences between simple
authoritarianism, on the one hand, and fascism, communism, or Islamic fundamentalism, on the other. The
crucial distinction between the two categories is the
lack in authoritarianism of a comprehensive monistic ideology. Authoritarianism exhibits a distinct dis-
interest in the ideological mobilization of the population. The authoritarian system is not intended to
penetrate all social and economic aspects of human
behavior, as long as they do not interfere with governmental control. Although the very name of this category of political systems denotes centralized governmental authority, these regimes exhibit a relative

neutrality toward many aspects of human life.[37] The authoritarian government is exclusionary—it excludes people from political participation in government, which it reserves for a set of elites. But this limitation of its sphere of activity, and its tolerance of many other spheres throughout society, permits social pluralism to some degree, in which extensive social control is exercised by other organizations. In essence these organizations exercise political authority within their own limited spheres.[38] Communist, fascist, and fundamentalist Islamic governments, like democracies, are inclusionary—mobilizing people to participate and, in the case of fully developed ideocracies, forcing them to do so and conform to ideological prescriptions in all aspects of their lives. In ideocracy, nothing is completely apolitical, although some aspects of life may be ignored at times by a government preoccupied with what it considers to be more important tasks.

Authoritarian government does not aim at converting people to its own faith; it desires only to rule them. Communism, fascism, or Islamic fundamentalism strives for people's minds and souls. For that reason, authoritarian systems are generally less durable than ideocracies and are often toppled very suddenly to the surprise of everybody. This was the case with the Soviet Union, which with the Gorbachev's reforms (e.g., "glasnost" and the transfer of political power from the Communist party to the Soviet state), became "deideologized" and changed its basic nature from ideocracy to authoritarianism. Stripped of its ideological legitimacy, it quickly fell apart. The limited reach of authoritarianism is well illustrated by its noninterference in scientific pursuits of individuals or groups, providing they do not in any way endanger its political rule. By contrast any reader of scientific literature emitting from a communist, fascist, or fundamentalist Islamic state, and especially that which in some way deals with humans, is painfully aware of the subjugation of science to ideology. The consistent scientific and technological lag of fundamentalist Islam, and of the communist regimes in the Soviet Union and China, behind Western democracies is partially explainable by this ideological straitjacket that inhibits human inventiveness.[39]

Finally, in human psyche itself we may distinguish between the open mind and the closed mind.[40] The open mind allows for the diversity of experience and the uncertainties of a changing reality. The closed mind must interpret all experience within a comprehensive conceptual scheme, rigidly subordinating new experiences to a prior understanding of the world. Democratic systems require tolerance by individuals of diverse perspectives. Authoritarian regimes allow some diversity of perspectives among different authorities, although they restrict freedom of thought in political sensitive areas. In ideocracy, however, the individual thought process must be subordinated to the authoritative interpretation of a comprehensive ideology. The closed mind is psychologically compatible with these requirements of ideocracy. Many Western scholars (mostly those who did not live or did not do extensive research in ideocracies) came to discount this psychological dimension of ideocratic politics and were prone to discount the relevance of the totalitarian "model."

Recently, after the collapse of communism in Central Europe and what used to be the Soviet Union, the debate over totalitarianism has been revived, partially because the prevailing theories of political science, when applied to new knowledge about these communist systems, were found wanting. Why were Western political scientists unable to predict these dramatic changes or even to recognize the rapid decline of these systems? Many quantitative studies were based on the assumed stability of the Soviet Union and its European satellites. What was missing in their analysis? Now Western scholars, groping in the "secret bowels" of previous communist regimes, have discovered that they were not simply *authoritarian*. Moreover, the people of Central and Eastern Europe themselves have insisted that they were, indeed, living under totalitarianism.[41] As a result, some political scientists have argued for the return to or a modification of the "classic" framework of Friedrich and Brzezinski.[42] Others have searched for a new and a more comprehensive paradigm.[43]

The debate over the totalitarian "model" of politics sharply illuminates many aspects of such polities. Scientific disputes, however, can be used to advantage only when the lessons learned are utilized for furthering the development of knowledge. Ultimately there is a need for a synthesis, bringing together many and often opposing views. In this Introduction we have examined the totalitarian "model" and criticism against it—charges that it is static framework, that it overly stresses terror, and that it fails to capture patterns of social change within the system. We have also explored the deficiencies of many narrower behavioral approaches, which fail to incorporate an adequate sense of these systems, which fail to acknowledge the perversive influence of a monistic ideology, and which subordinate analysis of these systems to an inadequate frame of reference, such as authoritarianism or a particular level of economic development. Now, we shall undertake to provide a synthesis of various perspectives in a new framework that applies to both traditionally acknowledged totalitarian regimes and other systems adhering to monistic ideology. We propose a new typology of political systems, in which forms of ideocracy are posed against forms of pluralism. Our analysis encompasses many of the characteristics of the totalitarian "model", especially those developed by Friedrich and Brzezinski, while incorporating other features that (1) broaden the category to include certain fundamentalist religious regimes, (2) include middle-range dynamics of social change, and (3) categorize fundamental patterns of systemic change associated with the inception, stabilization, and evolution of ideocratic systems.

Our analysis centers on the use of *ideocracy* as the organizing typological construct.[44] The term *ideocracy* originated in the writings of Nicholas Berdyaev on Russian intellectual history and the origins of Russian communism.[45] Sidney and Beatrice Webb in their writings on Soviet communism pointed out that the Soviet system was not just a dictatorship, but that "history records also theocracies, and various other *ideocracies*, in which the organized exponents of particular creeds or philosophical systems have, in effect, ruled communities irrespective of their formal constitutions, merely by keeping the conscience of the influential citizens."[46] In 1953, Waldemar Gurian conceptualized totalitarianism as political religion and argued that such regimes are better identified as "ideocracies." He asserted that totalitarian movements are actually "politico-social secularized religions."[47] He distinguished ideocracies that seek earthly salvation from traditional religions that recognize a deity and seek salvation in an afterlife.[48] His conceptualization of ideocracy is very similar to our own use of the term;

however, we extend its use to a broader family of political regimes. We believe that when fundamentalist religions come to dominate political systems, their drive to create an earthly utopia that prepares the faithful for heavenly salvation, establishes them as variants of ideocracy, with characteristics closely related to regimes traditionally labeled *totalitarian*. Our conceptualization of ideocracy includes this broader family of political regimes in a singular framework of analysis.[49]

We further propose a typology of political systems in which we distinguish ideocracy, which is associated with ideological monism, from pluralism, which involves the coexistence of multiple belief systems in a social order. In the first, a singular set of beliefs is considered to embrace all social life, whereas in the latter, competing perspectives on important matters support the semiautonomy of diverse groups in their own spheres of influence.[50] In our scheme, traditional authoritarianism is paired with democracy. We argue that, although the power of an authoritarian government may be repressive, it does not eliminate all competing bases of social authority and power. In democracy, on the other hand, the pluralism of the broader society extensively penetrates government and is formalized in electoral systems, which are designed to ensure the responsiveness of government to changing political coalitions emerging from society. Formal rights also protect disparate groups from governmental oppression. And thus, democracy and authoritarianism both lack the ideological singularity of monism, and their social pluralism affects the exercise of political authority.[51] We note with other analysts the possibility of gradual change from authoritarianism to democracy, as in a number of cases in Latin America (e.g., Argentina, Uruguay, Brazil) and in Asia (e.g., South Korea and Taiwan); and we observe the oscillation between military authoritarianism and partially developed democracy in Africa (e.g., Nigeria, Ghana). These systemic changes are possible precisely because of the absence of ideological monism.

However, the central focus of this work is upon ideocracy. We distinguish it as a unique form of political life and examine its dynamics. We explore psychological and social concomitants of its ideological foundations, and we delve extensively into the operations of ideocratic systems in action. In the early portion of the work we rely extensively upon what Max Weber called an *ideal type*.[52] This form of analysis explores the ramifications of an analytically integrated set of categories, describing a complex web of social relationship viewed in an exaggerated form, as if the logic of certain dominant ideas were essentially realized. We find that this allows the development of crucial insights in the analysis of what we call *ideocracies*. At the same time, like Weber, we recognize that social systems do not fully realize such extremes of coherence and ideological purity. Even in this portion of the work, we acknowledge contradictory patterns of social action that undermine ideocracy to some degree.

In our conceptualization, we recognize two fundamental types of ideocracy: (1) the totalitarian form, which relies extensively on the employment of physical force; and (2) the populist variant, which rests primarily upon the voluntary support of true believers in the ideology.[53] Between these two ideal types exist a number of plausible combinations and even a possibility of movement back and forth between them. This distinction allows us to recognize the essential similarities of and differences between traditional ideocracies and revolutionary ideocracies. It also enhances comparisons between regimes resting on beliefs that are virtually universal within their populations and those in which the force of terror is needed to remake society.

In the subsequent portion of the book we introduce a more dynamic form of analysis that explores phases of systemic change, associated with the inception, stabilization and evolution of ideocracy. Our consideration here takes the form of "average type" analysis in Weberian terms.[54] It recognizes the diverse contradictions to be found in all social systems that produce complex countercurrents of change. In this fashion, we examine ways in which real-world ideocracies move toward and away from the ideal type conception of ideocracy. Here the typology of political systems comes into play again, because their movements may be toward authoritarian or democratic forms of rule as time passes. Our discussion traces a variety of such changes, incorporating examples relating to the recent dissolution of communist regimes and the rise of Islamic fundamentalist politics. The work concludes with reflections upon how this approach to the analysis of politics illuminates the study of comparative politics more generally.

I

IDEOCRACY AS A DISTINCTIVE FORM OF POLITICS

What Is Ideocracy?

Ideocracy is a political system whose activities are pursued in reference to the tenets of a monistic ideology. More specifically, the legitimacy of the political system is derived from the monistic ideology, which establishes a universal frame of reference for the participants of the system.

The concept of ideocracy combines two root terms: *cracy* and *ideo*. *Cracy* is a Greek word meaning political rule. *Ideo* derives from ideology. Hence ideocracy involves political rule in the name of a monistic ideology. We may define *ideology* as an integrated set of assertions, theories, and aims that constitute a general program for the organization of social life.[1] It contains a view of the past, the present, and the future from which the program of political action is derived. Of course, every society and every political system operates in reference to some political ideology and an array of related beliefs, however imperfectly these may be defined. For example, the American political system involves a set of generally held beliefs that encourage a selective interpretation of history, present day reality, and the principles on which the system is founded. In the American case, this set of beliefs includes such concepts as rule by the people, government through law, the inalienable rights of human beings, the triumph of democracy, and so on. The conflict over the meaning of these beliefs and their application has abounded throughout American history.

But the ideology of ideocracy is of a specific character—it is monistic. Monism is the doctrine that reality may be understood as one unitary, indivisible whole; thus a monistic ideology posits that this reality can be interpreted by a universally true and exhaustive system of ideas. Although other ideologies are partial in their interpretative scope and tentative in their explanation of reality, a monistic ideology claims to be comprehensive and absolute. It presumes to explain *all* aspects of reality. In this regard, it rejects any separation between different realms of human behavior, including the separation of political, social, economic, ethical, and aesthetical spheres of human endeavor. Therefore the political sphere is seen to subsume all other spheres of society. Monism likewise rejects the need for tentative assumptions in the face of complexity and instead asserts an absolute knowledge of reality that overrides any more immediate sense of uncertainty.[2]

The legitimacy of an ideocratic system derives from the principles of its monistic ideology. It is assumed that the decision makers of the system have a strictly defined framework of reference that allows them an absolutely correct interpretation of events. Thus, their decisions are infallible. What sets ideocracy apart from other kinds of political systems is the fact that it claims to derive the legitimacy of specific programs of action *exclusively* from the tenets of the ideology itself. By contrast, in other systems the justification for political action involves reference not only to a specific ideology but also to standards stemming from other sets of rules—for example, norms governing ethical conduct, scientific inquiry, and artistic creation—norms derived from distinct realms of human behavior.[3]

Ideocracy Distinguished

Extending upon the previous discussion, a fundamental distinction may be made between ideocracy and all other political systems (see Figure I.1, classification of political systems). Thus, two polar types of polities are identified: the first, which we have termed *ideocratic*; the second, which may be called *pluralistic*. We have already defined *ideocracy*. Pluralistic polities conversely are all those systems that tolerate competing ideologies and other schemes of thought not withstanding adherence to a general ideology that supports the organization of the political system. This apparent contradiction is possible because the general ideology is not viewed as an absolute and comprehensive truth, as it is in an ideocracy.

FIGURE I.1

Classification of Political Systems

System of Beliefs	Type of Political System
Monism	Ideocracy
Limited Pluralism	Authoritarianism
Pluralism	Democracy

Note: By *democracy*, we mean a political system in which top political decision makers are chosen through election by the citizens, political participation is open to diverse and competing groups; and the rights of individuals are grounded in an established legal order.

Pluralism is commonly associated with participatory democracy. In fact this is not always the case. Indeed one can easily think of authoritarian systems that are somewhat pluralistic. They are characterized by a centralized political realm that is relatively uninvolved with many other spheres of human behavior. Most dictatorships and oligarchies fall in this category. We may also recognize an authoritarian form of political pluralism in which there exist many centers of political control, each characterized by its internal authoritarianism; for example, the feudal systems of medieval Europe and Japan. It is possible to distinguish various forms and degrees of pluralism in different authoritarian systems.[4] Thus authoritarian systems may be seen to fall on a continuum between ideocracy and democracy involving, as Juan Linz has suggested: "limited but not responsible political pluralism, without elaborate and guiding ideology but with distinctive mentalities, without intensive or extensive political mobilization . . . and in which a leader, or occasionally a small group, exercise power within formally ill-defined, but actually quite predictable limits."[5]

Although authoritarian regimes exercise centralized power, which may be more or less culturally legitimized, they lack the ideological scope of ideocracies or their drive to mobilize the entire population.

Two ideal types of ideocracy may also be distinguished. Many modern ideocracies have been totalitarian, with extensive physical control functions and the widespread use of political terror, as in the cases of Nazi Germany and the Stalinist Soviet Union.[6] While not denying the validity of the totalitarian variant, we would argue that there is another valid type of ideocracy—the populist ideocracy. This latter kind derives its voluntary acceptance from a high level of support for a commonly held monistic ideology. Some small, relatively isolated systems best approximate this type; for example, Calvinist Geneva, the Commonwealth of Massachusetts.[7] Further, as will be clarified later, mature modern ideocracies tend to become less totalitarian and more populist.

It should be clear from this discussion that ideocracy is based upon the existence of a monistic ideology and not upon a specific structure of political control within a political system. Therefore we have both totalitarian and populist variants of ideocracy, one essentially coercive and the other consensual, just as we have both authoritarian and democratic pluralistic systems.

Intellectual Origins of Ideocracy

Because ideocracies concern themselves with the existence of the absolute truth, they are in some ways similar to organized religions. Indeed, for some ideocracies, a fundamentalist religion forms the base for the monistic ideology upon which the system rests.[8] In both types of ideocracies, secular and religious, a considerable portion of the tenets must be accepted on faith. Only then may the rest of the system be logically deduced.[9] For example, an acceptance on faith of a specific view of historical necessity may lead logically to an attempt to create a particular social structure foreordained in that history; for example, a racially stratified political system may be sought because of a faith in the superior role of one chosen race (e.g., Nazi Germany).[10] Likewise, in a religion, belief in God may lead to social action intended to exemplify the believer's state of grace. But ideocracy

goes beyond traditional religion. Whereas the reli-
giously faithful adhere to their beliefs as individuals
and as a collective body of believers, the faithful of
ideocracy seek to *enforce* their views throughout a
politically governed territory. Religious views may be
spread by teaching and by example, whereas ideocratic views are backed by political action to enforce
them, as well.[11] Ideocracy typically involves either
fusion of religious and political beliefs, as in the case of
some militant religious regimes, or the substitution of
secular ideology for religious belief. Indeed some have
called ideocracies *secular religions.*[12] The classical
examples of ideocracies (Sparta, Calvinist Geneva,
Commonwealth of Massachusetts) as well as contemporary Islamic fundamentalist regimes (Iran and
Sudan), have involved the fusion of religion and politics. In these societies, social and political organization
has been designed to achieve salvation for the participants. Most of the contemporary Western or Western-
type ideocracies, however, have been of the secular
form, substituting historical ideology—completely
(Marxism) or partially (fascism)—for transcendental
religious beliefs. In these, the ultimate goal of an
earthly utopia have replaced heavenly salvation.

A general secularization of politics and society has
occurred in the Western or Westernized societies with
the advancement of technology and science. In these
societies, the religious content of earlier political ideologies does not appeal to the typical audiences, who are
more interested in economic and social advancement
than in eternal salvation. The underlying scientific revolution has encouraged reliance on theories relating to
the scientific method of inquiry and stressing innovative, rational problem solving. Secularized masses see
the tangible results of technological and scientific

progress. Increasingly, they expect political leaders to *engineer* clear-cut solutions to perceived social problems. No longer are they willing to accept references to the supernatural as justification for the real or imagined frustration of their desires. Hence, more contemporary Westernized ideocracies have employed ideologies that focus upon a monistic historical explanation of reality and contain a claim of scientific truth (communism, Ba'th socialism in the Middle East). Thus, the superiority of a particular ideocratic creed is justified by historical and pseudo-scientific evidence and not by a reference to the favor of God.

In the non-Western world, however, there is often a negative reaction to the secular influences of modernization and a revival of traditional values. This is clearly rooted in tradition and derives from sacred roots in the society. At the same time it selectively incorporates aspects of modern society, such as a communication network, mass propaganda, technology, and international economic connections, although it does so by severely subordinating these to the strictures of a religious creed. The result is an ideocracy rooted in the mass politics of the nation state, as are other modern ideocracies, but one that draws deeply on the premodern traditions and beliefs.[13] For example, the ideocratic creed on which Islamic fundamentalist regimes are based promises heavenly salvation and an earthly utopia. Strongly anti-Western, its message claims modernization leading to economic prosperity to be possible only within the prescriptions of Islam. This skillful blend of the traditional and the modern lends to its popularity among the Muslim masses and many of its intellectuals.

This is not to suggest that the secular ideologies are devoid of idealism. The followers are still expected to sacrifice for an ultimate perfection, which, it is claimed, will benefit the future generations. A metaphysical belief in the attainment of this future utopia lends a sacred quality to the ideocratic system of beliefs, creating thereby a secular religion.[14] Faith, grace, evil, and divine inspiration all have a place within the earthly historical drama. With the forces of good pitted against evil, the followers are expected to have faith in the righteousness of the ideocratic cause and in the divine inspiration of their leaders.[15] Ironically, the masses are again asked to sacrifice, now in the name of an earthly utopia rather than heavenly salvation, or in some cases both. All of this exemplifies the character of ideocracy, which combines a sense of religious dedication with a belief in the attainment of ultimate material goals. Hence, there are two kinds of ideological support for ideocracy— one strongly religious (e.g., Islamic fundamentalism) and the other based on historicism and science (e.g., Marxism or fascism).

It is often argued that totalitarian political systems result from the development of contemporary technology and the mass society.[16] Obviously, what we choose to call *ideocracy* existed before the industrial revolution as well. One must not deny, however, the profound impact of industrialization and the advancement of technology on all human societies and political systems. Urbanization, as a by-product of industrialization, has brought masses of people together. Rapid transportation and broadly developed mass communication have extended the mass public to the countryside as well. Urban and rural masses have become aware of contemporary events occurring not only in their immediate communities but throughout the world at large.[17] A century ago, the average

Indian villagers never expected to travel more than 20 miles from their places of inhabitancy and seldom met anybody from beyond this distance. Naturally, their social and political perspective was limited primarily to events occurring within that realm. Today, for better or worse, the transistor radio, movies, and increasingly television now bring them news and pictures from Paris, London, Moscow, Teheran, and Peking, opening their imagination to the world beyond. Formal education further contributes to this process. Mass transportation likewise increases their chances of travel in that broader world.

All of these developments lead to mass politics. Mass support can be generated—through communication and social interaction—from distant centers of political power.[18] The legitimacy of a political regime can be inculcated in a broad mass of followers. On the other hand, these same conditions enhance the capacity of revolutionary movements to develop geographically extended bases of mass support.[19] For these and other reasons, the masses cannot be ignored.

Except for the very smallest, political systems of the past involved the exclusive participation of small elites (nobility, mandarins, intelligentsia). Large authoritarian political systems of the past mobilized such specific elites only, leaving other strata of population uninvolved and unpenetrated ideologically, although they were controlled politically by the elites. In a sense, some of these were partially developed ideocracies, in that the elites were mobilized in reference to a monistic ideology.[20] However, the fully developed ideocracies of this earlier period were set apart from these larger political systems. They were small, highly mobilized communities, sharply isolated from contact with other social systems. Most primitive social systems were of this sort—tribes with fused religious and political organization, an integrated tribal world-view, and belief in a sacred status separating them from the rest of humanity.[21] Some early ideocracies were also formed by intense religious groups, which turned away from larger political systems in efforts to create isolated religious utopias.[22]

The rise of the masses is necessary as a precondition to mass politics, both pluralistic and ideocratic. This helps to explain similarities seen by some between mass democracies and modern ideocracies. The fact remains that the industrial revolution brought the masses into the political realm with the consequence that highly dynamic modern political systems must mobilize their support. In this sense all mass political systems involve broader patterns of political participation; however, this does not negate the fundamental distinction between pluralistic and ideocratic systems, which is rooted in ideological differences between the two systems.[23] The ideologies of pluralistic democracies explicitly recognize the legitimacy of diverse groups of participants and different realms of social life outside the sway of political control. Modern ideocracies bring all facets of social life within the scope of legitimate political control. Moreover, extended ideocracies of the modern world mobilize their masses with powerful monistic ideologies that pervade their systems of communications.

Organic and Mechanical (Pragmatic) Concepts of the State

Throughout history human beings have often asked, What is the state and why should I obey it?

Their primary allegiances have usually been given to their community; so, their answers to these questions have involved their conception of the relationship of the state to this community. Basically, there are two general conceptions of that relationship—one is organic, the other mechanical (pragmatic).[24]

The organic concept views the state is an extension of the community, and because the community (society, nation) itself is regarded as a living organism, the state also assumes organic qualities and becomes the organized expression of the whole. The community is seen as a collective body, with a continuation of its life through generations, and not merely as an aggregation of distinct individuals and groups. Whatever meaning individuals possess, they derive from this enveloping organic community. To express this vividly, the individual is to the community (and hence, to the state) as a finger is to the human body. The finger's meaning derives from the functions it performs for the body, in its organic unity with the body. The finger severed from the hand becomes a useless, dead object. Equally, individuals separated from their society (physically or psychologically) lose their *human meaning*, even if they continue to exist physically. To a degree, all theories of community have some organic characteristics; however, our discussion focuses upon the additional conception of state as the embodiment of that organism. Indeed, some conservative democratic theories view society as an organic entity but envision a limited role for government, which places them clearly in democratic tradition.

The mechanical (pragmatic) concept envisions the state as a mechanical device—an artificial creation—constructed by groups of individuals for specific purposes.[25] Individuals are not totally subsumed within the community, nor is the state the organic embodiment of that community. Hence individuals or groups of individuals can claim civil rights protecting them against the state. Although in the organic view the state is all-embracing, in the mechanical it is particular and limited in its purpose: the private realm of activity stands separate from and coequal with the public realm. Because of its limited purpose, the state must compete with other social organizations seeking the allegiance of the individual. By now it should be obvious to the reader that the organic concept of the society and the state is most consistent with the ideocratic form of politics. The mechanical view of society is more clearly at odds with monistic ideology.

Politics and Problem Solving

The techniques of problem solving in our two kinds of political systems, ideocratic and pluralistic, differ quite basically. In ideocracy, all techniques must be justified, in the last analysis, by reference to a monistic ideology. No sphere of specialized human activity is strictly neutral in relation to the all-embracing concept of reality. All problem solving techniques must be ideologically correct; that is, they must conform to the general ideological frame of reference. To some degree, realms of expertise will still have their own set of techniques and rules. However, their final product must be compatible with the tenets of the monistic ideology. On occasion, of course, the two will be found in conflict, and then the techniques themselves will be held to be ideologically deviant. To a considerable extent, the freedom of inquiry will be impaired, as the experts attempt to confine themselves to techniques that will produce ideologically acceptable solutions. Still, ideocratic politics does encourage concentrated problem-solving efforts, and hence it is often characterized by a spectacular growth in limited ideologically acceptable areas, while little or sharply confined attention is given to ideologically troublesome problem areas.[26]

In pluralistic politics no overall comprehensive ideology determines the legitimacy of all problem-solving efforts. The rules of the different spheres of inquiry are derived from their own specialized sets of principles. And therefore, science relies primarily on the tenets of scientific inquiry and is influenced only indirectly by other spheres of human concern, such as morality and politics. The products of science will still be judged by their usefulness to society, but the techniques of scientific activity will be evaluated by a different set of principles, including, of course, the ethical standards of the society, but only in regard to the most fundamental social conventions. The problem solvers are less constrained by the ideological considerations; rather, they are subject to standards and pressures derived from sets of principles appropriate to the subject matter. These principles develop within various areas of specialization within the pluralistic system. In this system, problem solving follows many avenues and is characterized by a wide dispersion of efforts. This is why the pluralistic systems are often seen as slow moving, although in fact they are highly flexible; for, diverse streams of problem-solving activity are only poorly related to each other.[27] Ideocratic systems are characterized by ideologically stimulated and constrained problem-solving activity. Pluralistic systems display a diversity in their problem-solving efforts that reflects the variety of coexisting standards on which the whole concept of pluralism is based.

Community and Ideology

The organic concept of community, which is philosophically crucial in ideocracy, not only conceives of the individual as an inseparable element of society, but equally important, conceptualizes society itself as absolutely distinct and separate from other societies. It stresses the unique characteristics of each fundamental social group into which the whole of humanity is divided. Further, the monistic ideology of an ideocratic system identifies its own community as a sacred collectivity, superior to other communities, which are regarded as either lower or often perverted forms of human existence (e.g., the master race of Aryans in Nazi ideology or Umma Moslemhood in Islamic fundamentalism).[28] Because ideocracy possesses this chosen quality, it has an undeniable historical mission to perform—at the least, to defend its own specific identity, or at best, to lead part or all of humanity to salvation as it defines this.

The pluralistic society, on the other hand, regards its community as an assemblage of groups, outside as well as inside the political community. These groups are related to one another by the possibility of mutual membership and overlapping concerns and by the mobility of individuals between the groups. Also the community is not an absolutely exclusive entity, because individuals and groups are permitted to divide their loyalties among different communities. In special circumstances they can transfer from one community to another, as for example in emigration.[29] No organization in the pluralistic community demands absolute loyalty of the individual in all aspects of one's behavior. The pluralistic community has of course an historical identity, but this identity is similar to that of other communities. Hence, the community has no basis for claiming a unique and superior historical mission, which it must perform.[30]

The essence of the pluralistic community is the recognition that the membership in it is created primarily by law or voluntary association and does not basically derive from biological origin or ideological identification.[31] This is expressed well in the Roman concept of citizenship, in which community membership depends on legal status and is dissolved by specified legal processes. Citizenship in this perspective, involves a limited association between the individual and the political community. In ideocracy, full membership is more fundamental, because it embraces the individual as a whole and involves a fusion of the individual and the community. The membership of the community is considered to be historically determined, because one is either born into the organic community or merges with it in response to historical or supernatural forces recognized within the monistic ideology. This process may involve individual conversion, but even this conversion is seen as preordained. Some participants straddle the gap between membership and nonmembership. Their historically defined characteristics are held to be such that they waiver between alliance with, and opposition toward, the ideocratic community.[32] At best, they may attain a partial, lesser membership in that community. Their impurity is such that they may, at any time, turn against the community.

Ideocratic communities are organized through one of four ideological sources of membership: the Nation, the Race, the Class, and the Culture.[33]

Membership in the national form of ideocracy derives from a combination of biological, cultural, and geographic characteristics that together make the individual a natural element of the national community. Individuals are regarded as members to the *degree* that they possesses these characteristics (e.g., in Fascist Italy).[34]

Racial ideocracy is founded on a common biological heritage. Persons are born as members of *the* superior, or of some inferior, race. In some circumstances, they may be acceptable to the racial community even if they are not of absolutely pure blood, but their level of perfection is only as great as their degree of racial purity. Therefore, those of impure blood can have only a limited membership[35] (e.g., in Nazi Germany).

Class-based ideocracy utilizes the economic division of labor (differentiation) of society for its definition of the membership. Individuals are members of an economic class because of their specific relation to the social forces of production in the division of labor. For example, if they contribute to production as workers, they belong to the working class as defined by the ideology (e.g., all communist ideocracies).[36]

Membership in the cultural ideocracy is not so easy to specify, because culture is difficult to define. Basically, it refers here to the set of socially transmitted ideas about what is characteristic of "a people."[37] Typically this set of ideas involves only part of the social life of the participants. However, in the ideocratic system, culture is considered to be all embracing in the sense that it provides a basis for the complete identification of the individual, the people, and the community. In other words, individuals are what they are because of their essential cultural identity. But because they are normally born into a culture, cultural ideocracy contains strong overtones of biological (race) community. Indeed, a cultural ideocracy often refers to itself as the *Volk community*. Various cultural ideocracies emphasize different aspects of culture, such as religion (e.g., in the Islamic republics of Iran and Sudan),[38] education or technological advancement (e.g., Republic of South Africa at the height of apartheid).[39] Philosophically, although not always in practice, the superiority of the community is held to derive from the superiority of its culture. Theoretically, other communities might eventually attain the same level, but at the present time they remain inferior. The culturally advanced community has the obligation of leadership and example, while at the same time it must be concerned with its own purity, which must not be compromised.

Ideocracy Described

Ideocracy is a political system that derives its legitimacy from the tenets of a monistic ideology. This monistic ideology presumes to explain all aspects of reality and requires the subordination of all realms of human behavior. The ideocratic decision makers rely on a general framework of strictly defined rules and hence claim the right to infallibility. Although ideocracy tends toward total control, not all ideocracies are coercive; in fact, some are consensual. In terms of intellectual roots, ideocracy can be compared with traditional religion. In both, the "Truth" should be realized within their realm, but ideocracy merges absolutist religious beliefs with political control over a territory. Many ideocracies involve complete or partial fusion between religion and a historical doctrine. The general secularization of many of the Western societies has led to the emergence of a number of secular ideocracies. They engage in the drive toward earthly utopias, which derive from secular metaphysical principles similar in many ways to the metaphysics of religion. This metaphysical character is also expressed in the supernatural qualities ascribed to their organic community. However, the recent appearance of fundamentalist regimes and movements in the Islamic world has led to the revival of religious ideocracy.

Ideocracies are found throughout the course of history. Many folk communities have had ideocratic characterisitcs, as have some intense religious sects that have attempted to leave broader societies to establish isolated self-governing communities. Furthermore, there have been partial ideocracies, which mobilized limited elites only, as in the apartheid Republic of South Africa. Most contemporary ideocracies, as all modern political systems, must rely on and therefore mobilize the masses. The use of technology in these contemporary ideocracies is critical, but it is no less vital to their operation than is the case in modern pluralistic political systems. In general, ideocracy is characterized by ideologically stimulated and constrained problem-solving activity throughout its society. In many ways this results from the view that ideocratic society is absolutely distinct and separate from other human groups, by virtue of the superiority of its nation, race, class, or culture. Such superiority imposes on the ideocratic society an historic mission; at best to lead humanity to a glorious future, at worst to defend its own purity. Therefore, individuals must subjugate all aspects of their behavior to the superior ideocratic goal. For, the sacrifice of their potentially deviant personal freedom creates the conditions by which the whole group can attain the freedom to perform its historic mission.

II

Psychological and Cultural Aspects of Ideocracy

Before proceeding further, it would be well to explore the psychological dimension of ideocratic participation. There is no one-to-one correspondence between certain psychological patterns and particular kinds of political action. It can be argued, however, that some psychological syndromes are *more compatible with* ideocratically "proper" (supportive) action than are others. Further, it can be shown that certain psychological responses may be associated with a full and active belief in an ideocratic perspective on reality. Thus, it is likely that particular individuals, or even large groups, would exhibit particular psychological traits because they are involved in an ideocratic political system.[1] Some psychological syndromes should be more often evident in ideocratic settings than in others.[2] It may also be asserted that the ideological strictures of ideocracy encourage certain psychological syndromes. Earlier efforts on the part of the Communist party in China to psychologically cleanse the populous involved public rituals in which participants were led to confess deviant behavior and seek rebirth as cleansed comrades.[3] This discussion of the psychological aspects of ideocracy is important for another reason. In considering the psychological syndromes discussed here, one may visualize the impact of ideocracy on the individual. This should provide some sense of how and why individuals adjust to the extreme demands of ideocracy. The initial discussion will describe the ideal type system in operation. Deviations from this pattern will be considered later.

Public commitment to an all-embracing ideology is required within the ideocratic political system. Participants are expected to become "true believers," dedicating themselves to a process of personal regeneration, through which a perfected individual will emerge.[4] All doubt, all contrary beliefs are to be purged from their minds, while the tenets of the ideology are incorporated within the structure of their thought processes. When fully regenerated, they will epitomize the idealized characteristics of the "new human." However, so long as they are still in the process of regeneration, their minds will be a battleground in which contrary forces of good and evil contend for control. Moreover, their personal struggles to regenerate themselves are an integral part of the broader social struggle to attain the ideocratic vision. Indeed, their psychological regeneration is necessary for the success of the social struggle, but likewise, their participation in the ideological social movement makes possible their own personal salvation. Thus, there are three aspects to their personal involvement in the process: absolute commitment to the monistic ideology, complete dedication to their own personal regeneration, and total submersion of themselves within the ideological social movement.

Certain psychological-behavioral traits may be generally associated with this kind of ideological commitment. They take the following form:

Participants will identify themselves completely with what they consider to be a sacred community of believers in the ideology. They will exhibit what has been called a closed mind in the general structure of their thought.[5] They will be absolutely committed to the tenets of ideology and will be closed to competing perspectives which challenge, or even differ from, ideologically "correct" views. They will seek personal regeneration through ideological guidance from ideocratic authorities, subordinating their beliefs and attitudes to their dictates.

This ideologically based sense of identity is of central importance psychologically, for individuals should perceive an absolute dividing line between their own self-realization within a sacred community and their seeming destruction in the world outside the community. No serious consideration of alternative ideas is possible for them with so much at stake. Their minds must be closed to such heresy. Therefore, participants are quite rigid in their general thought process and unable to cope with ideologically ambiguous questions.[6] They require absolutely correct answers if they are to avoid mistakes that might destroy their membership in the sacred community. Stereotyped ideas and action meet their needs quite well. Simple, repeatable forms of response can be learned and adopted as signs of ideological conformity, signs that prove their loyalty to other members and to themselves. This identification of the participant with the ideological community greatly stabilizes the ideocratic society, because properly indoctrinated members reject conflicting ideas and respond to new situations in stereotypical ways.

However, social adaptation to changing realities is a reoccurring necessity. This is true in all ideocracies, but is less pronounced in primitive systems with a more stable environment and less internally generated change than in contemporary times. The ideocratic political system requires some means of changing policies, of adopting new courses of action. Hence, someone must address ambiguous new problems and find ideologically correct means of solving them. Psychologically, the closed mind deals with the need for change by looking for *charismatic leadership*.[7] The sense of uncertainty caused by change can be overcome if only someone can be depended upon to have the right understanding of the situation. Thus, ideocracy meets the problems of change with a hierarchy of prophetic leadership. The most general societal problems are put in ideological perspective by the top-most leader, whereas lesser problems are dealt with by leaders at lower levels of hierarchy in the system. This process reduces the anxiety of both the leaders and the followers. Whereas followers gain confidence from the "truths" provided by their leaders, the leaders receive psychic support for the idea that, within their own spheres of competence, they can find the ideologically correct lines of action.

Within the process of ideocratic change, however, there is a need to correct past errors and to adopt new actions, which are often at odds with presently accepted views. For leaders, particularly those within the hierarchies of the system, there are nagging fears that a course they have justified will be found wrong by higher authority. Their pronouncements may sound absolute as they are passed downward to followers. Yet, these same pronouncements must be framed in highly tentative and technically restricted language when communicated upward to *their* own leaders. Likewise, followers adopt a seemingly contradictory approach to pronouncements, in that they accept contradictions in past policy pronouncements without questioning the validity of current policies. Their recognition of past errors does not lead them to question present wisdom, nor does confidence in current policy limit their willingness to accept later policy revisions. On the most general level, the monistic ideology must not be drastically altered, for it provides a general frame of reference for all participants. On the level of evolving policy, however, drastic alterations in the practical meaning of the ideology may be accepted by reference to historical change or to past human errors in ideological interpretation.[8]

Paradoxically then, a very powerful commitment to the general monistic ideology leads participants to accept serious contradictions in lower level policy. The closed mind reduces anxiety by compartmentalizing beliefs and refusing to deal with apparent contradictions. Thus, middle-level leaders need not reconcile their upward submission to authority with their downward assertion of absolute certainty. Nor need followers reconcile seemingly contradictory directives, given their belief in the divine mysteries of their faith. Therefore, the closed mind can combine ideological rigidity with tactical flexibility. An apparent amorality emerges in some areas of ideocratic action, but this is the result of adherence to the higher ideological morality that justifies the use of seemingly immoral means to attain ideological ends.[9]

A further psychological syndrome aids in ideological integration of the system—the need for self-purification. Rituals of self-purification (self-criticism, accusation, conversion, mass meetings) dramatically link individuals with the sacred community.[10] Individuals find within themselves the very forces that battle in the historical drama. Through purification, they gain a spiritual union with the sacred community as a whole. In this, they are touched by the mystical forces of the movement. But so long as the battle wages historically, they cannot be fully saved. Daily, they are assaulted by counterideological forces, and daily some part of each person responds to these temptations. Hence the members of an ideocratic community must be at war within themselves in a continuing battle against personal contamination. Only by continuing acts of purification can they prevent their corruption by the enemies of the community.[11]

The process of self-purification has generally functional consequences for the ideocratic system. It reinforces the aforementioned psychological syndromes— submersion of the self in the sacred community and subordination of the self to the concept of absolute leadership. On the one hand, individuals are driven to seek purification through good works. They will tend to see ideologically prescribed accomplishments as reflecting their personal progress. On the other hand, they will be plagued by a sense of guilt, which will erode their capacity to stand apart from their place in the system. In this situation rituals of purification will provide moments of ecstasy and renewal—of symbolic union with the ideological movement. And these rituals will further reinforce both their drive for purification and their sense of guilt. Correspondingly, however, rituals of excommunication from the movement will reinforce an underlying fear of ultimate contamination.[12] Thus individuals will be caught in an intense drama, containing the potential for ultimate salvation or damnation.

The extreme consequences of individual contamination are associated with some group or groups of people (or satanlike beings) who become scapegoats in the ideocratic system. In fact, these groups are seen as the major proponents, or carriers, of the foremost counterideology. They personify the forces working to undermine the sacred community, and so they are clearly labeled in the ideology—as heretics, bourgeois elements, agents of capitalism, Jews, Communists, American devils, Bahai apostates.[13] They provide individuals with stark examples of the evil forces at work, examples that, by contrast, help them define the moral order of the sacred community and recognize the practical steps that must be taken to defend that community.

Psychologically, the scapegoats also represent the forces that individuals must fight within themselves.[14] Through moral laxness, they may, symbolically or actually, join the ranks of the enemy. Thus, while the scapegoats of the system provide a target for aggressive community action, they also provide individuals with a group of culprits onto which they may project their own feelings of guilt. In aggressive attacks upon them, they are both engaged in creative community building with their comrades (actually or vicariously) and proving to themselves that they stand with the sacred community in its fight against the forces of evil. Individual guilt is purged from their minds by a sense of righteous hate. For both the participant and the onlooker, attacks upon the scapegoats of the system contribute powerfully to the psychological integration of the individual within the ideocratic movement.[15]

In a very practical sense, scapegoats also provide a convenient focus for the frustrations of the modern ideocratic community. The demands of ideocratic politics are great—idealistic goals are proposed, and fundamental processes of individual and social transfor-

mation are attempted. Severe social disruption is typically associated with such major processes of social
change. Submission of individuals within the ideocratic system helps to overcome the frustrations
attending this social disruption. However, the dramatic
rituals of scapegoating—mob or terrorist attacks on a
group of scapegoats; public trials, highlighted by
impassioned accusations and confessions; stylized
forms of punishment—provide additional means of
tension release for the participants. Blame for confu-
sion and failure is diverted from the ideocratic leadership and focused on the scapegoats.[16]

Traditional Culture and
Divergent Individual Propensities

Ideocracy, of course, does not operate within a
historical vacuum. Individually its participants have
highly diverse personality traits, which affect their
degree and manner of participation in the ideological
community. Further, the traditional culture of the society includes certain shared traits that affect ideocratic
participation. Some of these individual and cultural
traits—such as high levels of personal insecurity,
authoritarian family structures, and closed belief systems—may reinforce an ideocratic form of politics.
Thus, a particular ideocracy will easily incorporate
certain traditional relationships within its system of
action. Other individual and cultural traits (fatalism,
for example) will be only partially consistent with the
ideocratic system. In some ways they may be supportive while in others they will frustrate the full realization of ideocratic goals. Finally, some traits—such
as the tolerance for ambiguity, strong individualism,
family loyalty—are quite contrary to those psychologi-

cal characteristics generally required within an ideocratic community. Accommodations always emerge
within ideocratic systems between ideological ideals
and the contrary tendencies of individuals and groups.
These accommodations are quite complex and in some
ways unique to each system. It is possible, however, to
identify a simple threefold typology regarding the effect
of these traits on the system: supportive, mixed, and
contrary.

Individual and cultural traits may be supportive of
the ideocratic system if they contribute or approximate the psychological syndromes of ideocracy discussed previously. A high level of *personal insecurity*
may be related to both a learned fear of a hostile and
capricious world and a low level of ego development.
This sense of insecurity will contribute to the tendency
to seek self-realization in ideocratic commitment and
the submersion of the self within an ideocratic movement.[17] Such insecurity may emerge as individuals are
socialized to the world around them, from early child-
hood onward throughout their lives.[18] Disruptive social
and economic changes are also bound to increase the
number of insecure individuals (e.g., depression, economic boom, or fundamental social or environmental
change—see Chapter IV).[19]

The tendency toward conformity is another trait
that encourages ideocratic involvement. It may be
related to a sense of insecurity, but it may also result
from learned views regarding proper behavior and how
communities may survive the dangers of a threatening
world.[20] The conformist belief that individuals should
model their ideas and actions on those of others in
the community reinforces their subordination within
the ideocratic system. For them, independent thought
about ideas gives way to support for group approved

views. They may simply live highly conventional lives within a stable traditional community, but they may also become ardent believers in an ideocratic movement, when that normal pattern is severely disrupted.

Faith in an exclusionary belief system may be associated with the life of particular groups in a both authoritarian and democratic societies. Although such ideas contradict the norms of democratic society, they may still be held by relatively inactive portions of the population or by active but limited groups. Such exclusionary belief systems are quite common in traditional authoritarian systems, although these systems exhibit de facto social pluralism in the coexistence of groups with differing beliefs within the society governed by these political systems. The implicit faith of these groups in one correct vision of the world is quite consistent with the emergence of ideocracy, which may *incorporate* within it the views of these groups or may *convert* their followers. Thus, the tendency to see the world in singular terms is a psychological trait highly consistent with ideocratic rule. Ironically, such a belief may be held by some of the strongest opponents of a particular ideocracy. They do not challenge the principle of ideocratic rule itself, but substitute their faith for that of the ideocratic system in power (e.g., conflict between revolutionary and conservative ideocrats in Latin America or between Islamic fundamentalists and Ba'thists in the Middle East).

A number of individual and cultural tenets are generally mixed in regard to support for ideocracy. They often allow for, or even contribute to, ideocratic rule, but they frustrate the achievement of many of its higher ideals. Widespread support for ideocracy may be associated with a sense of *fatalism*, among those who do not believe the ideological creed, but who accept their own inability to contest the power of those who rule the system. These individuals will usually provide that level of support for the system required of them. Such support not only undercuts opposition to the system but further contributes to many of its working operations. Fatalistic support of this variety is quite common within many stable ideocratic (and authoritarian) systems. In these instances, the call for ideological zealotry is met with counterfeited commitment. From the perspective of the ideological zealot, however, this fatalism strikes at the heart of the ideological movement, for it may rob the movement of commitment to its utopian goals.[21]

To maintain a sense of separate identity while conforming to what is required of them by the ideocracy, many individuals develop a form of "double think" in which they create within themselves a "socio-ideological mannequin" through which they conform. At the same time, they may step back and examine the mannequin from the outside, thus maintaining a degree of separation from the conformist person. Dmitrii Nelidov, in presenting this perspective, distinguishes degrees of psychological separation ranging from "ideological infantilism at the minimum to cynicism at the extreme.[22] In *The Captive Mind*, Czeslaw Milosz asserts that this psychological separation may be associated, in practice, with diverse patterns of covert resistance. While appearing to fully support the demands of ideocracy, the individual engages in an Islamic technique called *Ketman*—one interprets the all-embracing faith in ways that preserve ones own separate identity.[23] Various forms of greater or lesser resistance may be presumed within this frame of reference. It should be noted, however, that this psychological separation is only partial (except at the extreme), and the sense of fatalism, coupled with an acceptance of the conformist mannequin, lends broad, even if imperfect, support to the ideocratic regime. As Walicki notes, ideocratic systems bring great pressure upon those who seem to waiver from the true path.[24] Individuals engaging in Ketman fool themselves that they resist the "evil" of ideocracy. In fact, they do not.

In the higher realms of power there is another trait, which may be called *Machiavellianism*, the cynical and ambitious use of authority by those lacking sincere ideological belief.[25] Such leaders may be central to the successful adjustment of ideocracy to changing environmental conditions. Lacking the inhibitions of true believers, they may be more flexible in considering various policy alternatives. Conceiving of the world as beset by desperate, but inconclusive conflicts and lacking adequate social norms, they may use the ideocratic system for personal ends, assuming that no better is possible (at least within the *present* world). Although these Machiavellians perhaps contribute greatly to the flexible stability of ideocracy, they are also a powerful barrier to its ideal realization. For them, the ideocratic ideals are useful as tools of power, but the actual realization of these ideals would frustrate the real aims of these Machiavellian leaders.[26]

It is also possible to identify a set of traits that are contrary to the maintenance of ideocratic rule. They have in common their association with what has been termed the *democratic personality* and more generally with "self-actualization."[27] These traits are indeed contrary to all forms of authoritarian control, for they encourage the independent assertion of the individual personality in creative action that often breaks the bonds of tradition and conformity.

Both the self-actualizer and the democratic personality have a strong "sense of self." They have iden-
tities rooted in a sense of individual attainment and
worth. Although they desire community with others,
they reject any subordination of individuals to highly
restrictive social organization, for this would destroy
the creative freedom they hold dear. Rather, they are
inclined to seek social relationships that embrace the
potential for self-actualization—those structures that
increase the individual's sense of self-determination
and, conversely, lower his or her need for ideological
certainty. Thus, a strong sense of self (in this psychological context) is contradictory to the psychological
syndromes conducive to ideocracy.

An open-trusting view of others is closely associated with the democratic personality and self-actualization. Such individuals have moved beyond that
sense of insecurity associated with a generalized dis-
trust of other people. They have learned from good
relationships with others that trust and openness
among human beings is both possible and highly
rewarding. Ironically, this means that they will not
give their trust to an authoritarian leader or a monistic ideology. For they are not driven, as is the dis-
trustful, anxious individual, to grasp at ideological
security, believing that warm, human relations have
failed or are not possible. Nor are they limited intellectually, as are most people in premodern settings, for
whom a singular world-view is part of their social tradition. Nor do they need scapegoats upon whom to
project internal feelings of guilt and generalized external anxiety. Leaders who argue for such views lose
their support.

Finally, a "general tolerance for ambiguity" runs
counter to those psychological syndromes that sup-

port ideocracy. A monistic ideology serves to reduce ambiguity by asserting a universal system of correct thought. But likewise it increases the insecurity of the "true believer" in the face of ambiguity, for he or she believes that there is a correct view that *should* be recognized and to miss it would be tantamount to alignment with the forces of evil. Self-actualizers do not need such sweeping ideological certainty to reduce their anxiety. In fact, their tolerance for ambiguity is integral to the creative portion of their lives. They can *explore* new ideas and complex problems precisely because psychologically they do not require immediate answers.[28] They can live with the ambiguity that attends the search for reliable answers to complex problems. As they find answers in various problem areas, they develop clusters of *standards* for evaluating similar questions. These standards differ from area to area in the world of activities, although each set or cluster is appropriate to experience *in that area.* Because of their tolerance for ambiguity they resists the appeal of a monistic ideology, which would integrate all standards in a universalistic system of thought.[29]

In this chapter, we have considered cultural and individual traits that, in varying degrees, support or counter the maintenance and development of ideocratic rule. Some clusters of traits provide the very fertile ground for ideocratic developments. Others may be incorporated within the ideocratic political systems only with some loss of ideological purity and zeal. Ideocratic systems must always be adapted to the existence of individuals with these and other traits in their social settings. In the process of this adaptation, ideocracies take on culturally specific characteristics, which make each system somewhat unique and ensure that each contains imperfections in its organization.

Although there is only some empirical research providing the quantitative evidence for these psychological traits in ideocracies (see the previous text, for examples), an ample anecdotal literature describes individual experience and presents case studies of ideocratic mechanisms at work.[30] Some understanding of these psychological syndromes is integral to an adequate understanding of the social analysis that follows in subsequent chapters, for within the individual adaptations to evolving social circumstances the politics of ideocracy may be understood in dynamic perspective. We shall now turn to a more thorough analysis of ideocratic politics in action.

III

IDEOCRATIC FRAMEWORK OF POLITICS

In the study of any complex subject matter, it is necessary to conceptualize its component parts and clarify relationships among them. General schemes of this sort may be called *frameworks of analysis*. In this chapter we will construct such a framework for study of the ideocratic system, which will focus our attention upon the most important characteristics of this form of politics. Our framework for the study of ideocracy is composed of elements that apply to any political system:

1. The foundations of political legitimacy
2. The organization of political leadership
3. The relationship between the political system and other social organizations
4. The scope and nature of political involvement

These elements of the framework may be used to describe the organization of political life within society, by highlighting certain of its dimensions. We will explore these dimensions in reference to the ideocratic political system and, in the process, develop a simplified, ideal type model of ideocracy. However, no political system is perfectly organized in real life. Therefore, we will discuss various conditions that prevent the full realization of this model in actuality.

The Foundations of Legitimacy

What distinguishes ideocracy from other political systems is its monistic ideology, which provides a universal frame of reference upon which the legitimacy of the system rests. The reader is reminded that an ideology is an integrated set of assertions, theories, and aims, constituting a general program for the organization of social life. A monistic ideology is distinguished by the assumption that reality is one unitary, organic whole that has been brought into clear perspective by the ideology.

Such an ideology consists of the following components. First of all, it contains an interpretation of the historical drama, in which the forces of evil battle the forces of good. Further, it foresees an eventual victory for the forces of good, which will lead humanity to a spiritual or material utopia; for example, paradise or communism. But before this victory is achieved, there are numerous pitfalls and the requirement of great sacrifice. Were it not for the efforts of the ideologically dedicated, the forces of evil could temporarily triumph. Therefore, active involvement in the struggle is required of all the dedicated.

Basically, there are two ideocratic conceptions of history. One assumes a continuous linear progression toward the perfect, so that, although there are reverses and setbacks, the forces of good will ultimately triumph completely. In the other view, the conception of the utopian ideal (e.g., perfect social harmony) is just as clearly defined, but the vision does not include the certainty that it will be *permanently* achieved.[1] Periodically the society will approximate the ideal order, but then it may again regress under the assault of the forces of evil. Both types require sacrifice and a continuing struggle for perfection. What distinguishes these as differing types is their relative optimism concerning the possibility of enduring success. The more prevalent type in recent history is the more optimistic one envisioning an earthly utopia, because in this progressive age, it provides greater potential for mobilizing the masses.[2] The less optimistic form of monistic ideology was more generally appropriate in the premodern world, when the belief in general progressive change was not widespread.

Both types of ideocracy involve the belief that an entire society can and should be fully organized to achieve an ideologically prescribed order. In this, they differ from less optimistic ideologies that envision a perfect order but deny the possibility of fully organizing society to achieve that order. Sometimes such ideologies lead to despair—the ideal may be seen by an enlightened person, who is, however, powerless to change a corrupted world and has no hope for salvation. Somewhat more optimistic is that religious ideology which envisions an ideal heavenly salvation for pilgrims, who must prepare *themselves* for this afterlife, although they are still powerless to fundamentally alter worldly society, which is, to some degree, corrupted.[3] Above this level of optimism, various forms of ideocracy begin to appear. First, there is that ideology which conceives of small withdrawn communities that will approximate the ideal, set apart from a broader corrupt world. The adherents lack the capacity to change that generally corrupted social order, but, if left alone, they can perfectly order their own isolated communities. This is the less optimistic form of ideocracy found usually in rudimentary cults and religious communities. Then, there is the ideology that envisions political rule by those who are ideologically committed to a predominant worldly order, but who feel that only a limited elite may be part of their ideologically perfected system. They rule broader groups of people, but tolerate their nonadherence to the ideology so long as they are dominated by the elite and provide limited but necessary support to the elite. This variant of the less optimistic ideocracy is associated with some historical empires, such as ancient Egypt and imperial China.[4]

The more encompassing variant of ideocracy involves an ideologically justified rule that not only establishes and protects the ideologically sacred community but seeks to *extend* this community throughout all of society. All within this society must be converted, controlled, or eliminated, for the ideal order has to be achieved. In the more limited ideocracies, this ideal is bounded by time and space, whereas in the more sweeping form, universal and eternal perfection is expected. The following discussion will focus primarily upon the more developed form of ideocracy, as it is more dramatic and more timely for our age. The analysis, however, applies basically to *all* ideocracies, because their drive toward an ideologically comprehensive social order separates them from other kinds of political systems. In short, a monistic ideology contains a coherent and singular view of history— an interpretation of the past, the present and also a vision of a future ultimate perfection. What joins the past and the future is an ideological program of action, which is derived from historical interpretation and designed to achieve the future state of perfection. In this sense, the utopian prescription of the ideology and the program of action derived from it are essential parts of an ideological continuum of historical development.

The monistic ideology may be divided logically into two components: theory and doctrine.[5] Theory is the statement of broad principles that underlie the movement of the historical forces. Doctrine is a more specific set of prescriptions for action that derives from the theory and includes the programmatic means to bring about the utopian goals envisaged in the theory. Both theory and doctrine are integral to the framework of reference of the ideocratic decision makers, theory determining the general direction of the movement and its ultimate goal, doctrine providing tools for the achievement of that goal. Together they establish for the system and its authorities the ideological foundation of their legitimacy.

Within the bounds of the monistic ideology, then, are certain generally prescribed courses of action and other forms of action that are forbidden: the first, because they are seen to be consistent with the theory of historical movement; the second, because they are bound to be contrary to the logic of the Idea. Between them exits a realm of permissible action, which is problematic in relation to the general frame of reference. Action in this realm is acceptable either because of ideological uncertainty or because of historical compromises made by the ideocratic leadership.

All general ideologies contain such rules for action (doctrine) that establish constraints upon the decision maker in the choice among policy alternatives. Monistic ideology differs from other ideologies, in that its constraints are more specifically defined and more comprehensive, limiting the decision maker in a more inclusive way. First, these constraints derive from a singular view of reality; second, they cover all aspects of social life; and finally they include a sharp and absolute division between virtuous and deviant behav-

ior. This is not to say that decision makers have no
freedom of alternatives. Although they must operate
within the outer boundaries of the theoretical and doctrinal prescriptions, they retain substantial freedom
of choice within this framework. Still, there are things
they absolutely cannot do and those they must do.
Violation of such principles would undermine the legitimacy of the system and, if broadly undertaken, would
destroy it. The boundaries, however, are not absolutely
immobile. They are subject to continuous reinterpretation by those vested with the authority to do so. Yet,
at the same time, even this process of reinterpretation remains within a generally established set of ideological boundaries. The decision maker must respect
the weight of general social norms, which are derived
from previous socialization under the monistic ideology. To a degree, the system is locked into its own
movement, given its own previous experience and
sense of direction. In general, this path can be
changed only with considerable difficulty. Thus, the
decision makers of an ideocracy are as much the pris-
oners of the system as they are the makers of its destiny. Their personal motivations may, of course, vary
from total ideological commitment to an opportunistic
cynicism. Nevertheless, they must operate in all cases
within the general confines of the *public* ideological
belief system. To do otherwise would be to undermine
their own legitimacy and hence imperil their authority
to rule. One does not question whether the Pope
believes in God, unless the Church has lost its hold on
the faithful.

Of course, lower levels of doctrine may be manip-
ulated by decision makers to legitimize even radically
new courses of action. Much of the apparent flexibility
of ideocratic systems derives from such doctrinal

manipulation. However, in no case would this be in stark violation of the general theory—the fundamental principles of the ideology—unless the ideocratic system were coming to an end. While the ideocratic system continues, its general historical course must be maintained.[6]

In many ways the constraints imposed on the decision maker result from the socialization of the significant participants of the system, whereby they internalize the tenets of the monistic ideology. These tenets are expressed through a set of symbols that represent complex ideas of the theory in simpler form. Within the ideology are concepts that depict the forces and actors involved in the historical drama, concepts that portray utopian goals to be achieved, and constructs that distinguish the means for achieving these ideological goals.

Among the concepts concerned with historical actors and forces, are the following: (1) the forces of evil, the enemies of the system, that are personified by specific human groups (Jews, capitalists, blacks, infidels); (2) the positive masses, groups that may be in darkness and should be enlightened and guided (the people, the proletariat, the superior race, the faithful); (3) the elect, whose destiny is to lead and fulfill the commands of history (the Communist party, the Nazi party, the Church hierarchy, the Ulama-Islamic "clergy"—people versed in Islamic prescriptions). These various actors themselves may or may not be absolutely conscious of their particular roles. However, historical forces work through and with them, as part of the general historical process, identified within the ideology (the historical dialectic of Communism, the movement of history in fascism, the historical combat of good and evil in a religious ideocracy, followed by the judgment of God). Some actors are chosen by history to play a central role in the fulfillment of the movement's goals, and therefore they are more creative and more self-willed forces than others (Communists, Fascists, Nazis, Islamic fundamentalists).

Another group of ideas deal with the utopian goals to be achieved: (1) the utopian community (Communism, the thousand-year Reich, the glory of the Italian empire, the Islamic state); (2) the new person (the new socialist human, the pure Aryan, the pure white, black, yellow, or red; the pure Moslem); (3) the utopian social ideals (human freedom, perfect human progress, human salvation).

The doctrinal portion of the ideology focuses primarily on the means by which ultimate perfection is to be achieved. It will specify (1) the organization of the actors (the dictatorship of the proletariat, the Movement, auxiliary groups); (2) the means to destroy or conquer the enemy (revolution, war, terrorism, evangelism, propaganda); (3) the forms of temporary compromise (alliance, coexistence, acceptance of limited capitalism in socialist states and moderate Westernization in fundamentalist Islamic states); (4) the ways to construct the perfect society (direction of the economy, control over socialization, leadership of the Movement).

These various kinds of symbols, which are mental signals expressing complicated ideas, are used for communication between the decision makers, the implementors, and the mass audience. The decision makers issue directives by use of these symbols; hence, the implementation of their commands depends on the specific meanings these symbols have within the system. Drastic and precipitous changes in the ideology would disrupt meaning of the concepts used in this communication process, because the signals sent from the top would take on new meanings incomprehensible to the implementors. Just as the symbols are rooted in the ideology, the whole system of communication depends for its effectiveness on relatively constant reference to that ideology. To be sure, change in the interpretation of the ideology is possible, but this requires time, because the implementors must be retrained to understand the new meanings of the symbols. This process permits systemic changes over time but restricts the decision makers in their short-term choice of alternatives. In specific periods of extreme tension, the meanings of particular groups of symbols (especially doctrinal concepts) can and will be sacrificed for higher goals. Some symbols will change overnight, such as those defining strategy and tactics in those particular historical situations. Still, most of the symbolic structure of the ideology must remain intact. The implementors will be retrained subsequently to understand the new situation (e.g., with the announcement of the secret Soviet-Nazi Pact in 1939, a pact of cooperation between two mortal ideological enemies, the Soviet society had to be quickly indoctrinated to view the Western capitalism as the most threatening enemy at that time).

In summary, the monistic ideology provides the ideocratic system with a general sense of direction toward the achievement of ultimate perfection, as the culmination of the historical process. Further, the ideology provides legitimacy for the creation of political authority empowered to organize the society for the ideological struggle. The nature of this task requires the total mobilization of society and the elimination of all opposition to ideological development, including those human groups of conscious or historically determined opposition.

The Organization of Political Leadership

Most characteristic of all ideocracies is the existence of a single political movement (party or elect group) that is the center of all political power.[7] Because the movement is seen as the primary organizational vehicle for realizing the tenets of the monistic ideology, it must theoretically possess an absolute hegemony of political power. All other political (and social) organizations must either derive their functional purpose in relation to the movement or exist as illegitimate opponents of the system.

The movement itself includes only the most dedicated and ideologically committed elements of the society. Hence, the movement is not normally a mass organization in terms of its size: rather, it has a strictly elitist character. In some small religious ideocracies (church) membership extends to all the faithful, but still the core of the leadership remains elitist. In some other systems, when the general movement grows beyond its initial elitist core, a new elite core is created by the leadership.[8] Furthermore, the movement itself is usually divided into a strictly defined top leadership and a general membership. There is a tendency for the top leadership, in time, to be organized around one single dominant leader and a group of his lieutenants.

The Top Leader

The emergence of a top leader derives from the logic of monistic ideology. As argued earlier, such an ideology involves a unified view of reality. However, the actual conditions of historical reality change over time in unexpected ways. The ideology, therefore, must be continually reinterpreted, while preserving the integrity of its monistic image. For a large group of followers, the single preeminent leader is the most practical means of maintaining symbolic coherence in critical periods of ideological reinterpretation. For, if there were more than one permanent leader, and hence more than one potential source of interpretation, the monistic unity of the ideology would be destroyed, eventually creating competing ideocratic movements or one pluralistic system.[9] For example, as long as the top Soviet leader was automatically considered to be the leader of the international Communist movement, the ideological unity of that movement was preserved. The rise of other sources of Communist authority (e.g., in Yugoslavia and China) effectively destroyed this ideological uniformity. Still, a collective leadership (for example, two coleaders) can arise at times of succession. In this case, the leadership will most likely adopt a fairly conventional ideological position and even denounce the previous leader for his innovative interpretations.[10] As social problem-solving pressure mounts, increasing conflict within the collective leadership will lead either to the reemergence of one dominant leader or, as argued previously, to a dissolution of the system. The transition from collective to singular leadership was witnessed on six occasions in the Soviet Union, first in the succession from Lenin to Stalin, Stalin to Khrushchev, Khrushchev to Brezhnev, Brezhnev to Andropov, Andropov to Chernenko, and Chernenko to Gorbachev.[11]

The major functions of the top leader include authoritative interpretation of the ideology and commitment of political resources in the programmatic realization of ideological goals. As has been suggested, the top leader is the most general source for the authoritative interpretation of ideological theory and doctrine. All other analyses of reality must be consistent with, and derivative from, this source. Even analyses quite removed from ideology, such as those undertaken in science, will still seek justification in the pronouncements of the top leader and his ideological forbearers. For example, a book on budgets of the local administration in a communist country used to have, and still has in such countries as North Korea, a first chapter devoted to the link between the author's concepts and the pronouncements of Marx, Lenin, and the contemporary first secretary of the Communist party.[12] The same book in a fundamentalist Islamic state would have references to Quar'an and Shari'a, teaching of Muhammad, and in the case of Iran also to Khomeini.

The major commitment of political resources occurs within the top leadership of the party, which is the conversion point between policy formulation and policy implementation. In fact, the top leader, himself, is expected to make major policy decisions, arrived at in conformity with the ideology and in response to impulses sensed by him within the system. Those decisions become directives for implementation. Thus, the top leader combines in his person the roles of top legislator, executor, and adjudicator in the system. He is for all practical purposes above the law because he is the immediate source of law, but he is not above the ideology, which is the recognized source of all authority. This role, as the foremost interpreter of that ideology, leaves him some degree of freedom even there. However, the ideological constraints discussed earlier impose fundamental limitations on him and permit him only piecemeal alteration of the doctrine and even less revision of the theory at any one time. Many of the basic tenets must not be violated, even by him.[13]

The Top Leader and His Lieutenants

The group of lieutenants surrounding the top leader provides a link between him and the lower levels of authority in the system. As representatives of the leader's authority, they direct major organizational elements of the system, such as the movement (party) and the various sectors of state administration. They form, as it were, the cabinet of the top leader. Many of his decisions are based on information supplied by them and on their advice. To some degree, they can be compared with influential members of the American president's cabinet, in combination with his personal staff of advisors. They have considerable power derived from their control of the organizations under their directorship and from their critical position in the topmost decision-making processes. For example, they are in some command of patronage, because they exact a degree of control over appointments in their specific administrative sectors. These appointments are made both on their own authority or on the basis of their advice to the top leader. Their manipulation of this patronage permits them to build their own factions, which they can utilize for the aggrandizement of their own personal power. In specific circumstances, they can even limit the authority of the top leader. In most instances, this power is expressed by a subtle bargaining relationship with the top leader, in which the lieutenants try to obtain more allocation for their own sectors or to diminish the influence of other contenders for power. The question of succession to the top leadership is always prominent in the minds of the actors, perhaps because the system does not really provide an institution for this process. In an extreme situation, a cabal of lieutenants may depose the top leader (e.g., Nikita Khrushchev in the Soviet Union in 1964, Ahmad Hasan al-Bakr in Iraq in 1979).[14] On the other hand, the very authority of the lieutenants is delegated to them by the top leader. At any time, this trust may be withdrawn. Aware of the possibility of their challenge, the leader attempts to balance the power of his lieutenants against each other. Also, the status of the top leader is normally foremost within the group, so that cabals are not often likely. Unlike the case in pluralistic systems, ideocracy lacks legitimate independent bases of power on which the lieutenants' opposition could be founded.[15]

The Leader and the Movement's Organization

The movement's organization is the primary vehicle of political control. It normally consists of the supreme leader, his lieutenants, other paid functionaries in the movement's hierarchy and the general membership. Typically the organization of the movement is divided into national, territorial, and local levels in large ideocracies. Below the supreme leader and his lieutenants, functionaries staff the central, provincial, and local offices of the movement. The central offices are typically organized as a secretariat, or office of the president, which is the executive branch of the supreme leader. The major work of the secretariat is directed by a few lieutenants who provide the links between this body and the supreme leader. The departments of the secretariat are divided into two functional categories: those dealing with the affairs of the movement (e.g., finances, membership, propaganda) and those involving supervision of the state administration (e.g., economics, public security, defense, foreign affairs). The dominance of the single, exclusive movement over the units of government organizationally distinguishes the ideocratic government from that of a pluralist system. Most of these departments have offices at the territorial and local levels. The organization of these units is led by one foremost leader, supported by an executive committee and an executive office. In appearance, the local organization is a copy of the national level, with the local leader, his or her lieutenants and lesser functionaries staffing the executive office. The similarity is only structural, however, because the power of the local leader is more circumscribed. For one thing, his or her authority derives from the supreme leader, and further, many of the local lieutenants have direct functional or personal ties to the lieutenants of the supreme leader. Like the central bodies of the movement, the local leadership not only administers the work of the movement, but also supervises the performance of the local state administration.[16]

Ordinary members form the cells of primary organization and are constituted either in geographic locations (a village, a city block) or in places of employment (a factory, an office, a large farm). The cell is led by the leader who takes directives from the higher party leadership. Only the functionaries of the movement are paid officials, and they compose a small percentage of the total membership. Most of the work performed by the movement is done by unpaid voluntary members.

In addition to the administrative structure of the movement, there are, at each level, assemblies composed of delegates from lower levels of the movement's organization. Thus, the primary cells send delegates to the territorial assembly, which in turn send representatives to the national assembly. These assemblies are granted formal legislative power in terms of movement's rules and programs. However, in practice, they are used as symbolic bodies, which in no way can reverse the policies of the top leadership. They provide enthusiastic support for programs announced by the leadership before them, and they project an image of absolute unity. The delegates are typically lower level leaders and other luminaries, plus a sprinkling of the "common folk." Nomination for this membership signifies an honor bestowed on an individual by the movement.[17]

The overall organization of the movement is designed to perform the following political functions: (1) to organize all political participation, (2) to formulate all political programs, and (3) to control the use of all political power.

The organization of political participation is limited to activity in the movement itself and in other specified structures (state and social) subject to strict control by the movement.[18] The movement is the central vehicle for the transmission of political directives. It is also the most important upward channel of information on the performance of the system and the attitudes of the population. Thus, the capacity to affect the flow of information is one of the primary ways by which the membership and, even more, the movement's lower leadership influences top level political decisions (another being their impact on policy implementation). All information in its progression through the communication system is subject to selective transmission, which gradually narrows its scope and meaning.[19] The party members at all levels can and do manipulate the information to their specific advantage. They attempt to promote thereby the interests with which they are identified—interests associated with personal status, locality, profession, production unit, and so forth.[20] As already discussed, all political programs are theoretically formulated by the supreme leader or by leaders on lower levels in regard to specific programs within their authority. In fact, no leaders make decisions in a vacuum. Indeed, they rely on the information supplied to them in the upward channels of communication. Further, they consult with their lieutenants and specific technical advisors, either individually or in council. Finally, they may call for additional information or even specific advice from the lower levels of the movement and other organizations.

The process of policy formulation is also affected by problems associated with policy implementation. As already stated, the movement exerts dominant authority over government and other agencies of political control. It does so as an extension of the authority of the supreme leader. Of course, all programs originating from the supreme leader are entrusted to the state and other organizations for implementation. Therefore, constant supervision must be exercised by the movement to ensure proper implementation of the programs. Ultimately, the aim of this control is to maintain consistency between policy implementation and the theoretical and doctrinal principles of the ideology (as interpreted by the supreme leaders). However, such oversight is not fully effective. Those who implement policies make decisions regarding the relative emphasis to be given a particular policy and the means by which it is implemented. In some cases, even noncompliance is an option. The implementors thus wield some power of their own in this process. They can consciously obstruct the implementation if they regard the original policy as mistaken. To protect themselves against the accusation of sabotage, they will present technical arguments. Yet, often there is a close relationship between these arguments and the doctrinal aspects of the ideology. Thus, technical positions can be used for political effect, but also on occasion they may be dangerous for their proponents. Ideological conformity remains a continuing concern for the ideocratic movement.[21]

The Movement and the State

All units of governmental administration are brought into one centralized and unified system. All formal autonomy is eliminated or restricted by the control of central ministries. This centralized state organization is in turn controlled by the movement (party), which staffs most of the state executive positions with its own members. The movement reserves to itself veto power over appointments to all vital staff positions within state administrative bodies. Above certain levels, nobody can be promoted without the formal and specific approval by the movement (in the communist ideocracies the list of these positions is called *nomenclature*). Further, the movement can reverse all decisions of the state administration, because the movement is seen as the central vehicle of ultimate political authority.[22]

With the growth of technology, the modern state administration increases in importance within the system and develops a certain degree of independence from strict control by the movement. This is simply the result of the growing complexity of problems to be solved and the technological sophistication of specialized knowledge necessary to deal with them. The state administrator must become more and more the technical expert. In the face of this specialization, most of the movement's leaders and functionaries who are initially generalists (e.g., old revolutionaries, ideologues) must rely on the opinions of the experts. Gradually, even among movement's members, two distinct groups develop with fundamentally different orientations: one the generalist wing, the other what may be called the *techno movement*. This leads to an oscillation in movement's platforms between pragmatic-technological positions and more general ideological ones. It also influences the implementation of movement's policies by the state, with the state specialists often taking a more pragmatic-technological stand in opposition to what seems to them unrealistic idealism. To the degree that pragmatic-technological standards gain autonomous recognition, the monistic ideology is undermined and the system takes on a proto-pluralistic character.[23]

The Penetration of
Political and Social Organizations

The ideocratic perspective envisions an organic social community in which all spheres of social action—political, economic, cultural, and even ethical—make up an integrated whole. Hence, all the organizational elements of the community must be integrated within the ideological program of development. In the final ideal society, these organizational elements must be brought into a state of perfect harmony. Toward this purpose, it is essential for the political leadership to dominate the development of all social organizations. Not only must these organizations be prevented from interfering with ideological programs, but further they must contribute to ideocratic development. In ideocracy no sphere of human life is apolitical.

In practical terms, such dominance requires that political control penetrate all social organization. In other words, the internal decision makers of social organizations must be sufficiently indoctrinated that they *choose* to pursue goals set by the political leadership. Even more they must play their assigned roles in the general program of ideocratic development. The means of political penetration take the following general forms: (1) administrative controls, (2) economic devices, and (3) social controls.

Administrative controls constitute, first of all, the elimination of those organizations that, for political or social reasons, cannot be incorporated into the system (e.g., oppositional political parties, dissident religious organizations, uncooperative elements of the mass media, army, and police).[24] Those that *are* brought into the system are constricted, modified, or expanded, depending on their usefulness to the ideocracy. Their leadership is purged and infiltrated by movement members, who are designated by the movement to direct their work. Conglomerate organizations are created with a monopoly in their particular sphere of action, which on the one hand, ensures their dominant position in that sphere, but on the other hand, permits easier control of them by the political system. In some cases, this monopoly is enforced by the allocation to the conglomerate organization of some of the administrative functions of the state, such as, for example, licensing. (Thus a craft association issues licenses to practice the craft. This is also true of all professionals and artists. Only those who are members and who are licensed can engage in a given craft, profession, or art.) The performance of these organizations is constantly monitored by the movement in regard to their achievement of the goals assigned to them within the movement's program. First of all, they have their own special functions resulting from their character (e.g., trade unions involve the organization of workers and some degree of control over productivity and working conditions). Second, they engage in transmission of the movement's programmatic goals to those portions of the general public with which they are associated. Finally, they indoctrinate their own membership in the official ideology. The movement has special departments to monitor these activities, and they develop techniques of assessment (e.g., statistical measures, scrutiny of the minutes of the meetings, interviews with selected personnel).

The economic devices of control involve criteria for the allocation of funds from the state budget for organizational programs, including the remuneration of leaders and functionaries. Thus, both financial support for the organization's activity and economic benefits for its members depend on the performance of the organization as judged by the movement. Organizations throughout the society gain their allocation of resources from the state. This allows the state to use general economic plans as a means of controlling general social development. To a substantial degree, investment in preferred areas of development is expressed in state budgets. Likewise, areas that are downgraded in importance are allocated fewer funds, and their personnel are transferred to other jobs. Such economic tools offer a powerful means of controlling social and political development (because, for example, among other powers, they determine personal careers and incomes of individuals).

Social controls include the allocation of various privileges and penalties to leaders and lesser members of social organizations. The leaders of successful organizations are brought to the central council of the movement and may even become lieutenants of the supreme leader. The members of the organization may receive group recognition at political rallies and parades, special feast-days (the Day of Trade Unions, Youth Day, Women's Day, Teachers' Day), medals, badges, blessings, uniforms, and standards. Groups engage in competition in particular tasks and the winners are given wide public acclaim. Hence, organizational performance is linked to the status of individuals and groups within the ideocratic system. This may give an appearance of pluralism, but in fact it is highly controlled and orchestrated.

Control by the movement, although extensive, is not all inclusive. The political organization of the movement overlays preexisting social organization. The traditional patterns of activity may be only partially consistent with the dominant ideology. On the one hand, the political leadership must build upon the traditional patterns, but on the other, it will attempt to change many of these over time. To some degree, even the ideology itself will reflect traditional cultural patterns in the society (e.g., militarism, nationalism, authoritarianism, religiousness). All of these conditions make absolute ideological control impossible, and so compromise between the new and old will emerge in various organizational sectors of the society (e.g., a compromise with traditional religious congregations in ostensibly secular ideocracies, such as that made during thirty-three of the forty-two years of Communist rule in Poland;[25] or alternatively, accom-

modation in religious ideocracy with nonreligious organizations within, as in the Islamic Republic of Iran).

Old, as well as new organizations will maintain
and develop their own interests, which are rationalized
to include goals consistent with ideological doctrine
(e.g., the commercial interest of the bazaar-market-
place in Iran).[26] Often these goals will not be in complete accord with the program of the movement. It has
been suggested by some authors that, over time, these
groups become the equivalent of pluralistic interest
groups.[27] The difficulty with this assumption is that
pluralistic interest group theory views most interest
groups as reflecting private interests that are politically independent from the government. The politically
active organizations in ideocracy cannot claim such
independence, because they are subordinate agents
of the political leadership. They cannot openly challenge the political leadership. They can manipulate
the leadership only covertly from within the system
(e.g., by transmission of biased information and influ-
encing the implementation of policy). They are comparable to the so-called agency (official) interest groups
in pluralistic systems, although they lack much of the
autonomy often accorded even governmental agencies
in these polities.[28]

Finally, some organizations survive that are not
penetrated to any great extent by ideocratic control.
They may be called *islands of separateness.*[29] Their
survival results from their strong traditional roots
within the community (e.g., church, family, ethnic
organization). Ideocratic leaders may not feel immediately strong enough, or may not be determined
enough, to bring them under their full control.
However, the assumption is that, in time, they also
will merge within the ideal organic society, both

through physical pressure (coercion) and through education of the "new person." For the time being ideocratic leaders have to bargain with them, exchanging a
degree of tolerance for a degree of support (e.g., both
Nazi Germany and the Polish Communists with the
Catholic Church). These organizations approximate
more closely the status of private interest groups:
although they do not have formal political legitimacy
within the system, they, in fact, maintain independence in their own limited spheres and thus are capable of exerting external political influence upon the
political leadership. Within a few areas of social life,
then, there remain real interest groups, so long as the
government does not feel strong enough to destroy
them.

The Nature and Scope of Political Involvement: Total Mobilization

The ideocratic program calls for total mobilization
of society in pursuit of utopian ideals. Because the
ideocratic vision of reality consists of a continuing historical drama in which the forces of good battle the
forces of evil, ideocracy must assign roles to its members within this eternal struggle. Individuals must be
enlisted in ongoing battle, but additionally, they must
be transformed into perfect members of the future
utopian community. These individuals are soldiers for
the Idea, but further they must reeducate themselves
in the teachings of the Idea. Both of these purposes
are to be accomplished through total mobilization,
which enlists action, changes attitudes, and regener-
ates personality.

Many forms of indoctrination are used within the
ideocratic system; all of them aim at properly socializ-

ing the participants. In this setting, political socialization provides individuals with a general set of political attitudes, beliefs, values, and behavioral patterns,
which are related to the tenets of the monistic ideology, tenets that require their total mobilization.[30] Three
groups of techniques are common to the process of
ideocratic political socialization: (1) persuasion, (2) participant activity, and (3) coercion.

The whole educational system from grade school
through higher education is enlisted in the service of
ideocracy. In those historical situations in which the
educational system is limited, ideocratic politics
requires spectacular educational expansion (as in
Cuba, China, Syria, and Iraq). The selection of teachers and other educational personnel is undertaken
with considerable care that candidates reflect the
proper ideological zeal and social consciousness. It
goes without saying that unreconstructed members
of the old staff are weeded out. The same process is
applied to all textbooks, which are rewritten in conformity with the tenets of the ideology and further
rewritten following changes of ideological doctrine or
purges of leading political figures (e.g., the burning of
books in Nazi Germany, the change of textbooks in
all schools in the Soviet-type communist states after
the succession of a new leader, or the purge of many
Western books in Iran after the Islamic Revolution).
Even purely scientific literature is subject to these ideological constraints. Many authors and subjects are
put on an index and their literature may be confined
to the closed sections of the libraries.

The purpose of education is twofold: technical
preparation for functional performance within the
society and ideological training for political socialization. The progress of students in both areas deter-

mines their educational standing within the system. The movement itself is intensively involved in the educational process through its directives, in the active participation of its personnel (cells in educational institutions), and through the movement's youth organization. Again, like other social organizations, all educational institutions participate in competition and are rewarded according to their performance.[31]

In technologically developed societies, the media of communications become major vehicles of socialization, and the movement assumes an absolute monopoly of control over all their operation. In less developed societies, religious sermons may play the same role (e.g., Friday prayer meetings in Islamic fundamentalism). The media indoctrinate the mass public in the ideology through political programs (speeches, discussions, plays), and through the selective interpretation of the news. The political reliability of the media is ensured through strict censorship by the movement. Nor do the arts escape political control. The movement develops ideologically consistent standards governing the form, as well as, the content of all artistic expression (literature, painting, sculpture, music, theater, movies). Those artists who comply with the ideocratic standards (Aryan art, socialist realism)[32] are cultivated and rewarded; those who do not are repressed and ultimately denied the right to practice their art.[33]

The nature of the ideocratic ideal requires that members of the society not only become convinced of the rightness of the ideological principles, but further that they actively participate in building a new society based on these principles. Hence, it is a goal of ideocracy to involve a great mass of citizens in political action through a wide variety of mass organizations.

Widespread mass participation is a striking characteristic of ideocracy. It is important to recognize that such mass participation is a central *means* of ideological socialization as well as an ideological end in itself. Through participation, individuals come to identify with the system for which they are acting. Also, they are seen as agents of the system by other members, thus encouraging a "bandwagon" process of recruitment.[34]

There are three kinds of individual participation in regard to their relative location within the power structure of the system: membership in the movement, membership in mass organizations, and participation in spontaneous action. First, members of the movement are the spearhead, breaking through the lines of resistance and leading the way for other portions of the system. These people are normally conceived to be the most committed and dedicated adherents to the goals of the ideology. Second, the members of mass organizations are seen as builders of the new community in their respective spheres of social construction. Their work requires more patient and less dramatic dedication to the central ideological goals. Theirs is not the heroic task of path finding, but the consistent nurturing of social development. Finally, spontaneous action of the masses allows them also to participate in the total drama. In specific instances, their task is to root out deviants, spur on lagging elements, and generally regenerate the sense of purpose within the system. Usually, their spontaneity is covertly organized and controlled by the leadership. For example, actions may be taken to attack scapegoats who are seen to personify the forces of evil. And thus, following the 1979 fundamentalist revolution, the American Embassy in Teheran was repeatedly subjected to mass demonstrations. Eventually, it was occupied and its staff members were taken hostage, with highly symbolic meaning for the revolution. Alternatively, an urban population may be mobilized to help with the harvest when agriculture lags behind, as with the sugar cane campaigns in Cuba. Likewise, youth may be activated to revive the ideological commitment of the movement when portions of its leadership are viewed as losing their revolutionary zeal, as in the Great Proletarian Cultural Revolution in China (1966-1970). All these actions involve a dramatic departure from ordinary life for the participants, and they create a strong sense of involvement in the major events of history.

The purity of the system and the dedication of its members are also enhanced through the application of coercion. Coercion takes many forms. Here we would identify economic, social, and physical pressure. The system of ideocracy includes political control of the economy, and hence the political leaders of the system determine the economic well-being of its members. They control, directly or indirectly, all employment of, and career possibilities for, the people. They also have the ability to deny educational opportunities at all levels. This power is used to compel the people to submit to the requirements of the ideocratic state. The reader must recognize that the loss of a job or career opportunity is an extreme sanction against the individual in such a system. The more technologically advanced an ideocracy, the more it may rely upon economic coercion for the manipulation of its members. As career opportunities become greater, economic sanctions become more effective, especially because they can be applied against the members of one's family as well (e.g., one's children).

As ideological mobilization spreads through the society, social censure becomes a more important tool of socialization. To be different is to be indecent. Thus, the process of socialization becomes self-generating. The more closely a society approaches the total mobilization of its members, the more difficult it becomes for the skeptical individual to resist social demands for conformity. Individuality in all social groups is somewhat suspect because it brings into question the norms of the group. Submission of the individual in the group is almost total in mass action.[35] In ideocracy, these norms are held to be absolute and all inclusive. Hence, any defiance of specific ideocratic norms brings into question the entire way of life.

From the very beginning of an ideocratic system, the committed portions of the society accept the justification of physical coercion as a form of socialization. Many theorists argue that destructive terror is one of the most important characteristics of what they choose to call *totalitarian systems*.[36] Such physical coercion can be both a method for destroying enemies of ideocracy and a means of socializing members of the system. Yet, terror is seldom used for the sake of terror alone. It is more often designed to accomplish the following purposes: removal of irreconcilable opponents, definition of the limits of permissible criticism, creation of a prophylactic atmosphere of fear, and identification and isolation of symbolic enemies.[37]

In the initial stages of an ideocratic system, immediately after a revolution or takeover, the society has large groups of clearly identifiable opponents. Although many efforts will be devoted to the reeducation of these groups, some of their elements (e.g., their leadership) will be isolated or destroyed. The intensity of physical terror will be great and the brutality of the regime quite pronounced. The scope of physical terror is closely related to the intensity of the struggle through which the system has been established. In some circumstances, such as when there is a more evolutionary emergence of ideocracy, banishment will be more evident than physical terror (as in Fascist Italy). The gradual destruction of opposition leads to the decline of overt physical terror and an increase in the use of other methods of coercion. Mature ideocracies are characterized by a low level of terroristic activity.

All political systems must permit some internal criticism to effectively meet emerging problems. Ideocracies are no exception, as the preceding discussion has suggested. However, criticism is not allowed to overstep the bounds of ideological conformity—it must be restricted to technical and limited doctrinal matters. These boundaries, although quite distinct in general terms, are not clearly defined in many specific instances. Here, the role of the terroristic organization (political police) is to prevent individuals from committing ideological heresy. The methods of terror vary from a friendly visit by police functionaries to nightly interrogations and short periods of detention. These methods are designed to warn individuals and bring them back into the fold, rather than to destroy them as an incorrigible. Like preventative medicine, this terror is designed to prevent the spread of ideological disease.[38]

Terror performs a more general social function, as well. The very existence of a terroristic organization, with its widespread network of secret agents (ordinary citizens recruited for this job), creates a general atmosphere of fear. This has a prophylactic impact on the society in two ways: first, it stimulates the self-discipline of citizens, preventing them from overt acts against the regime (e.g., private criticism of the leaders); second, it makes the individual more receptive to indoctrination. Individuals seldom admit that they act out of fear. When, in fact, they do, they are psychologically prone to assume that they act from more positive motives, such as belief in the tenets of the ideology.[39]

The ideocratic concept of reality includes the forces of good and the forces of evil. For total mobilization, the forces of evil must be identified in physical terms. Therefore, ideocracy selects a scapegoat, which is the personification of evil: usually a distinct minority group of people within the society, defined in terms of such categories as race, religion, or social class, or an external group, such as a nation or a group of nations.

From this perspective, the application of terror to scapegoats is designed to socialize those who wield it and those who witness, and often applaud, its use. It reinforces their identification with the system by allowing them to participate, even vicariously, in the dramatic struggle against the forces of evil.[40]

The Major Components of Ideocracy

The major characteristic of the modern ideocratic polity is its monistic ideology. This ideology contains an interpretation of historical drama that distinguishes a continuum of development from the past, through the present, and into the future, envisioning a goal of ultimate perfection. This theory of universal progression is made concrete through a doctrinal program of political action, prescribing a set of tactical and strategic means and identifying the characteristics of the enemy. It contains clusters of fundamental symbols: terms defining the enemies, the positive masses, and the destined leaders of the movement, who in their action provide the means of alerting and mobilizing the faithful. The utopian goals of ideocracy include a vision of the perfect community, a conception of the reborn human, and a conceptual scheme harmoniously linking the individual with the community and the universe. This ideal vision suggests the appropriate means for organizing the actors of the drama to destroy the enemy and construct the perfect society. The monistic character of the ideology determines the general organization of the polity as a pyramidal hierarchy with, at the apex, a single dominant leader and his lieutenants, and a descending order of power through a movement constituting a dedicated ideological elite. This hierarchy is extended downward through various layers of organization to the local level of social life. Its web of control is likewise spread outward to cover all governmental units and most other social organizations. Indeed, the intent of the leaders is to penetrate all major social organizations, to control these, and to use them in the ideological struggle. The struggle, however, must be carried on the individual level as well. Mobilization of all the members of society is attempted through an extensive effort at mass political socialization, ranging from reorganization of the educational system, through control over all mass communications, through the development of widespread participant activity, and finally to various forms of economic, social, and physical coercion.

In effect, the social system is dominated by one embracing political organization, legitimized by an absolute ideology, and guided by an omnipotent leadership. All realms of social organization have been

penetrated and reconciled with the ideological program; all participants have been mobilized in the
struggle to achieve the utopian vision. This ideal
model, of course, overstates the degree to which the
ideocratic system is totally organized. Analysis of the
dynamics of ideocratic development (Chapter IV) and
evolution (Chapters V and VI) will balance this exaggerated model. The model is useful, however, because
it identifies characteristics that set ideocracy apart
from pluralistic political systems and it expresses the
essential thrust of the ideocratic vision—a vision that
incorporates this perspective: "In the last analysis, the
battle between the forces of good and the forces of evil
is an all embracing battle for the minds of men."[41]

IV

CAUSES OF IDEOCRACY

In searching for the causes of ideocracy, it is necessary to distinguish the factors that produce the breakdown of a prior social and political system.[1] Following such a breakdown, ideocracy may emerge as the result of a new constellation of social and political forces. In this chapter, we shall examine first the social institutions that normally maintain stability, second the conditions that challenge this equilibrium, and third the processes that lead to the breakdown of the political system. Against this backdrop, it will be possible to consider the emergence of new political forces that create ideocracy.

Stability

The analysis of the previous chapter involves the assumption that all social systems contain a complex network of social controls. Because the interaction of individuals and groups often produces social conflict, a stable society develops social customs that moderate much of this discord (e.g., good manners require politeness even to those whom we dislike). Further, authoritative institutions develop for the resolution of more serious conflict (e.g., the intervention of government in some kinds of private disputes). In more technical terms, adequate social organization includes the following types of social control: (1) social integration, (2) socialization, (3) regulation, (4) mobilization, and (5) repression.

Social Integration, in this context, involves the spontaneous adjustment of individuals and groups in the process of daily life.[2] For example, many potential conflicts are avoided because the parties involved realize that the struggle would be equally debilitating to both sides.[3] As classical economists realized, much social adjustment may be based on rational self-interest of the involved parties. Such a general realization often leads to the emergence of customary social norms (e.g., shaking the right hand to show that it does not contain a weapon), which all participants are expected to respect. Through *socialization*, these norms are inculcated in the members of the social system. This involves a variety of means—family upbringing, formal education, peer group pressure, and the influence of the mass media. Individuals are taught to respect particular social customs of interaction. The enforcement of these norms is often accomplished through the private action of individuals and groups. Organizations, as well as individuals, undertake activities that involve mutual adjustments to adapt to changing circumstances in socially acceptable ways.

Social control is also achieved through more formal means of action. For example, *authoritative regulation* may be seen as the use of specially designated social organizations, which are formally responsible to see that rules are uniformly obeyed (e.g., use of police to enforce the rules of the road). Social organizations are likewise affected by authoritative regulation, which restricts their activities to within acceptable limits. The legal system is the central institutional structure designed to maintain such regulation. Some social goals require more positive action. The *social mobilization* of new efforts by groups of individuals may be realized through the initiatives of leadership. Therefore, groups of individuals are mobilized for specific social purposes, as with major community projects or in defense of the nation.

In all societies, however, some individuals and groups will be intent on the violation of important social norms and authoritative regulations. Their deviant activities are often met with authoritative sanctions aimed at *repression*. These sanctions vary in severity from small fines through intermediate forms of punishment, such as social exclusion (prison), and finally reach the extreme of capital punishment. Repression, as a mode of social control, is needed only where other forms have failed. Societies usually develop a complex mix of all these forms of social control, with formal controls complementing the more informal social mechanisms. To an important extent, then, social control is ingrained within the participants of social system; thus, coercive repression is necessary only in the exceptional situation.

In a pluralist political system, the government plays a delimited role in maintaining social stability, because it coexists with a host of other social institutions that also contribute to social equilibrium. To be sure, the government takes the lead in those areas of social control that involve political action in the spheres of regulation, mobilization, and repression. But its activities in these spheres complement those of other social and economic organizations, whose mutual adjustments help to maintain the integration of the social system as it adapts to changing circumstances. Moreover, the very legitimacy of the political

system is rooted in the beliefs individuals are socialized to hold. The leadership of the political system,
therefore, participates with leaders of other organizations in meeting new challenges and does so in the
context of widely held social beliefs.

All social systems experience some evolution in
their activities and beliefs. These alterations create
disturbances in the network of social control. However,
in normal circumstances, they are met by processes of
social adjustment. These adjustments renew the network of social control by integrating new patterns of
activity with the existing social structure. In some
cases, the process is gradual and not particularly disruptive, although often producing substantial change
over time. In other instances, the disturbance is more
intense, impairing social control within a limited and
specific area of social activity, over a particular period
of time (e.g., as in the adjustment of the communities
in a geographic area to the departure of the major
industry). Systems vary in their ability to cope with
such change, but in all systems there exist some
thresholds of disturbance beyond which the normal
patterns of social adjustment fail and widespread
social disruption results. In this context, *severe social
disruption* is defined as a widespread breakdown of
social control that affects a relatively large portion of
the population and undermines the effectiveness of
some of the major societal institutions.[4] For example,
the American Civil War brought formal legal equality
for blacks in the South; however, the enforcement of
this equality by the North was exceedingly difficult to
implement, because it involved severe social disruption
of traditional social control in the white South.
Eventually, the reassertion of white social control
brought quick repression of virtually all those activities

that were based on the premise of racial equality. Often, significant social disruption will linger for some time in a society that continues to function, but its presence substantially increases the potential for the cumulative spread of social disruption, which may result in a general breakdown of social control, that is, a systemic breakdown.[5] Such cumulative disruption is often catalyzed by war, rapid economic change, or a general social realignment.[6]

Types of Social Disruption

We have been arguing that serious disturbances, which are not adequately met by social adjustment, may lead to social disruption. What are these disturbances, and what kinds of social disruption may they produce?

Most patterns of social disruption are rooted in gradual historical change, often extending for years or even centuries. For analytical purposes, we can distinguish four types of such historical change: demographic, technological, economic, and environmental, even though they typically interact with each other.[7] Some of these processes are limited to the affected societies themselves, whereas others take place in the broader regional or even global context. They effect changes in the fundamental conditions of social life, thus altering the existing patterns of social activity and thought. In the process, traditional norms and values may lose their relevance given the new environment and the new conditions the society faces.

Such instability is often the result of demographic changes. These can involve a general growth of the population,[8] which, although unremarkable for sometime, eventually outpaces the sustaining capability of a country at its traditional level of technology and trade.

The typical example here has been China. For centuries, the empire was relatively free from external or internal war, well-governed, and with sophisticated medical and culinary skills. Under these conditions, the population grew steadily, and by the nineteenth century it had exploded beyond the political or economic capacity of the country. Today over 1 billion Chinese people, or one fourth of the humanity, lives on the territory roughly equivalent to that of the United States. However, only about 15 percent of Chinese land is suitable for agricultural use. Even now China is adding 20 million to its population every year. This overpopulation continues to be a grave concern of Chinese government. It will likely persist in the future whatever political system develops in that country.[9] A general decline in population can be equally disturbing to the established social patterns. There are historical examples of communities or even whole nations devastated by an epidemic (black death). Uganda fits the bill in the 1990s. Ravaged by war and an AIDS epidemic, the country has many families headed by youths of fourteen or even younger. Population also can change in its age composition, either becoming younger or older. Younger people are generally more daring, vigorous physically, less reflective, and more open to radical change.[10] A large number of old people, unable to work, places a burden on declining numbers of working-age cohorts. Generally, with economic diversification, there are population shifts from rural to urban centers, creating new tastes and values. All of these demographic changes can create disruption in the prior social order.

When considering technological change, we normally assume that it accompanies social progress to a level of higher material wealth. In fact, societies can also decline technologically, as European society did after the disintegration of the Roman Empire during the fifth century A.D. Technological advancement can be centered in the means of production (better tools, better machinery, or even better organization). It can be in the system of distribution through changes in transportation and communication, involving not only goods, but also information. And it can occur in the production of new goods. A critical element in technological development is often the creation or acquisition of new weapons that can be used by a society. Technological development may be balanced, generally improving the conditions of life in the society, or unbalanced in that only a narrow sector of technology develops. Many contemporary Third World societies have incorporated the technology of modern weapons without similar technological advancement elsewhere in the society. In many circumstances this has led to much more extensive bloodshed than would have been true with weapons matching their general levels of technological development (e.g., civil wars in Angola, Mozambique, Kampuchea and many others). Many communist and ex-communist countries, provide further examples of unbalanced growth. Building their industries, they typically have neglected to develop their transportation and communication networks. The result has been the inability to move the goods produced and a failure of communications within market channels. Different regions of the world may be affected differently by changing global technologies. For example, the invention of a combustion engine eventually created a great opportunity for the oil-producing nations. Equally, wide use of the electrical car could devastate them economically, socially, and politically.

Of all the evolutionary changes that affect society, economic change is most widespread and noticeable.[11] Sustained economic growth is considered by many political scientists to be the necessary foundation for a stable society.[12] But even such continuous growth has its disruptive effects, partially because its rate is seldom the same in all parts of a country, a region, or the world. Some areas grow faster, while others stagnate or even decline. For example, in the twentieth century Northern Italy generally has prospered while poverty persisted in the South. In most communist countries, industries expanded rapidly while their agricultural sectors declined.

Slow economic decline is usually unnoticed initially, as the standard of living of the population only deteriorates gradually. Eventually this creates general frustration and dissatisfaction with the system (e.g. to some degree we are experiencing this today, in the United States, with our minimal growth). Since, as Marx stated: "Man must eat to live," the performance of the economy has a profound impact on all societies.

Many kinds of change in the natural environment may affect the stability of a country. This may result from a change of climate, often over a long period, which would obviously influence agricultural, but also practically all other aspects of human life (e.g., clothing or transportation). During the period of Roman Empire, North Africa was the bread basket of Italy. Now large part of this area is the Sahara Desert. Pollution caused by humans plays a destructive role, damaging, sometimes permanently, the fragile ecological balance of an area (e.g., in Poland 95 percent of all surface water is unfit for human consumption and 42 percent is not even suitable for industrial use).[13] Natural disasters, such as hurricanes, floods, and volcanic eruptions, spectacular during their occurrences, often have a long-term ecological impact. They are likely to lead to changes in the affected societies.

Against this backdrop of historical change, various mechanisms of social control allow societies to adapt, while maintaining their stability. Different social organizations adjust to meet the new environmental challenges; new generations are socialized to cope with evolving technologies; governments mobilize societies to overcome depressions. But sometimes, there are basic flaws in the mechanisms of social control themselves. In the sphere of social integration, new groups may emerge with novel interests and demands, and this may effect a realignment in the relationships of older groups as they react to the new situation. This disturbance may result in social disruption when particular social groups, new and old, lose confidence in the existing modes of social accommodation, some groups because they intend to challenge the system and others because they do not trust the system to provide a necessary level of security from such challenges. At the extreme, a society splits into two polar groups—radical and conservative.[14]

The process of socialization is subject to disturbance when the norms of complex social systems become incompatible with the experience of a prominent group (e.g., a new generation). In some circumstances, latent inconsistencies in the structure of norms provide the basis for group conflict. These inconsistencies are of two types: structural and categoric. Structural inconsistencies result from the conflict between norms of *different portions* of the social order, such as the family, school, business, and government. These inconsistencies force individuals to adjust to the demands of conflicting norms in different parts of their lives. For example, ideals taught in school may be in serious conflict with those required in business. Categoric inconsistencies originate from the conflicting views of *different groups* with contrasting characteristics, as for example different economic classes or different religious, age, and racial groups. The recognition of structural inconsistencies often brings together diverse categories of individuals and unites them in common intellectual cause. Highly diverse student protest groups are often motivated by the recognition of structural inconsistencies (e.g., conflicts between the norms of their upbringing and those of major social institutions). We may suggest, in fact, that disruption of socialization becomes much more serious when structural and categoric inconsistencies are combined in composite groups.[15] In other words, categorical groups such a workers, with specific normative complaints, come together with groups such as students or intellectuals that have identified fundamental structural incompatibilities in the normative organization of the social system. This is true also of peasants and rebel priests, as in Latin American revolutionary movements.

Serious disruption in social regulation may be produced by the adherence of authorities to outdated rules, by the active pursuit of unenforceable reformist regulations, or by the inability of authorities to meet problems in critical areas of social concern.[16] The first kind of difficulty is exemplified by the quandary of the French king, Louis XIV, who, prior to the French revolution of 1789, maintained the privileges of the French nobility and the clergy to the dissatisfaction of the new, rising middle-class, which was spawned by the evolving economy. U.S. prohibition laws offer an example of the second condition. Although perhaps justified to some on moral grounds, these laws were widely violated and produced, as a by-product, widespread bribery and corruption. Finally, the authorities' inability to meet problems may result from the lawmakers' failure to predict the effects of their policies. For example, the action to stabilize economy, although well-intended, may fail to improve the situation, as was the case with the government of the Weimar Republic in Germany (1918-1933). Its economic policies were completely undermined by the world depression of 1929. When such ineffective regulation or policy seriously reduces adherence to the law within a significant portion of the population, it creates a major social disruption in the structure of authoritative regulation.

A failure in social adjustment through authoritative mobilization may occur in three contexts: (1) when there is a strong opposition, for whatever the reason, to the specific mobilization efforts of the leadership; (2) when there is an overextension of mobilization activities, which thus demand of people more than they are willing to contribute; and (3) when there is a general loss of confidence in the leadership and hence a refusal to be mobilized at all. In the first case a large portion of the public rejects a particular program of action, (e.g., U.S. military involvement in Vietnam). In the second instance, the public may be simply tired of continuous demands on its time and efforts, as in the case of frequent local elections, where the percentage of voters drops to insignificant levels.[17] The third case involves a general erosion of faith in the capacity of a government to lead the society. Therefore, the population simply refuses to be mobilized for most governmental programs. Such a situation developed in Tsarist Russia during World War I (1914-1917). Originally, there was a high enthusiasm for the war against Germany, but eventually the population lost faith in the government's capacity to bring war to a successful conclusion. The soldiers deserted and the home population refused to bear sacrifices for the war effort. In all these cases, the process of adjustment through mobilization becomes inoperative, and this, in turn, undermines the government's capacity for constructive action.[18]

The last aspect of social control under consideration involves the ability of a society to repress deviant behavior. This capacity may fail for three basic reasons. A part of the society may be in sympathy with the deviants and hinder their pursuit by the authorities (e.g., the sympathy for criminals within urban ghettos). Second, there may exist a general sympathy for the underdog, which is part of the folklore of a given society (such as the American public sympathy for ruthless killers such as Bonnie and Clyde). Third, the authorities may seemingly overreact in their repression of a relatively small group of deviants, who in no way can be assumed too seriously threaten the system itself. Such repressive action often harms innocent parties as well and may create a general revulsion against the action and support for the deviant group. Examples relating to the suppression of small guerrilla bands abound. Perhaps the most striking example involves the efforts of the Batista government in Cuba to repress Castro's guerrillas.[19] Thus, efforts at repression may ironically lead to further social disruption.

We have been discussing various areas of social control and the emergence of numerous disturbances within these areas as a society evolves over time. In most instances, these disturbances are met by processes of social adjustment. However, as we have shown, these processes of social adjustment sometimes fail, and there patterns of persistent social disruption emerge; that is, in limited, but strategic areas of social life, social control has broken down. In most situations, societies can tolerate some areas of social disruption without the general loss of social control; however, in some situations, there is a cumulative aggregation of numerous discreet areas of social disruption. Difficulties emerging in specific areas of social control spill over into other areas and reinforce already existing conflicts. In other words, a breakdown in one area of control may highlight the problems and conflicts in other areas, which up to that time remained latent or contained. If this aggregation spreads unchecked it will eventually lead to an overall systemic breakdown of social control. In this situation some portion of the society may retain its means of control but their effectiveness is severely limited by the erosion of the broader social system. For example, the social norms of a village may remain effective, but the national system may fail to supply essential goods and services. Therefore, the village may turn inward and come to rely on its own resources, but this very act reflects and accentuates the general breakdown of the larger system. This often happens in countries with protracted guerrilla warfare, such as China (1927-1949) and Vietnam (1945-1979).[20] At the end of these struggles, the government controls only few urban centers. An overall systemic breakdown destroys the intermediate social institutions between the individual and general society. There develops a general disaffection or alienation from the social sys-

tem, which has failed, and a growing feeling of desperation or despair. Some will engage in desperate
action to save themselves and their worlds; others will
despair that any action would suffice. Chaos and anar-
chy spread throughout the social system. There is a
nearly complete breakdown of old norms, conventions,
and institutions.

Multipliers of Cumulative Disruption

The forces of history sometimes produce rapid
change and fundamental challenges to the social
order. When they do so in a society already facing
severe social disruption, the problems of social control
may intensify and spread across the society leading
to a systemic breakdown. We analyze multipliers of
social disruption that stimulate a process of cumulative disruption that concludes in a breakdown of the
social system. From among the forms of historical
change already discussed, we shall highlight war,
rapid economic change, and major social realignment
as multipliers that move a society with areas of severe
social disruption toward systemic breakdown.[21]

Of all the multipliers, war (whether external or
internal) is the most vivid in its impact on society. It
profoundly disturbs the normal patterns of social life,
economic activity, and politics.[22] The basic social unit,
the family, must adjust to the departure of men—
fathers, husbands, sons, brothers, or more recently
in some nations of few women as well—to the armed
forces. Often the women of the family must take on
roles performed in more traditional societies by men,
including working full-time jobs on the home front.
As a result, normal family relationships are altered.
Children, deprived of parental guidance, fend for them-

selves and indeed in many cases prematurely assume the roles of adults. All members of the family develop greater independence from the family unit and are placed in a situation similar to that caused by legal separation of the parents. Of necessity, the traditional socializing role of the family is greatly diminished. This often creates, especially in children, a feeling of insecurity and a need for alternative sources of social solidarity.[23]

Moral norms and institutions (e.g., religion) are equally subject to disruption by war. The norms of war stand in sharp contrast to those of peaceful social life. In fact, two separate and distinct sets of standards emerge: there is one for interactions among one's own people and another for the enemy. Inevitably, the two standards cannot be kept wholly apart. The violence of war intrudes, to some degree, into the civil society, often with brutalizing effects upon its members, especially those involved in armed combat. The supreme effort and sacrifice of a major war encourages intolerance for nonconformist behavior. All those who seem to stand apart from the war effort are regarded by loyalists as dangerous deviants, if not outright traitors. Even more, those in a position of moral authority (e.g., clergyman, social leaders) are expected to lend inspiration to the cause of war, further complicating the distinction between good and evil. Prewar restraints are substantially loosened.

Other social institutions are altered, as well. The significance of formal education is altered during wartime. Training in liberal disciplines and for strictly civilian occupations gives way to development of skills needed in war, such as those required for armed combat or arms production. War requires new standards of success—daring, resolve, ruthlessness—and thus changes the criteria by which accomplishment is measured. New heroes emerge and are emulated. Participants develop extreme dependence on the group and fellowship with it. Extreme sacrifices of the war heighten expectations that social ideals will be realized in the postwar period. In effect, the war educates individuals to expect a world strikingly different from their prewar experience.

In addition, war changes the group structure of society itself. People from diverse backgrounds are thrown together in many wartime activities. Strict class distinctions are blurred by the close interaction of the participants. The various symbols of class prestige are undermined. In some ways, the individual is set free from previous group restraints. Greater flux in group membership and in intergroup relations results.

The economic effects of war can be seen in both the production and distribution of goods and services. Of necessity, production changes substantially from that which satisfies peacetime needs to that which meets the requirements of combat. The well-known view that one must choose between guns and butter applies here. Not only must production be controlled, but scarce productive materials and energy must be rationed. A labor force, composed substantially of women, old men, and youths, is marshaled to undertake crucial tasks. The discipline of labor is greatly increased by the rigor of the effort and by wartime regulations (e.g., a ban on strikes). Changed production influences the process of distribution, which is now accomplished according to different criteria. The free movement of goods and services is restricted. Profits are regulated. Abundance in areas considered vital to the war effort is accompanied by a general shortage of most consumers goods. Furthermore, these shortages are aggravated by sporadic distribution, due in most cases to military calls on transportation. War, of course, may involve physical destruction on the home front as well, reducing the productive capacity of the nation and its means of distribution. In guerrilla warfare, the leadership usually understands the need to undermine the economic vitality of the nation and hence attempts to disrupt it (e.g., Vietnam, Nicaragua, El Salvador, Guatemala, Peru). Moreover, seldom is any substantial investment made in new equipment, excluding that which produces armaments. Equipment becomes outdated and wornout and it must be replaced after the war. In this context, both the discipline and the deprivation of the effort must be borne by the populace, during the war and for some time afterwards, until the system returns to normal peacetime performance.

The advent of war brings a vast increase in the activities of government, which assumes major responsibility for mobilizing participants, goods, and services. It enlists people to perform the various tasks of war; it reorganizes the economy; and it suppresses hostile elements within the population. In this last sphere, all opposition to the war effort is viewed as an act of hostility undermining the national resolve. Demonstrations and controversial public meetings are typically outlawed. In fact, some suspected groups of nationals and aliens are detained, on the assumption that they might act against the state if left free.[24] Overt forms of treason, such as espionage, sabotage, and conspiracy, are dealt with by summary forms of justice—detention without trial, military courts and executive orders. More generally there is a sharp restriction of civil rights that were normally guaranteed, intrusion into private lives of the people through mobilization, regimentation, and the limitation of their civil rights. (The cold war produced some of the same effects.[25])

Hence, war destroys traditional patterns of life by reducing former family and group ties and by altering moral and intellectual perceptions. The war likewise creates new criteria of success and new patterns of identity. These effectively undermine the old patterns of socialization and inspire a new intense feeling of belonging, a sense heightened by the common rigors and deprivation of the experience. This new wartime identity is temporary, however, and it ultimately ends with war weariness, defeat, or the simple emergence of peace. The ideals and the sense of involvement in the war must be replaced either by the return to the somewhat changed prewar system or by the search for a new and more ideal alternative. The extreme experience of the war may encourage the expectation of radical solutions to the peacetime problems. Further, the political conditions of wartime regimentation, the restrictions on civil rights, and the centralization of governmental control are now more acceptable as means of solving social, economic, and political problems. In most historical situations, social institutions are equal to the task of adapting to changes wrought by war short of defeat. Political systems adapt to the demands of the effort and new wartime groups, economies are reorganized, schools take in large groups of veterans, and other social institutions adapt to changing times.

In systems characterized by severe social disruption, war accentuates the divisions of society. In Russia, World War I gradually sapped support for the repressive government. Alienation from the war effort left masses of people ripe for new leadership. In China, the disruption caused by the Japanese invasion dramatically weakened the Kuomintang government, providing the Communist insurgency with the opportunity to mobilize vast portions of the countryside against both the Japanese and the Kuomintang. Guerrilla war in various settings, such as Vietnam and Cuba, exposed weak and corrupt governments to an increasingly alienated population. At some point, the spreading disruption in these societies led to a systemic breakdown. Thus the rise of revolutionary forces was paralleled by the growing disarray of the dominant political, social, and economic system. The system, itself, was ripe for revolutionary change.

The second multiplier of cumulative disruption is rapid economic change, which may take the form of either an economic depression or an inflationary boom. Depression is marked by economic conditions that include declining production, widespread unemployment (serious loss of purchasing power), and general financial instability (e.g., bankruptcies). The economic system is caught in a downward spiral of increasing unemployment and declining production, encouraging widespread pessimism and a general loss of confidence in the system.[26]

The impact of depression on the social subsystem takes many forms. The basic social unit, the family, in many cases experiences a rapidly declining standard of living, which, apart from other consequences, places a heavy strain on the authority of the traditional breadwinners (parents), who are unable to provide for the family's necessities. The family is no longer a haven from the harshness of the outside world. People without jobs lose their sense of confidence and ability. Both spouses must often join in their desperate search for employment, leaving children to their own devises. The normal pattern of family life is destroyed, introducing a high degree of insecurity for all its members. More broadly, the whole moral order is brought into question. The good person is no longer rewarded. The major institutions are no longer effective. Throughout society, people search for new moral alternatives. Some try to find consolation in religious involvement, others turn away from traditional religion and may embrace the ideology of radical movements. This altered moral consciousness is also reflected in rising crime rates and changes in the character of crime, which often takes on semipolitical overtones.[27]

Economic depression generally shortens the period of formal education. Often, young people must seek employment earlier and thus forego their original career plans. They are diverted from the preparation for higher professions by the need for immediate jobs. And even those who manage to go on find few opportunities for employment, as most employers reduce their staffs. As "careers open to talent" diminish, the talented must seek other outlets, finding themselves in manual jobs far below their earlier expectations.[28] Many attempt to regain their status through involvement in radical causes. Visions of a basically reorganized society abound in study groups, radical theater, and the arts in general. New education in radical action is experienced by many. Class conflict is sharply intensified, with an increase in downward mobility and the apparent isolation of the rich. The middle class, the traditional stabilizing element in all industrialized societies, diminishes in numbers and function. Many of its members decline to the lower levels of society, losing contact with the more affluent and often providing leadership for the radicalized masses.[29]

There are two typical reactions of the political system to depression. The government may drift hopelessly with a resulting loss of confidence in its ability to avert economic disaster (e.g., Hoover's administration in the American Great Depression). When this loss of confidence is coupled with a severe pattern of preexisting social disruption, it may instigate a process of cumulative disruption, as was the case just before the beginning of the French Revolution. Alternately, the government may intervene and attempt to expand its control over the economic system (e.g., the Roosevelt administration after 1932). This expansion of the political control may be consistent with political tradition, functioning in effect as a reform that conserves that system. However, if combined with the use of sweeping authoritarian leadership, this political control may be used to intensify preexisting conflicts associated with a realm of social disruption, thus stimulating a process of cumulative disruption within the society. Another possibility is that government intervention ends in the failure to revive the economy. Then, the government is blamed for making matters worse.

Depression also causes the state's revenues to decline drastically exactly at the time when its expenditure should increase to stimulate the economy and support the unemployed. The only answer is borrowing, which, if not carefully managed, may create an excessive national debt. The debt can, in time and by itself, impede recovery. According to Brinton and Goldstone, the state's financial crisis, preventing it from performing its functions and providing its service, is one of the major causes of revolution.[30]

At the other extreme, an inflationary boom also creates difficulties in social adjustments. In the economic subsystem, a rapid expansion of production brings full employment and rising prices. The benefits of the boom are, however, distributed unevenly within the society. Some groups enrich themselves overnight; others are bypassed by the prosperity.[31] Those with capital to invest benefit greatly from the expansion in production and constantly rising prices. Those on fixed incomes and those with limited savings suffer an erosion of their standard of living and their general economic security. Even those who do not immediately lose ground experience a sense of heightened insecurity due to the general turbulence of the whole system. The class structure becomes more fluid with rapid upward mobility for some. Traditional class values, with their stabilizing norms, are undermined by the new standards of success, the visibility of new wealth, and the fear of potential failure in the quickly evolving society. The new rich often lack the sense of social obligation and propriety held by the more traditional upper classes. Their dramatic success appeals to people who believe that they themselves may be successful, while at the same time their new wealth is resented by those who see themselves as failing. On the one hand, rising expectations lead people to assume that "great things" are possible; on the other hand, few of them are really that fortunate. Many remain frustrated, and their disappointments are heightened by periodic economic failures.[32] The general boom impels them to search for alternatives and scapegoats for their own lack of achievement. Much of the middle class is caught up in this feeling of frustration, which is aggravated by their sense of insecurity in the rapidly inflating economy. As in depression, the middle class loses its role as social stabilizer and indeed some of its members join radical movements (as in the case of Iran).[33]

In this context, other traditional bonds are giving way as well. Many families experience internal disruption when some of their members advance rapidly up the social ladder. Many more young people emulate the new ways and become critical of traditional family values. In general materialistic criteria for success replace the more ordered moral values of the prior society. In education, as well, more pragmatic career training replaces the traditional reflective education. This makes society more receptive to the idea of engineered change and lowers its commitment to traditional values and ways of life. As a countertrend, there is an increase in the number of fanatical religious groups. (This phenomenon was particularly evident in the Iranian Revolution.) Likewise, secular groups will appear that offer radical moral visions set against the materialistic ethos of the period (e.g., the Nazi movement in 1920s Germany and the New Left in the United States in the 1960s, leftist terroristic groups in the 1970s and 1980s in Italy and the Federal Republic of Germany).

In politics, a government that has little control over the economy will tend to be left behind by the general economic boom, and it will rely upon the traditional power elites. In this context, the new economic elites will demand greater participation in the system and attack the government for its lack of recognition of their claims.[34] Equally dissatisfied with the government's performance will be those who do not benefit from the economic upsurge. Conversely, the government with considerable control of the economy will either originate the boom (and, we may add, the inflation itself) or will join with the economically successful. In this case, the new economic elites will have no problem with access, but the government will be identified with all the negative aspects of the boom by those who feel left behind (Iran, again). Their number may rise substantially if the boom continues for an extended period of time. The negative image of the government is sharpened by the perception that government officials have been corrupted by the wealth. Indeed, because public salaries often lag behind those in business, the propensity for bribery is considerably increased (as has been often the case in American politics, e.g., in the 1980s). Ironically, an extended boom, like an economic depression, undercuts the traditional social order, while spreading seeds of discontent. It may act as a multiplier of social disruption, especially if it leads to a period of general economic crises, which often follows the uncontrolled boom (or what economists call the *overheated economy*).[35] Given the prior existence of severe social disruption, such an economic boom and the following crises can lead to cumulative disruption and a systemic breakdown.

Potentially, the process of social realignment can contribute to the crisis generated by war or by rapid economic change. In some cases, however, it is the central multiplier in and of itself. There are situations in which important, newly organized groups appear on the social scene. Their rise cannot be attributed with certainty to any specific cause but is rather a result of slow historical evolution. Such groups include a growing economic class (e.g., workers) or a national ethnic or religious minority (or even a subjected majority, e.g., Republic of South Africa). These groups have existed for some time within the particular society, but what makes them of new importance is their growing awareness of their common identity and interests and a sense that their interests cannot be realized within the system, which they view as unresponsive to their special needs at a critical time when they have come to feel capable of demanding a place in the sun.[36] The catalytic potential of their demands depends on the reaction of the system.

The system may accommodate these groups thereby reducing their disruptive potential. The partial accommodation, however, may sometimes lead to further and more extreme demands. On the other hand, the system may repress the new group. This often leads to violence on both sides. The terrorism of the group being repressed may spread and bring a coalescence between the new group and the other dissatisfied parts of society. Violence may also spread among groups attempting to counter the rise of the new group. For example, the popular belief in 1933 Germany that the Communists burned down the parliament building as a signal for the start of their revolution permitted the Nazis, who themselves instigated the fire for that purpose, to destroy their opposition.

Governmental violence also leads to the suspension of normal civil rights and increases the acceptance of terror as a normal expression of political power (as is more and more evident in India). On both sides in the conflict, the extremists win over, or neutralize, the moderates and argue that only the acceleration of violence will attain their higher goals (e.g., increased bombing of populated places by political extremists as by the Irish Republican Army in Northern Ireland and Great Britain). The spread of violence in itself indicates the degree to which the social order is breaking down (as it was in South Africa). Soon this pattern of social conflict may extend through all major social institutions. Some families choose sides, some are torn apart by dissension, and others withdraw from involvement. Northern Ireland is an excellent example of this as the whole society is polarized with the Protestant and Catholic extremists at the two ends. The system is kept together only by the thousands of British troops stationed there.

All of these multipliers—war, rapid economic change, and social realignment—when combined with prior patterns of severe social disruption lead to a cumulative disruptive process that concludes in systemic breakdown. Their common effect is that they impair the general patterns of social control and adjustment within the society, while at the same time intensifying and combining patterns of disruption already in existence. The result is a spreading chaos that engulfs the system as a whole. Violence is often a visible expression of this chaos, at the same time, it increases the systemic polarization. At this stage it appears to many that the system is beyond repair and that revolutionary change is the only answer.

Leadership, Ideology, and Organization

Obviously systemic breakdown could lead to many different forms of social disintegration or regeneration. Here the question of an emergent leadership group is crucial.[37] If such leadership is to lay the foundation of the ideocratic rule, it must mobilize individuals and galvanize them into a political movement. The leadership must transform large numbers of disgruntled and apathetic men and women into dedicated, self-sacrificing, and disciplined groups. This leadership must convert sporadic and disorganized protest and violence into conscious and recurrent attacks on the existing system. (In Iran, tapes of Khomeini's speeches were spread through the country and the Islamic clergy provided the organization to the movement.) To succeed in these tasks, the leadership must inspire the masses to believe in the ultimate truth of its own solutions to the existing social chaos. Therefore, it creates a powerful vision of a new, reconstructed and unified future community (e.g., Islamic republic). It identifies those who are assumed to be guilty of causing the present disaster (e.g., the Shah) and those who exacerbate it (e.g., today, Hosni Mubarak, president of Egypt in the view of the Islamic fundamentalists of that country). The clear identification of the individual villains personifies the causes of social breakdown, and this helps to unify support for the ideocratic movement.

All forms of social regeneration seem to require leadership of the sort described to this point. However, regenerative change leading to ideocracy must employ the vehicle of a powerful *monistic ideology*. Because the revolutionary movement must utilize broad masses, direct physical contact between the foremost leader and the followers is impossible. The ideology serves as the basic language of communication with which the leader inspires the masses to action. No partial ideology will have such a broad potential for mobilization. The monistic ideology specifies the nature of the targets to be assaulted. These targets include specific scapegoats to be eliminated, because they personify the ideologically defined contaminants that permeate the social fabric. In other words the scapegoats are specific enough to be identified as individuals, but these individuals represent the universal forces of evil, which require the total mobilization of the forces of good. If the leaders are to sweep away the old system, which they consider absolutely corrupt, they also require a profound ideological vision of the new order to replace the old. The advocacy of partial reforms cannot suffice to mobilize the masses for the total regeneration of the society. Thus, the ideology must contain a model of absolute perfection in which the "reborn mass" constructs an earthly paradise. Only then can the followers be expected to make a total commitment to a fundamental revolution.

These utopian ends are the ultimate conclusion to the historical drama that unfolds according to the underlying forces of history. Therefore, the followers of the movement can be certain that history is on their side and ultimate victory is theirs. Within this context, programmatic means are well-defined and can give certainty to those engaged in tactical action. For the ideology is assumed to prescribe an exact set of tactics for all contingencies, although the final interpretation is left to the supreme leadership. Without such a powerful ideological vehicle, which includes an interpretation of history, a vision of future utopia, and a set of tactics to achieve it, efforts at social regeneration would not take an ideocratic form. Rather they would result in more limited forms of social change ranging from various kinds of partial reforms to limited forms of revolution (as in the American War of Independence). The monistic ideology is a crucial element in the construction of an ideocratic system.

Successful political programs are transformed into action through a political organization. The sweeping regeneration of society advocated in the monistic ideology requires the eventual penetration, by the ideocratic movement, of all the institutional sectors of society. Such penetration is critical for the capacity of the movement both to undermine the remaining elements of the existing system and to organize the building blocks of the new ideocracy. In effect, the organization of the movement increasingly becomes the model of a future society, while it is pursuing the struggle with the old.[38] Thus, the evolution and development of the movement is at the same time the emergence of the fledgling ideocracy. The very capacity of the movement to provide a coherent alternative to the prevailing chaos makes it such an irresistible force. This is exactly the quality that attracts individuals lost in the disintegrating system and searching for new alternatives. It sways them away from the seemingly ineffective reformers, who are basically defending the old system. It also provides a vehicle for those already engaged in fragmented rebellions.

The organizational structure of the movement is composed of a well-defined leadership, a core of dedicated members, and the cluster of front organizations in which marginally involved individuals are linked with the movement. The movement leadership provides the tactical command center and the authoritative interpretation of the ideological theory. The core membership constitutes the army of absolutely committed individuals, unquestionably following the orders of the leadership. Many of its members are in fact full-time paid professional revolutionaries grouped into either political or paramilitary units. The political cadres are charged with the indoctrination of the movement's members and the conversion of "nonbelievers" to the cause. They also disseminate propaganda to the society at large. They provide leadership for the front organizations, creating new ones and infiltrating the old. They are active in study groups, the educational system, local government bodies, professional and religious organizations, and other socioeducational groups. In these, they are responsible for gradually instilling the "correct" ideological perspective and weeding out deviant views.[39] The paramilitary units engage in disruptive violence designed to accentuate the weakness of the existing system. They also combat and attack opposition groups. Finally, they exercise physical coercion against wavering elements in the movement itself. They are, in fact, the seeds of the repressive organization in the future ideocratic system. The front organizations are associations utilized for specific purposes, focusing on particular goals of the movement (e.g., women's associations, youth groups). In many cases the association of the fronts with movement is disguised and the bond between them and the movement is maintained only through the front's leadership. The fronts permit a much broader penetration of the society than that which would be possible under the conditions requiring total commitment of all participants to the monistic ideology. And thus the movement can utilize for its own purposes social groups that only partially agree with its goals or means.

The movement is in competition with other political and social forces throughout the society. Some groups are clearly identified as the enemies of the movement, and as such they must be destroyed. The major contours of programmatic action are determined by the evolving conflict with these enemies. Other groups are caught somewhere between these two extreme opponents. The leadership of the movement will attempt to penetrate and capture some of these groups, ensure the neutrality of others, and finally destroy those considered potential allies of the enemy. The attempt of the movement is to eventually force all individuals to take sides.[40]

As the movement expands, it spreads a network of organizational control that mobilizes increasing portions of the society.[41] The chaos of social breakdown is progressively replaced by order, which is given a revolutionary form consistent with the ideology. It should be understood that the movement itself fosters social chaos externally to increase the very social disruption it can then replace with the certainty of its own coherent organization.[42]

Scenario of Ideocratic Revolution

What we have described in this chapter is a sequence of stages leading to the emergence of ideocracy. After considering the operation of social controls and the processes of adjustment in a normally functioning society, we examined fundamental patterns of historical changes that challenge the ability of a society to adjust successfully. Through maladjustment, societies often experience certain patterns of social disruption that impair the ability of the system to regulate social conflict in important and specific institutional areas. Societies can often endure limited patterns of social disruption for a considerable period of time. However, certain kinds of rapid and intense social change—such as war, severe economic depression or rapid economic development, and social realignment—aggravate or multiply the patterns of social disruption, causing its cumulative spread throughout society and leading to a systemic breakdown of that society. In this context, there may exist, or now appear, a powerful political movement with a leadership committed to total regeneration of the social system. Such a movement usually adheres to a monistic ideology that includes a sweeping utopian vision of the new social order. Employing organizational means to intensify social disruption in all parts of the society, such a movement penetrates all major social

institutions. It mobilizes the population for the process of social reconstruction, and it eliminates or neu-
tralizes all opposing powers within the society. If such
a movement gains dominance, the initial foundations
of ideocracy have been established.

V

IDEOCRACY IN DYNAMIC PERSPECTIVE: INCEPTION AND STABILIZATION

Introduction

Change affects all human institutions, including, of course, those of ideocracy. Our model in Chapter III largely ignored this fact. As an ideal type, it presented a logically exaggerated and static picture of the ideocratic system. Such an abstraction is useful for clarification because it permits a comprehensive framework of analysis. Reality is never so clear or so orderly. Although our model simplifies and elucidates reality with some degree of accuracy, it also ignores special variations in concrete political systems, which only somewhat approximate the model. Furthermore, it omits the characteristics of dynamic change, which move these systems both toward and away from the "ideal type".

We shall now consider the evolution of ideocratic systems, recognizing the interplay of contradictory forces that are found in real life situations. This view will highlight the mixed characteristics that all political systems possess: characteristics that make them more or less ideocratic and more or less pluralistic. This permits the examination of ideocratic development over time and allows, as well, a comparison of ideocracy and pluralism in relative terms. For this purpose, we must recognize the characteristics of ideocracy as variables rather than constants. Therefore, it is possible to conceive of ideocracy and pluralism as polar extremes along a continuum composed of the major variables we have distinguished—ideology, leadership, penetration, and mobilization (see Figure V.1). In reality, systems fall between these extremes, exhibiting varying combinations of these characteristics. To the degree that ideocracies vary from the ideal, they lose their ideocratic identity, becoming in fact somewhat pluralistic. Eventually, it should be possible to specify typical mixtures of these variables (average type models), but for the present we are proceeding more loosely. We identify intermediate situations, and we trace general processes of change that affect the evolving systems. Figure V.1 illustrates a continuum in regard to each of the major variables of ideocracy.

In ideocracy, a sacred dogma is given a singular interpretation by the top leadership. Conversely, in pluralism, diverse belief systems are promoted by multiple authorities. In an intermediate situation, limited ideological tolerance may be found, both in some acceptance of ideological diversity and in the coexistence of some rival interpretations of the ideology. Between the concentrated leadership of ideocracy and the dispersed leadership of pluralism, situations are found in which some spheres of partially autonomous leadership coexist with a dominant political authority. For example, the top leadership may be collective and that political authority may be somewhat dispersed along lines of functional expertise (e.g., in Iran, the Grand Ayatollah gives religious-ideological interpretation, while the president heads the Islamic Republic). Further, penetration in the mixed system is less than total in the sense that, at the least, some

FIGURE V.1

Indicators of Political Organization

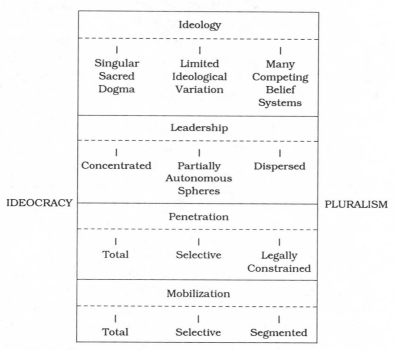

islands of separateness are ignored by the regime and, at best, some independent groups are allowed their own spheres of public authority (e.g., the Catholic Church in previous Communist Poland). In the mixed case, mobilization likewise is imperfect and allows limited freedom for psychological withdrawal from commitment, nonparticipation in regime sponsored activities, and even privately or obliquely expressed heretical views (e.g., Slavomir Mrozek's plays in previous Communist Poland).[1]

Use of these variables permits us to describe the political development of particular ideocracies, in

terms of both their stable patterns and their dynamics.
For this purpose, we shall identify three periods in the
life of ideocracy—inception, stabilization, and later
evolution—and we shall distinguish typical processes
of change that create differences among them. Again,
these processes have an important influence on the
degree to which the evolving systems actually approximate our ideal type model of ideocracy.

Inception of Ideocracy

Ideocracies are established in three general ways
following the disruption of a previous system: civil war,
takeover, or the founding of an isolated colony.

Civil War

Actual civil war occurs where the proponents of
ideocracy and their opponents are more or less equally
matched. Early phases of guerrilla-based insurgency
fall more into the category of what we have called
severe social disruption.[2] At some point in the development of a successful insurgency, cumulative disruption causes a systemic breakdown. Prior to all of
this, the insurgency has yet to become a genuine civil
war.

For convenience, we have identified civil war as
emerging when the opponents are approximately
evenly matched.[3] Much of the general populace is often
uncommitted. In a civil war, both sides control different portions of the territory and its population. The
widespread military conflict is combined with a life
and death political struggle for the allegiance of the
population. This political aspect of the struggle neces-
sitates considerable flexibility in the tactics of the conflict. Ideologically, while maintaining the general his-

torical dogma, the ideocratic movement must permit loose interpretations of specifics of the doctrine. For example, the enemy is prominently identified, but at the same time in terms that are purposely vague to accommodate possible converts. This ideological imprecision permits a loose revolutionary alliance that contains many groups of supporters (e.g., Marxist revolutionary groups and liberation theology Catholic priests in Latin America).[4] The interpretation of ideology is not rigidly assigned to one exclusive source, and some debate on its current historical meaning is permitted.

The relative coherence and drive of the ideocratic movement in the civil war situation is often related to the charismatic qualities of a single dominant leader. His power, however, is not absolute, but depends to a large degree on his ability to manipulate and inspire his followers (e.g., Lenin in the Russian Revolution, Mao in the Chinese Revolution, and Castro in the Cuban Revolution). Furthermore, his leadership must be shared with other leaders, who are only somewhat subordinate to him. Some will be separated from him by territory, others will rely on their personal following within the movement and the general population. The movement, operating in a semiconspiratorial manner and with a highly idealistic and dedicated membership, may be divided into factions reflecting underlying ideological differences, fragmented leadership, and territorial separation. As more area is won, the consolidation of leadership proceeds. The discipline of the movement increases in the base areas, while still remaining loose in the territories of guerrilla operation. (The most perfect examples are the Chinese and Vietnamese revolutions in which the Communists fought for twenty-two and thirty-two years, respectively, gaining more and more territory over time.)[5]

The penetration of social and economic organizations likewise varies with the degree of physical control. The emphasis is on covert penetration and the sponsorship of fronts in areas of marginal and contested control. In the base areas the movement will attempt more substantial penetration, but even here the process is designed not to aggravate potential supporters, until the victory in the civil war is just about assured.

The intensity of the conflict guarantees substantial mobilization of core members of the movement, who are absolutely dedicated, even to the point of death. In many ways their devotion is crucial for victory in the civil war. However, the same degree of mobilization is not required of the sympathizers, who support the cause in varying degrees and for different reasons, extending from belief in parts of the ideology to opposition to the other side (e.g., support of Fascists due to the hatred of Communists, support of Marxists due to the hatred of a military regime, or support of Islamic fundamentalists because of the dislike of the West). In many ways the movement attempts to increase the number of supporters in the enemy's territory and, at the least, neutralize those who cannot be converted. The movement will emphasize recruitment drives to fill its own ranks as well as the front organizations. While the movement must be composed of highly dedicated individuals, large front social organizations recruit less devoted participants from the masses. Of crucial importance here is the revolutionary army and guerrilla units, mobilized essentially for the military struggle and less for the development of ideological commitment. The armed forces support only those portions of the ideology that have broad popular appeal, and they are often unaware of the utopian goals to which the core of the movement adheres (e.g., Tito's communist partisans in World War II Yugoslavia, many of whom joined to fight the hated Nazis).[6] In general terms the civil war requires ideological and organizational flexibility in which penetration and mobilization of a group vary with the degree to which it exercises territorial control and its proximity to the core leadership. Both the absolute dedication of the movement's core and the broad support of the masses are essential for victory.[7]

Takeover

The ideocratic system is often established through an evolutionary process of growing support culminating in a brief coup d'etat or in an extralegal assumption of dictatorial power by the previously elected leader of the government. In this case, cumulative disruption does not lead to the polarization of forces into two armed camps waging a civil war, but to a proliferation of struggling political groups in a situation of system's breakdown, which permits the ideocratic movement to eventually capture a powerful political plurality. In other words, the ideocratic movement emerges victorious because of its ability to become the strongest political force in a situation of political fragmentation, a force composed of a highly dedicated core of supporters and a set of peripheral allies. The battle lines between the contesting groups are not as clearly drawn as in a civil war, and the situation demands even more flexibility on the part of the ideocratic movement. Various alliances are formed with many and often opposing groups, which are themselves contenders for power, although they are willing to form a coalition with the ideocratic movement. And thus, the ideocratic movement attempts to gain support from the rich and the poor, from the conservatives and the revolutionaries, all at the same time.[8] Crucial to its ability to do so is the process of cumulative social disruption that affects all groups within society. In the face of this social disintegration, the clear sense of purpose expressed by the ideocratic movement provides for many a semblance of security and reassuring answers to the existing social, economic, and political problems. The movement is propelled to power by the spreading disruption, which it manipulates, to a degree, through the use of selective violence. This violence increases a general sense of systemic breakdown; at the same time, it is used to emasculate and further divide the opposition.[9] As the victory of the movement becomes apparent, this creates a "bandwagon" effect, in which increasing numbers of individuals and groups join to enjoy the fruits of victory.[10]

In this stage of the ideocratic revolution, ideology is extremely flexible, to the degree that some ideocratic movements have been accused of not having an ideology at all, such as the Fascist movement in Italy.[11] In fact, the negative aspects of the existing system are well-articulated. The causes of social disruption are well-specified and the enemies and scapegoats clearly identified. Indeed, violent attacks on specific individuals or groups are central to the political program. On the other hand, the future objectives of the movement are not yet so well-formulated, although they include a utopian goal that, because of its extremism, appears to be no more than a vague propaganda device, taken seriously only by a core few in the movement itself.[12] This picture contains little of the program of social reconstruction required to realize the utopian goals. In this sense, the ideology is abstract and a seemingly naive, romantic vision. The real social goals of the movement remain secret, except for the group of the most initiated; for example, neither Hitler nor his followers initially claimed that *Mein Kampf*[13] contained a necessary program of social reconstruction, although eventually all its points were pursued with fanatic commitment. The real importance of the ideology for the core of the movement is hidden from both its allies and enemies during this period of political struggle.

Strikingly characteristic of this process of takeover is the centrality of the charismatic leader. Indeed his genius and personality symbolize the unique qualities of the movement, drawing a huge group of supporters to it. More than at any other time, "the movement is the leader, and the leader is the movement" (a Nazi slogan). His power stems not only from his control of the movement but also from his appeal to the broad masses. He is either the founder of the movement, or he takes over an existing organization and makes it in his own image. He is creator of the ideology and the political hope of the movement. His lieutenant's recognize, without reservation, his superior authority. They and the members of the movement idealize and revere him.[14] The movement itself, for reasons of open competition, gradually grows into a mass organization, composed of a dedicated core of participants who are totally faithful to the leader and, at the opposite extreme, nominal members who join for opportunistic reasons. The movement attempts to participate within the existing political system, and in that sense, it becomes a political party and penetrates the government both by recruitment of government officials and by placing the movement's members within crucial governmental positions, of which the most important are internal governmental administration, communication facilities, the armed forces, and the police. Experience shows that the armed forces, due to the socialization process of the officer corps, cannot be so easily penetrated. Nevertheless the movement must assure their sympathy, or at least their neutrality, and it must attempt to recruit some of its top leaders.[15] Concentrating on the development of short-run political power, the movement avoids responsibility for foreign affairs and other specialized administrative activities, such as the judicial and economic affairs. Indeed, the control of economic ministries is shunned because it might prove embarrassing in view of the widespread economic disruption. In essence, the movement attempts to assume control of the major instruments of internal communication and repression in preparation for the total assumption of power. When that time comes, the movement controls these vehicles of state power and thus deprives the opposition of important means to prevent the takeover.[16]

In the social realm, the movement attempts a broad penetration of the major organizations of social control. Of special attention are the mass media, the educational establishment, and particular professional and trade organizations. In addition, individuals with control of private financial resources are induced, by promise of rewards or threats of coercion, to supply funds for the movement and to deny support to the opposition. Even religious organizations may be penetrated and utilized to integrate the movement within the broad cultural patterns of the society.[17] This is not to say that all these organizations become fronts of the movement, but they are willing to ally themselves with the broad goals of the movement. In many ways, such alliances accord the movement the necessary degree of respectability, which it must have to assume power by legal or semilegal means. Its penetration of social institutions is selective, simply because of the scarcity of resources and the varied importance of different groups for the purposes of the movement. Through this penetration, the movement builds a base of broad social support, which will assist its rise to political power and aid it in its eventual assumption of total control.

Likewise, mobilization is selective and partial, concerned immediately with building a needed coalition around the core of the movement. The movement attempts to expand its strongly committed membership and, at the same time, mobilize various groups of supporters operating on the fringes of the movement. A high priority is assigned to extensive propaganda through mass media, mass rallies, and even the arts. (A novel approach to this was used in Iran where, as mentioned before, Khomeini's supporters circulated tapes with his speeches.) A longer term concern involves mobilization through the educational system with programs of study that are made consistent with the movement's ideology. In all these efforts, special emphasis is placed upon using scapegoats, in which enemies are clearly identified and attacks on them communicated throughout the population. This effort is combined with the selective use of violence, often extreme, aimed at the elimination of the political opposition, the unification of participants banded together by violent acts, and the intimidation of those who are wavering. Mobilization through propaganda and violence aims at expanding the sense of social disruption and potential systemic breakdown, all of which is contrasted with the vision of ideocratic regeneration. The image presented is one of a decisive political program with clear-cut solutions, compared to the wavering and uncertain political opposition.

Preparation for an ideocratic takeover requires that the movement be built within the context of an already existing political system, and hence the movement must adjust to some of the characteristics of that polity, while progressively undermining it and providing an alternative solution. Therefore, the movement relies on flexible ideology and selective penetration and mobilization, while coalescing around a dominant charismatic leader and a core of fanatical supporters. This tactical flexibility enhances its strategic victory.

Founding an Isolated Colony

In a sense, founding an isolated ideocratic colony differs strikingly from the other patterns of inception. Here, the general society experiences no severe social disruption and no systemic breakdown. In fact, its repression of the ideocratic movement within its territory may be part of its processes of social control and adjustment in response to its deviant behavior. The sense of severe social disruption is limited, in this case, to the membership of the movement itself. This may be borne by the participants for some time. If they come to believe that this repression will destroy their utopian dream forever, this situation becomes the functional equivalent, for the group, of cumulative disruption. It can be corrected only by radical separation from the dominant hostile society. Of course, this separation is predicated upon the availability of territory for settlement and the chance to leave the established social system; for example, the migration of the Puritans from England to America, (1620), the Mormons' move to Utah (1847), the Dutch, German, and French Calvinists' settlements in South Africa (from 1657), and the emigration to Guyana of followers of the Reverend Jones (1978).[18] It is the hope of the migrants that they will be able to create their envisioned utopia in separation from the hostile forces of their former society.

Naturally, the unifying force of the group is a powerful, well-defined, and uncompromising ideology with a singular dominant interpretation. Their ideology usually has strong religious overtones, in which the concern of the believers for their salvation negates the possibility of pragmatic accommodation within the existing society because this would be damning to their souls.[19] The ideology draws a strict distinction between the purity of the faithful and the contamination of nonbelievers. Finally, the ideology is comprehensive, in the sense that the utopian goal is linked with precise rules of social behavior and a general program of ideocratic development. Like other ideocratic movements, the group unifies around a single leader, with a strong prophetic quality. However, his appeal is limited to the members of the movement and is not broadly projected outward through the society at large, as it is in other ideocratic movements. The leader has a direct personal relationship with all his followers; at the same time, there exists a well-defined hierarchy of authority. Typically, the leader is assisted in his functions by a tight group of close disciples—elders—to whom he delegates responsibility for routine matters.[20] In religious movements, the church itself performs ideocratic, movementlike functions, involving both elite and mass participants in its activities.[21]

In all ideocracies of this type, the leadership has the broad consensual support of the entire movement. It has total penetration of all social organization within the group and generally has mobilized all members of the movement, although to different degrees of active involvement. There is variation in the extent to which these movements attempt to proselytize outsiders. Some engage in extensive attempts at conversion, but with little success due to their unwillingness to compromise. Others view outsiders as absolutely unredeemable. Internally, all these movements emphasize the continuing moral regeneration of their followers, who may fall away from the faith. Violence for organizational purposes is minimal and coercion is mostly of a psychological character, in which the guilty willingly submit to punishment. The founding of an isolated colony is at once a simpler political process than that accompanying other patterns of ideocratic inception and, at the same time, a more consensual one.

All three forms of inception involve charismatic leadership and a dedicated core of followers. In instances of civil war or takeover, appeals are made to broad masses of the population, requiring a flexible ideology, concern with the tactics of the struggle and the need for varied messages to different audiences. The violent conflict of civil war leads to a clear definition of the movement and its general enemy. Although these are less clearly defined in the takeover, here the scapegoat assumes a clear focus and significance, because this scapegoat is blamed for the disruption. All three forms, in their different ways, lead to the establishment of ideocratic rule.

Stabilization

Once power has been assumed, the system takes on specific characteristics associated with its own stabilization. This process may take some ten to fifteen years for completion. The leadership drives toward the expansion of ideocratic control over society and the purification of the movement, which was contaminated during the period of heroic struggle. The stabilization process discussed here, does not apply uniformly to an ideocracy established as an isolated colony, because that system has already consolidated, in many ways, as it settled in its new territorial home. In other types, attempts are now initiated to actually construct the ideocratic system envisioned in the ideology. A broad expansion of developmental activity occurs in all those areas distinguished by our model of ideocracy—ideology, leadership, organization, penetration, and mobilization.

The ideology is formalized and becomes highly dogmatic, with theory and doctrine brought into closer relationship with one another. Parts of the theory, however, are given primary emphasis, in terms of priorities in the process of development toward the utopian goal. The achievement of other ideological tenets is relegated to a secondary level of importance. For example, economic development was given priority in the Soviet Union over equality, while preparation for war and extermination of the Jews were given high priority in Nazi Germany.[22] Such chosen portions of the ideology become the central focus for political action and constructive social development. At the same time portions of the ideology are elaborated to cover most areas of social behavior. During this same period, the elimination of rival ideological positions is ruthlessly pursued, under the direction of a singular authoritative center for ideological interpretation. Initially, the ideological clashes are quite intense, until eventually factionalism is destroyed and an absolute orthodoxy is established.

This process of ideological purification emanates from the top leader, who eventually assumes the absolute power of authoritative interpretation by purging all those who might challenge his preeminence. At this stage, the movement's leader invests his authority in the bureaucracy of the state. This does not mean that he is hamstrung by its procedural limitations, because the legitimacy of bureaucratic action originates in the leader's interpretation of the ideology and not in the rules of bureaucratic organizations. Indeed, the leader becomes deified and changes from a prophetic comrade in the struggle to the elevated and secluded position of a priestly autocrat (e.g., Hitler or Stalin).

The leader's group of lieutenants is purged of the more individualistic members.[23] Only those absolutely faithful to the leader are left. They are assigned to the top organizational positions of the new system. These new bureaucrats assume control of the social system along functional lines: they run government ministries; they continue to lead the movement; they assume control of major social and professional organizations. They struggle among themselves for their leader's favor, and he skillfully balances them, one against another, thereby preventing any direct challenges to his authority.[24]

However, the lieutenants, at this point, start building their own bureaucratic empires, which become somewhat distinct bases of power for them. A system of patronage develops in which some lieutenants have a growing number of followers who are dependent on them for their careers. The success of these fiefdoms is affected by the struggle among the lieutenants for scarce resources. Coalitions begin to form among them in support of their factional claims, which are opposed by other groups of lieutenants. At

the back of everybody's mind is the question of succession to the top leader, should he die or otherwise
lose control of the system. This struggle for power
varies considerably from the unity envisaged in the
ideocratic ideal.[25]

The movement is drastically reduced in size. All
independent or ideologically impure elements are ruthlessly purged. The movement becomes a exclusive
elite, absolutely loyal to the leader and seldom larger
than about 5 to 8 percent of the total population. Like
the whole system, the movement becomes internally
bureaucratized and divided into a small core of
salaried, full-time functionaries and a mass of ordinary members. The functionaries become the lifeline of
the movement, through which orders are transmitted
downward and information upward. The movement
resembles a pyramid, with the top leader at its apex
and below him the lieutenants, then the movement's
functionaries, and eventually the general membership
at the base. The movement obtains the permanent
control of the state's machinery, and the state bureaucracy becomes subordinate to the bureaucracy of the
movement. Indeed, the movement can always overrule
the rulings of the state bureaucracy. Here, the movement's dominant position derives from its role as the
guardian of the ideology and the direct transmitter of
the top leader's rule-making authority.

The character of the movement changes drastically from that of a group of dedicated, idealistic, and
self-sacrificing individuals to an organization composed of career-oriented, self-serving members. They
begin to manipulate the system for their own personal
interests, forming factions along functional bureaucratic lines under particular lieutenants, discussed
previously. The party becomes a set of ruling cliques,

increasingly corrupted by its own power, employing the ideology to maintain its own legitimacy.[26]

Now the movement's aims include the total penetration of all social and economic organizations, so that all institutions of social control are subordinate to its directives. In each sphere of social activity, a single organizational structure is established, with a monopoly of control. All other organizations in that realm of social life are either outlawed or integrated into the official body (e.g., these organizations include trade unions, professional organizations, youth groups, education and religious organizations). The movement demands that appointments to leading positions within these organizations receive its prior approval. This, in fact, means that most of the leadership positions are filled by members of the movement or by equally loyal individuals. In the economic sphere, the leadership exercises two types of control: direct nationalization, with administration by the state of all sources of production (communism, e.g., China or North Korea); or indirect control through umbrella organizations that oversee privately owned enterprises, regulating their activities in specific spheres of economic endeavor, such as agriculture, manufacturing, or trade. Exercising state authority within their spheres, these regulatory agencies are subject to overall control by state ministries and are led by members of the movement.[27]

Although this penetration of social and economic organizations enhances control, it also fosters a duality of interests among party members leading these organizations. Their allegiance to the movement becomes diluted by the recognition that their careers depend on the success of these organizations. Also, over the years, they begin to identify the goals of the system as equivalent to the interests of their own organizations. In a way, although the movement formally controls the organizations, the interests of the organizations infiltrate the decision-making processes within the movement as well.[28]

Initially, penetration is connected with a general purge of those specialists considered to be opposed to the system. Soon, however, it is learned that complex social and economic functions cannot be performed without some degree of expertise, which only the specialists hold. Their services are again employed, introducing some nonideocratic criteria into the decision-making process (e.g., a dramatic example of this was the employment of the Tsarist officers in the Red Army in 1918 and the use of the Shah's officers by the Islamic Republic in Iran in its war with Iraq, 1980-1988).

The fundamental objective of the ideocratic system is the total regeneration of society. For this purpose, a total mobilization of all citizens is attempted. These individuals are mobilized through the movement, as well as through all other organizations, which assume a political character (e.g., even recreational and sport organizations will engage in political indoctrination). Neighborhood cells and work study groups are constituted throughout the country (the best example of this is the establishment of the Committees for the Defense of the Revolution in Cuba). In addition to this general mobilization, different publics are mobilized for specific purposes, as dictated by the current ideological emphases of the leadership (as, for example, "peace movements" in the Soviet bloc countries were used to attack the stationing of American short-range missiles in Europe.) It goes without saying that the whole educational system is utilized extensively for socializing youth for the new life. Indeed, the educational system is committed to conversion of the youth to the their ideocratic world-view. Mass media, and even the arts, become the tools of indoctrination.

The capacity of the system for total mobilization is not without limitation. The constant barrage of calls for action dulls the senses of the public, many of whom go through the motions of participation while, in fact, doing the minimum that they believe to be required. Overmobilization, on occasion, creates disturbances within the system, as it interferes with the normal processes of management. (Examples would include workers' attempts to take over factories in the early days of the Soviet Union, during the Cultural Revolution in 1966-1969 China, and in 1968 in Czechoslovakia. Even the birth of the Solidarity Independent Trade Union movement in Poland, in 1980, could be related to efforts toward social mobilization by the then first secretary of the Polish Communist party, Edward Gierek.) The effectiveness of mobilization varies from group to group, and touches, to a lesser degree, peripheral individuals such as those in ethnic minorities, marginal religious communities, some institutions of higher education, specialized professions, artistic groups, artisans, and peasants. These persist as "islands of separateness," which continue to defend their traditional way of life. Finally, those in charge of mobilization find themselves, of necessity, appealing to the traditional culture of the society, thereby undermining the central purpose of mobilization, which aims at transcending many of the existing patterns. In fact, the culture is the most serious stumbling block to ideologically pure mobilization and the most persistent force counteracting ideocratic regeneration. For example, secular ideocracies experience

great difficulties in their attempts to uproot traditionally established religions.[29]

Frustration arising from the mixed results of
mobilization leads to the spread of political terror.
Terror aids mobilization by removing opponents and
some who waiver and by forcing others toward greater
conformity. The leaders of prior hostile or independent social organizations fall victim, but neither are
previous allies immune to persecution. Terror, also,
solidifies the society by seemingly cleansing it of ideological impurities. Violent attacks on scapegoats highlight the sense of unity among the mobilized masses
and justify the purpose of mobilization itself.

Terror creates specific problems for ideocracy,
however. It destroys individual initiative because it
inhibits unorthodox views and speculative actions. It
overloads the command lines of communication
because it creates a tendency to refer all matters to top
leadership, which alone feels secure from terror.
Furthermore, terror destroys trust among individuals. Although this encourages psychological subordination to the system, it also impairs the smooth operation of organizations. Organizational effectiveness
relies upon a certain degree of trust necessary for open
cooperation and effective communication. Terror, to
the contrary, distorts the truthfulness of reports to
superiors. Likewise it reduces the willingness of equals
to share potentially damaging information with each
other. More open communication is found mainly
among individuals in informal cliques that are concerned primarily with self-protection.

In addition, terror often feeds upon itself, in the
sense that the confessions of its victims implicate
broader and broader circles of further suspects, leading finally to the emergence of a psychosis in which all

are suspected. Increasingly terror is promoted for its own purposes. In this case, the terroristic organization overpowers the movement and deflects the system from its original pursuit of ideocratic goals, exercising an undue claim on its human and material resources.[30]

In general, the process of stabilization witnesses an intensified effort to realize the ideocratic utopia. At the same time a small band of idealistic revolutionaries must now face complex problems associated with maintaining a society. As a result, the movement becomes bureaucratized, and the ideology is skewed toward addressing issues concerned with the operation of the state. The old cultural patterns not only persist but also require accommodation, because the old ways provide vehicles for accomplishing immediate goals and for enhancing the legitimacy of the new system. In many ways, these older cultural norms are likewise the best available normative means for rebuilding social cohesion destroyed by the widespread disruption of the revolutionary period.

The system assumes a life of its own, profoundly affected by the inadequacy of centralized decision-making processes. The channels of communication are not sufficient to provide the information needed by central decision makers. Furthermore, information may be sharply distorted in its upward movement through the bureaucratic hierarchy; however, this cannot be independently verified, as the system has previously destroyed all external media of communication. In the absence of adequate central decision making, many new activities develop without real oversight from above. Furthermore, bureaucratic agencies, at all levels, begin to express their own self-interest and manipulate the implementation of central decisions to their own advantage.[31] The degree of central control is further eroded by infighting among the lieutenants, who jockey among themselves for resources and power.

In many areas, total mobilization fails in the face of persistent opposition of culturally based "islands of separateness." The system finds itself compelled to accommodate various centers of independence which have roots in the traditional society. Also many individuals retreat into nonparticipation or adopt a Machiavellian stance of calculated cooperation.

As with other political systems, ideocracies have varied degrees of success in addressing the problems of their societies. Although, on the surface, the vigor and concentration of these efforts brings spectacular short-run results, existing social cleavages may continue to persist. Eventually new systemic problems may be created by the overly zealous activities of ideocracy itself, particularly in areas of strong ideological commitment. Efforts to convert ethnic and religious groups often lead to resistance and occasionally outright rebellion. This saps the energy of the system and diverts it from other serious problems. Further, the extreme centralization of authority, the inflexibility of the ideology, and the closed character of communication networks make the ideocracy vulnerable to new challenges. For example, ideocracies have difficulty in adapting to technological change and to develop new technology themselves. All of these forces are seeds of further evolution beyond the initial stage of ideocratic stabilization.

VI

THE EVOLUTION OF IDEOCRACY

All societies are caught up in processes of evolutionary change. Even those systems that are relatively stable maintain their equilibrium through varied and continuing adjustments to internal and external change. Ideocracies are no exception, in spite of their seeming ability to enforce their order. Their lack of open debate concerning fundamental alternatives lends the impression that they are highly durable and in control in their courses of development. In fact, this is not the case. In our prior analysis we have shown that the establishment of control is never complete. Various contradictory influences continue to play within the system, undermining its stability. As with other political systems, ideocracies evolve in a wide variety of idiosyncratic ways. We conceptualize, however, three general paths of ideocratic evolution: self-destruction, peaceful erosion, and systemic regeneration. As a consequence of this evolution, some ideocracies are transformed into pluralistic political systems, whereas others revive their ideocratic purity.

Self-Destruction

The process of self-destruction results from either the failure of the ideocratic movement to maintain its unity or its inability to adequately penetrate and mobilize the society. In the first case, the growing ideological cleavage between factions within the movement leads to its division into clearly defined warring camps, which ally themselves with different portions of the society. This can result in an outbreak of civil war, which either destroys ideocracy or reestablishes it in a new form. To a limited degree, such was the case with the Chinese Cultural Revolution and is now in evidence in a number of republics of the former Soviet Union (e.g., Georgia, Tajikistan, Moldova). Despite the recent examples, this possibility is likely only in unusual circumstances. Cleavage within the movement is usually resolved internally, because the movement understands that its survival depends on its superior position vis-à-vis society at large. It has also proven true in China in the Great Leap Forward Movement (1954-1958), the Great Proletarian Cultural Revolution (1970-1976), and the Tiananmen Square Massacre (1990). It seems that, in the Soviet Union, Gorbachev failed to understand the rule, permitting the division within the party to spill over into a broader society. This was, no doubt, one of the reasons for the eventual demise of the USSR.

In the second case—that of a failure of penetration and mobilization of the society—self-destruction may occur either in terms of a military coup (e.g., Peron's Argentina, 1955), a popular rebellion (e.g., Poland, 1989), or a combination of the two (e.g., Romania in 1989).[1] In most cases, a military coup has the greatest potential for success. The armed forces, when permitted to develop their own cultural identity, which is essential for their military mission, can become frustrated with their subjugation to the movement and disaffected from the dominant ideology. Three general conditions create the potential for military coup: (1) when the military perceives itself denied the resources to carry out its mission (especially in the case of war); (2) when the military regards the government as highly inefficient in the pursuit of political, economic, and technological development; and (3) when the military perceives national prestige to be rapidly declining (e.g., the military takeover in Poland in 1981).[2] All ideocracies are aware of this danger and attempt to counterbalance the power of the military with the armed forces of the movement. Prominent examples were the S.S. troops in Nazi Germany and the KGB units in the Soviet Union. However, seldom can such a force defeat the military once the military decides to move (e.g., the military coup in Ghana against Nkrumah, 1966; in Portugal against Caetano, 1974; and in Romania against Ceausescu, 1989).[3]

From one perspective, the likelihood of popular rebellion is closely related to the stagnation of the ideocratic system, in which the demands of the population outstrip its ideological or economic ability to satisfy them. A well-developed security apparatus, should prevent a gradual preparation for a popular uprising. As a result rebellion must be spontaneous in nature. What it most likely achieves is a modification of ideocratic rule under the leadership of a new party faction. Most of the known popular rebellions in East-Central Europe were quelled by external Soviet force or threat of such force (e.g., German Democratic Republic, 1953; Hungary and Poland, 1956; Czechoslovakia, 1968; and Poland, 1970, 1976, 1980-1981). These rebellions succeed in overthrowing ideocratic rule only when the instruments of suppression are substantially undermined. In East-Central Europe, rebellions were victorious only after the threat of Soviet intervention was removed following Gorbachev's accession to power.[4]

Generally speaking, ideocracies exclude some portion of their societies, viewing them as representatives of counterideological forces (e.g., Jews in Nazi Germany; former bourgeoisie in communist countries; blacks, colored, and Asians in South Africa). If these groups are relatively small or lacking in internal cohesion, they are easily subjugated by the system. In these cases, popular uprisings may be acts of desperation with little chance of success, as was the anti-German Jewish uprising in the Warsaw ghetto in 1943. However, a large suppressed minority (blacks in South Africa) can mount a substantial rebellion and, in some circumstances, destroy the system, especially if aided by those from outside the society. This potential is heightened if the ideocracy has expanded to bring colonies or satellites under its rule, such as the Ethiopian rebellion against the Italian Fascists (1942), the Yugoslavian guerrilla campaign against Nazi rule in World War II, the anti-Soviet unrest in East-Central Europe, or the guerrilla war against the Soviet-backed communist government in Afghanistan.

Ideocracies are absolutist in their ideologies and therefore deal with their external environment in one, or both, of two ways: first by territorial expansion and conquest of their ideological enemies (e.g., Iraq's attack on Iran, 1980, and on Kuwait, 1990), and second by the rigorous restriction of intercourse with external systems. In either of these cases, their utopian goals, coupled with hostility toward the external world, encourage other nations to fear their aggressive potential. Sometimes this fear reflects reality and sometimes it does not.

Depending on their ideologies and leadership, some ideocracies have a real propensity for aggressive territorial expansion, either for simply extending their ideocratic dominance or for liberating their ideological brothers, seemingly oppressed by other systems. This aggression against other countries can involve direct military attack (as in Iraq's attack on Iran and Kuwait), terroristic acts, or the promotion of internal rebellion (as by Iran or Libya). In all three cases, but especially that of military aggression, this can lead to the demise of ideocracy, because its uncompromising view of reality encourages an overextension of its forces. This overextension undermines its capacity to control its expanded territories and often stimulates a powerful coalition to counterattack, (e.g., Nazi Germany, Fascist Italy, and Japan in World War II; Iraq's invasion of Kuwait in 1990).

Ideocracy may also be destroyed by attacks from the outside. A country may engage in such an intervention because of sympathy for oppressed within the ideocracy, fear of ideocratic aggression, and finally fear of ideological conversion of their own population. This may involve subversion, in which potential internal enemies of ideocracy are provided the means for rebellion (e.g., the U.S. support of guerrillas in Afghanistan, "Contras" in Nicaragua, and Kurds in Iraq).[5] Alternatively, it can lead to direct military action, which is often regarded as preventive war (the allied military intervention against the "Reds" in the Russian Civil War of 1917-1921).[6] During the World War II, the Allies eventually sought the complete eradication of the Nazi, Fascist, and Japanese ideocracies.

Thus, certain tendencies of ideocratic systems, toward intense conflict and the adoption of extreme ideological positions, contain the seeds of self-destruction. This does not mean that most ideocracies are destined to end in such a way. Indeed, other characteristics impel them toward contrary patterns of evolution.

Peaceful Erosion

The principles upon which ideocracy is created address extreme crises of collective life. They require heroic efforts to gain distant utopian visions—visions that appeal most easily to those who are critically disturbed by profound personal crisis and social disruption. Eventually, some achievements of regeneration and stabilization create a sense of satisfaction in the social and economic spheres. New generations are born for which the revolution is only a historical event. The society moves well beyond the period of severe social disruption and conflict. New generations become socialized to broadly accept the system, with an increased interest in its daily maintenance. More concern with individual prosperity and careers becomes evident. All this creates a relaxation of the intense ideological commitment that attended the inception of ideocracy. Such normalization increases the tolerance of differences in the system and creates a general tendency toward pluralism. In ideocracies that experience considerable technological development, there is a marked increase in the complexity of the system. In some ways, the employment of technology facilitates centralized social control, by its ability to bring the leadership and the people into closer contact through improved communications and transportation.[7] At the same time, this technological development brings increased specialization and organizational complexity.[8] These, in turn, greatly magnify the volume and diversity of decisions that must be made to maintain the system. In fact, the centralized system of controls tends to fragment, as many specialized centers of decision making appear and gain functional authority. It becomes increasingly difficult to control such centers and their highly technical membership.[9] All these tendencies deflect the system from its utopian goals.

This is particularly evident in the increased gap between the theoretical and doctrinal parts of the ideology. Doctrine becomes adjusted to the pragmatic processes of problem solving, especially in regard to concerns not directly treated by the original ideology. Arguments emerge that ideology is a living thing, evolving over time. More and more spheres of activity are defined as nonideological and controlled by other criteria, such as scientific and aesthetic standards. Theory, although still asserted strongly, becomes more general and highly abstract, as contrasted with its more precise application during the process of stabilization.[10] This theoretical abstraction eventually encourages ideological controversies, which are increasingly distant from the pragmatic decisions of daily life. Serious ideological disputes are relegated to the chambers of the ideologues and philosophers, while the politicians engage in ritualistic references to the tenets as justification for their particular policy preferences. Eventually ideology erodes to the degree that it loses both its function as the central legitimizer of social action and also its exclusive monopoly in the realm of ideas.

The charismatic leader of the heroic period and the absolute dictator of the period of stabilization changes to the consummate bureaucratic politician, whose leading role derives from his position in the bureaucracy of the movement. His function is more and more that of a chairman of the board, in which he arbitrates claims of various groups and interests with the advice and consent of his lieutenants, who form with him the top political council. The security of the top leader's position depends on his ability to maintain a sense of governmental effectiveness and social well-being. The lieutenants are appointed to their offices for their ability to manage specific portions of the system. For this reason, they gain increased independence from the top leader, and when his failures become apparent, they may even remove him from power (e.g., Khrushchev in the Soviet Union in 1966, Gomulka in 1970 and Gierek in 1980 in Poland, and the remaining "old" communist leaders in Central Europe in 1989-1990: Kadar in Hungary, Zhivkov in Bulgaria, Husak in Czechoslovakia, and Honecker in East Germany).

The movement becomes more like a traditional oligarchic elite, composed of career-oriented members interested in system maintenance and bound together by political patronage. Its power becomes independent of the top leadership. The movement, as a collective body, exercises a growing influence on the decision-making process, including the selection of the top leaders. Within it, legitimate functional elites develop, which realize an increased degree of autonomy in their spheres of functional authority. They are allied with nonmovement specialists, some of whom are even permitted to hold executive positions. This alliance reflects the aforementioned decline of ideological intensity. Furthermore, concern with technical expertise allows more freedom in debates over policy alternatives and permits dissenting opinions on the grounds of technical knowledge.[11] In general, the leadership becomes more diffused and differentiated along functional lines so that separate bureaucracies exercise a considerable degree of autonomy under the umbrella of the general policies of the movement. The arbitrariness of policy decisions is now constrained by a body of pragmatic rules and regulations that are claimed to be consistent with the precepts of the ideology. They are now regarded to be essential for the maintenance of a stable system. An increased emphasis is placed upon legality and precedent, in contrast to the prior revolutionary contempt for procedural restraints upon action.[12]

Political decision-making now has to respond to competing interests. Leaders engage in the pragmatic calculation of political gain or loss. The ideology becomes more and more detached from reality, although it still serves to justify courses of action that have been taken. This leads to a growing sense within the population of the hypocrisy of the leaders, whose proclamation of exalted standards poorly masks seemingly self-serving actions. Growing cynicism throughout the system undermines its effective functioning.[13] This is highlighted by a growing reliance on officially tolerated black markets, which pervade the economic system and complement the growing corruption in the state bureaucracy and in the movement.

Although all social organizations are subject to political penetration, the changed nature of the movement leads to the greater identification of the members with those organizations in which they participate. The organizations themselves begin to assert independent political power—in extreme cases even challenging the hegemony of the movement publicly (e.g., trade unions in Czechoslovakia in 1968 and the official trade unions in Poland after 1981 military coup). Also, specific organizations assume freedom in the selection of their own personnel, especially in scientific and technical fields. Career patterns depend increasingly upon educational qualifications, in addition to the membership in the movement. The surviving islands of separateness are brought into the system by acceptance of their deviant views and activities, which, in fact, become less extraordinary as the ideocratic system moderates its extreme standards (e.g., representation, from 1956, of Catholics in the parliament of the Polish People's Republic). As ideocratic regulation of the system relaxes, diverse social and economic organizations take on decision-making powers within their own spheres. Many centralized controls give way to decentralized adjustments among diverse social organizations and through their cooperation in alliances of mutual interest. Thus, power is increasingly dispersed among numerous centers in the society, undercutting the effectiveness of political penetration. Personal incentives are increasingly prominent in all social actions. The stress on system maintenance and efficiency highlights the individual's interest in economic well-being, which, in turn, further undermines the relevance of the ideology. Given new career requirements, the educational system gradually moves away from ideological indoctrination to the teaching of scientific standards and technological applications.

The terroristic organization, so prominent in the period of stabilization, is now reduced in size and in its role as a vehicle of mobilization and regeneration. It becomes one of the many information channels, and it collects data on general performance, as well as violations of legal standards. The legality of its actions, rather than political expediency, becomes increasingly the dominant criterion for its operation. Its earlier purview, which included the sweeping matter of individual commitment to the utopian vision of ideocracy, is now reduced to focus primarily on overt attacks upon the system as it is presently constituted. Again, its earlier reliance upon physical coercion gives way to the employment of psychological and economic pressures. It is often argued that psychological tools exemplify the sophistication of the security apparatus and that they are a more effective means of control than physical coercion. However, such tools can be applied to only a small number of individuals and cannot create the same degree of fear as the direct application of physical terror. The realm of private freedom expands, in the sense that only repeated public expressions of deviant ideas are considered criminal attacks upon the system. There emerges the semiofficial recognition of competitive points of view and philosophies, so long as they are kept out of broad public view. Neither the intellectual privately expressing heretical opinions nor the drunken individual cursing the regime risks arrest by the political police.[14]

In the mass media the concern for ideological orthodoxy competes with a growing emphasis on the influence of popular interests. The increasing autonomy of different media organizations spurs their competition for audience attention. Although the media still mobilize support for the general system, more time and space are devoted to entertainment, art, human interest, and popular education. As the intensity of ideocratic rule diminishes, the social system becomes less isolated from the international exchange of ideas. With the flow of visitors and writings from abroad and penetration of the system by foreign news sources, the national media are compelled to give more truthful reporting of events and more sophisticated interpretations of their significance (e.g., ability of most East Germans before the unification of Germany to watch West German television and of East-Central Europeans under communism to listen to Radio Free Europe). Individual media personalities vie with one another for public recognition and fame. Recognition flows most quickly to those who are most controversial in their presentation or performances. Various organizations use both their own organs and the general media for presentation of their particular points of view. As the channels of public information contain increasingly diverse and sometimes conflicting views, the media became a battleground of competing interests and policy alternatives. The top leadership, as well as individual politicians representing organizations and localities, appeals to the public for support of their policies. Sometimes new programs are debated prior to their adoption to ascertain public reaction. In addition, the media become vehicles for the collection of public opinion through letters to the editor, opinion polls, talk shows, and so forth.[15] Even previous islands of separateness are allocated time and space in the general media and allowed to distribute their own publications, expressing their particular viewpoints within an expanding realm of ideological tolerance (e.g., in Poland under communism, the Catholic Church's weekly and monthly publications and, since 1980, Catholic mass on the radio). The growing freedom of expression in media contributes to the erosion of the ideocratic system.

Artistic expression develops in two directions, both of which lessen the ideological function of the arts. In the first of these there is a tendency toward the cultivation of art for art's sake, undermining the use of art to convey an ideological message. The second trend, of more immediately damaging consequences, regards the view that art should be a vehicle of social criticism and innovative ideas. Although the first comes to be broadly tolerated, the second is periodically restrained in its most extreme attacks on the system. The growing freedom of aesthetic experience stimulated by the first trend increases the popularity of the expressive freedom associated with the second. Outstanding individual artists gain a widely recognized fame (both internally and abroad) and, hence, a certain immunity from political suppression. They may become leaders of the opposition to the ideocratic rule (e.g., Vaclav Havel, a playwright, eventually a president of Czechoslovakia and, from 1993, of the Czech Republic). Art in general becomes more universal and certain foreign artists gain broad popularity. During this period, the form becomes more abstract, thus the message is increasingly veiled and difficult to control (e.g., plays by Slawomir Mrozek in Poland in the 1960s and plays by the aforementioned Havel).[16] The competition for public acclaim, as well as the concern for creative artistic expression, brings an innovative dynamic to artistic endeavors. With the declining use of art for ideological mobilization, the governmental subsidies are gradually replaced by market sources, which in turn, increase the independence of art from the political system. In general terms, the system becomes less concerned with the form of artistic expression and relaxes its controls over the content.

All of these changes in the system affect the performance of the economy. Initially, the lessening of central controls and the increasing reliance on pragmatic solutions stimulate general economic growth. The development of the economy shifts from expenditures on the military, related to the earlier expansionist policies to the satisfaction of internal needs. Subjected to less indoctrination, mobilization, and terror, the population seeks satisfaction in personal consumption. Although the expanding economy responds to this desire, the rising expectations of the people eventually outstrips the capacity of the system to sat-

isfy them. This leads to a growing sense of deprivation, contributing to a further decline in support for
the system.[17] Alarmed by this, the leadership will
attempt to continue the economic expansion.

Continuing growth of the economy becomes
increasingly problematic due to the relative exhaus-
tion of natural and capital resources. It is partially
because the conversion from military to civilian production is more difficult than initially assumed. More
and more the leaders rely on foreign borrowing and
deficit spending to meet popular demands. Eventually
the system outstrips its ability to service the rising
debt and prevent economic decline. The resulting
chronic economic crisis further undermines the ideocracy. In conclusion, the net impact of these developments—the decline of ideological fervor; the fragmentation of political power, the corruption of the
bureaucracy, the emergence of semiautonomous
social and economic organizations, and the spread of
materialistic interests, the increase in cultural pluralism, and the stagnation of the economy—is the
cumulative erosion of ideocratic control and the evolution of the system toward pluralism. This does not
necessarily mean the immediate democratization of
the system, but quite likely, the emergence of the
more authoritarian form of pluralism—oligarchy (e.g.,
the Soviet Union in the late 1980s). Some balance of
power develops between the central political leadership and diverse centers of organizational power. This
occasions new forms of decision making by accommodation among these contending powers. However,
the process of political change may not stabilize at
this point, but it may continue toward the emergence
of democracy or may result in a break-up of the system into independent states.[18]

Regeneration

Either of the preceding processes, self-destruction or peaceful erosion, may be arrested by a new thrust toward the regeneration of the ideocracy. This may occur either through piecemeal attempts to reverse the trend toward dissolution or by a sweeping wave of activity, sometimes violent, aimed at reinfusing the fervor of revolutionary ideocratic commitment. This regeneration requires reinterpretation of the ideology to meet the current threats to the ideocracy. If the disruption of the system is sufficiently fundamental, there may be a shift to an alternative monistic ideology (e.g., from communism to fascist nationalism or religious fundamentalism). Often the some vehicles of ideocratic control are employed within the new system (e.g., hiring the previous Gestapo officials by the new communist government of the [East] German Democratic Republic, 1945-1946).

We have described processes that lead to the disintegration of ideocracy through self-destruction and peaceful erosion. In the midst of these processes, various kinds of situations can trigger the process of regeneration. The disintegration of ideocracy releases previously suppressed elite, class, ethnic, and religious animosities. If these cause conflicts of considerable intensity, often combined with extreme violence, the leadership can reimpose extreme ideocratic controls, often welcomed by the majority. A variety of different factors can cause the same response. These include widespread corruption and crime, collapse of the economy, the emergence of groups demanding greater political freedom, and the threat of hostile outside forces (many of these conditions exist today in the successor states of the Soviet Union and Yugoslavia).

The process of regeneration may be initiated by a group within the movement, who are still intensely committed to the utopian goals and form a new faction aimed at revitalizing ideocracy from within its ranks. Such a group can combine with one or more personas among the top leadership of the movement (e.g., the Red Guards and Mao Dze-dang in the Great Cultural Revolution of 1966 in China). Equally likely, the top leader may attempt to reverse the dissolution of the system by marshaling portions of the system to reinvigorate the whole. Given the vast organization of the system, the top leader may pursue this goal without the creation of a new revitalizing faction. Instead, he elevates one of the existing organizations or a part of it as his agent of regeneration (e.g., the armed forces and police apparatus, as General Jaruzelski did in Poland in 1981).[19]

The means of regeneration are essentially the same as those used during the periods of ideocratic inception and stabilization. Above all, an extensive purge is instituted to cleanse the system of the uncommitted and the corrupt. This is combined with an intensification of terror, involving the renewed use of scapegoats. Certain groups and top leaders are singled out as primarily responsible for the corruption of ideocratic purity and the perversion of organizational power. They are forced to confess their sins, and other individuals are allowed to recommit themselves to the renewed ideocratic vision. The movement once purged, heightens its activity within the system, penetrating anew all social organizations replacing much of their previous leadership with individuals rededicated to the new goals. The legitimacy of all these changes is derived from a newly intensified and focused ideology in which theoretical and doctrinal levels are again brought together. In the case of an extreme transition, a completely new ideology is adopted. The whole society is mobilized to defend the system against the newly perceived dangers. The islands of separateness are pushed to the periphery of the society. (This was very much the case in Hungary, 1956, and Czechoslovakia, 1968, after their liberal reforms were reversed by Soviet invasions.) Generally speaking, this is either a period of retreat from external contact or one of adventuresome aggression. In both of these cases, a heightened perception of external enemies is generated.

In conclusion, various evolutionary problems in the development of ideocratic systems bring about a response toward regeneration by an intensely committed movement combined with, or initiated by, elements of the top leadership. These attempts at regeneration are further stimulated by systemic instability, which increases the responsiveness of various groups to the regenerative efforts. Thus, there emerges a general process of regeneration, which spreads involvement and furthers intensified ideocratic commitment. Such regeneration, of course, entails many of the same problems and limitations as those experienced during the initial periods of ideocratic inception and stabilization.

Conclusion: Ideocracy and Processes of Dynamic Change

Earlier in this study, we presented an ideal-type model of ideocracy. In discussing its applicability, we examined both patterns of thought and action that conformed to it and those patterns that contradicted the purity of the model's logical structure. In Chapters V and VI, we noted various processes of change that sometimes intensify ideocratic characteristics and, at other times, substantially decrease the extent to which these systems approximate the ideocratic ideal. We have systematically related typical processes of social change to the major variables of our model of ideocracy—ideology, organization of political leadership, penetration, and mobilization. We have shown how these processes affect the movement of ideocratic systems along a continuum with pure ideocracy and pluralism at its polar extremes. Furthermore, we have distinguished three general phases of ideocratic dynamics—inception, stabilization, and subsequent evolution. In all these phases, contradictory forces were shown to be at work, so that the net processes of change in one direction often set the stage for further swings of the pendulum in the opposite direction.

We have said that evolution of ideocracy can lead either to its demise, through violent or peaceful means, or to its regeneration. In reality, particular systems evolve in a variety of ways over time. Thus, periods of violent change intermingle with those of peaceful transition, and efforts toward regeneration are periodically undertaken. The history of any one system will involve a unique evolutionary pattern. All communist ideocracies have witnessed periods of peaceful erosion and attempts at regeneration. The Soviet Union and its Central European satellites were eventually altered to the point that they were transformed into essentially different systems. The ways in which this evolution has occurred are theoretically instructive.

Ideocracies can evolve into either an authoritarian or a democratic from of pluralism. In some cases, as noted previously, they can also regenerate as some new form of ideocracy. Alternatively, those with substantial ethnic, religious, or national divisions may

actually break into separate countries. Indeed, conflict over the nature of the subsequent political system
is often a strong stimulus for territorial disintegration.
The previous Soviet Union has broken into a variety of
different states. The Central Asian Republics seem to
be choosing an authoritarian solution. Latvia, Estonia,
and Lithuania are pursuing a democratic road. The
Russian direction is still in doubt, with significant conflicts among different elites and territories very much
in evidence. Georgia, Tajikistan, and Moldova are in
the throes of civil war; and Azerbaijan and Armenia
are fighting over the disputed territory. These examples illustrate the various theoretical outcomes
described above.

CONCLUSION

In this work, we have employed the concept of ideocracy to explore a wide range of political systems that have appeared throughout recorded history. Although our discussion concentrated on recent ideocracies, associated with the modern or the modernizing world, earlier examples abound in history. Our emphasis upon monistic ideology as the distinguishing feature of ideocracy is the key to recognizing the commonality among this historically diverse set of political systems, ranging from highly consensual, traditional systems to revolutionary systems racked by political terror.

By posing ideocracy against different forms of ideological pluralism, we have been able to distinguish ideocracy from authoritarianism, a political form that stands midway between the political pluralism of democracy and the all-encompassing monism of ideocracy. In our dynamic analysis of ideocracy, we have considered an array of social forces at work that affect the evolution of all political systems. In certain circumstances, these forces make likely the emergence of ideocracy in prior authoritarian or democratic polities. In others, they may bring changes that stimulate the emergence of authoritarian or democratic impulses that undermine ideocracy.

Our typology classifies political systems in regard to the principles on which their authority rests. This approach is not inconsistent with other common classifying schemes. In fact, further clarification of our analysis can be found in discussion of them. The classical typology of Aristotle distinguishes political systems by three criteria: the number of rulers, their original social position, and in whose interest they rule. Like authoritarian systems, totalitarian ideocracies are ruled by one or, at most, a small coterie of leaders. Traditional populist ideocracies share more dispersed leadership with democracies. By condensing the other two Aristotelian categories, we may distinguish conservative ideocracies protecting an idealized status quo (e.g., the Islamic fundamentalism of Saudi Arabia) from revolutionary ideocracies pursuing utopian future perfection (e.g., the Islamic fundamentalism of Iran).

Another generally accepted approach classifies political systems as either traditional or modern. We have argued that some folk societies have been nascent ideocracies. Their incorporation in larger political entities typically results in traditional authoritarian rule (e.g., hereditary monarchy). In our times, ideocracies have often appeared in the transition from traditional to modern societies—from systems governed by centuries old norms and values to those characterized by considerable social pluralism, coupled with rapidly progressing science and technology. This transition, especially in periods of severe social disruption, has often occasioned the emergence of ideocracy, in either its conservative or its revolutionary form. The dislocation caused by industrialization and urbanization, accelerated by the multiplier effects of World War I, led to the revolutionary ideocracies of the Communist Soviet Union, Fascist Italy, and Nazi Germany, and the conservative state Shintoism of Japan. Today, some Islamic countries, destabilized by Westernization, combined in few cases with sudden oil wealth, have become ideocracies: radical fundamentalist governments of Iran and Sudan and the Ba'thist socialism of Iraq and Syria.

Our analysis of ideocracy should broaden our understanding of nonideocratic political systems. Notwithstanding its distinctive commitment to a monistic ideology, ideocracy does share many characteristics with other political systems. In these concluding remarks, we shall consider some of the political phenomena of significance in our times in their relationship to ideocracy.

In the modern world, the dominant political units are nation states, subsuming lesser social groups in national political systems. These are held together by the sense of common belonging expressed by the assumed common biological origin and the community of language, customs, religion, and culture, occupying a definite territory, under one sovereign government. In fact, few of the contemporary nation states exhibit all of these characteristics. Nevertheless, successful states override a multiplicity of powerful political, religious, and ethnic loyalties of social group within their territory (as with the United States or the former empire of the Soviet Union). In others, nation states reflect the predominance of one historical group, as in the case of Germany, France, or Thailand. The political power of all nation states is associated with the influence of a dominant political ideology with which the masses identify. This ideology has the characteristics of a "civic religion" in that it supports the sanctity of the nation state in claiming the life and death loyalty of its citizens.[1] However, the modern nation state is associated with a highly complex society, which holds within it very diverse groups and their varied beliefs. Where pluralism is present, the civic religion does not encompass all social life. Some social subsystems, with their attendant social norms, are tolerated and ignored within authoritarian political systems, whereas diverse social subsystems are actually integrated within the political systems of democracy. However, the civic religion of ideocracy is monistic and, thus, excludes all competing systems of ideas.

It should be recognized, however, that various expressions of authoritarian nationalism may be extremely aggressive externally and inhospitable toward internal ethnic minorities without being ideocracies. Identification with an exclusive "volk" or ethnic group is consistent with support for ideocracy, but may not be accompanied by the existence of a full-blown monistic ideology. Instead, traditional ethnic hostilities may be sufficient to support repressive political measures, even ethnic cleansing. Indeed sharp ethnic conflicts are often found in the histories of pluralist systems as well. It has been shown that marginal ethnic groups often have to force their way into positions of influence in democratic systems.[2] Further, democratic systems often exhibit a "paranoid" style of politics as they respond to unsettling social change by striking out against imagined apocalyptic conspiracies.[3] In the extreme, democracies may give way to ideocratic movements, as was the case in Weimar Germany with the Nazis. Violence and social conflict are found throughout the spectrum of political regimes.

On the surface, contemporary ideocracies, like authoritarian systems, share with democracies many institutions. They have executive, legislative, and judicial branches; however, these serve different functions in an ideocracy. They are fully subordinated to the central leadership and must operate under the tenets of the monistic ideology. For example, elections in democracies provide mechanisms for the expression of pluralistic interests, whereas in ideocracies they serve only to demonstrate approval for the existing monistic system. In most, a single candidate is chosen by the movement for each position. In populist ideocracies, they may be a contest among ideologically committed candidates. Equally so, the legislature and the judiciary give expression to the dictates of the leadership under the auspices of the monistic ideology. Although the institutional framework is similar to that of democracy, its functions within the system are quite different.

Nor are extensive political efforts to integrate national socio-political organizations into the political system exclusive to ideocracy. It is true that extensive controls over these organizations (the armed forces, religious bodies, employers, and labor) are integral to the operations of ideocratic government. However, in the global economy of the twentieth century, nations with diverse political systems have sought political control over their developing societies in the effort to modernize or to further enhance a modern economy. Such "corporatist" political systems are to be found throughout the world.[4] These systems have significantly extended the reach of political control within the society and have incorporated a vision of social and economic progress within the dominant political ideology. A wide variety of political regimes—from ideocratic (communist) to authoritarian (Mexico) to democratic (Japan)—have adopted this approach to social and economic development. It may be expected that the economic success of corporatist political systems in an increasingly competitive global economy will see their continuing adoption in further political systems. The critical issue in regard to ideocracy is whether corporatism is accompanied by the emergence of a monistic ideology that is employed to suppress ideological and social pluralism throughout the society. In many instances to date, this has not been the case. But in some, corporatist organization is integral to an ideocratic system (fascism).

The fact that ideocracy shares these various characteristics with other types of political systems allows analysis with concepts common to them all. But in each case the analysis of a particular characteristic is misleading without reference to the broader political system in which it is found. And, therefore, our typology of political systems has provided an illuminating context within which to examine particular aspects of the entire spectrum of systems.

As already indicated, we have not seen the end of ideocracy: such systems continue to emerge and to depart from the world scene. Our framework of analysis has allowed us to identify a wide range of them. We have noted their existence throughout history and across diverse cultures. Our analysis has also revealed the dynamics through which ideocracies emerge, stabilize, and transform. The forces at play in all of these phases are fundamental to social life in a wide variety of historical settings. As already noted, radical Islamic fundamentalism, extremist ethnic nationalism, fascism, and the remains of communism provide monistic ideologies that still support the emergence of ideocracy. Ideocracies under various banners continue to pursue policies of total dominance in nations such as Iran, Iraq, and North Korea. We expect to witness no drastic decline in the incidence of ideocracy. Instead, it may be expected to emerge and recede and emerge again as complex historical circumstances dictate.

In modern times, ideocracy has involved the search of humans for perfection. It is a product of their response to seemingly overwhelming threats to their social well-being—a romantic response to periods of intense human crisis. However, the underlying forces of history and the limitations they impose on human designs frustrate the grand schemes of ideocracy. Although many ideocratic plans are realized, the unsuccessful pursuit of its utopian goals intensifies contradictory social forces. Eventually these undermine ideocracy. In some cases, they are met with renewed ideocratic vigor, whereas in others, they lead to a transformation from ideocracy to authoritarianism or even democracy. In essence, humans must build their schemes within an environment which they mean to control, but only imperfectly understand. Thus, their efforts must be ever again renewed, as they are met with only partial successes and recurring failures.

NOTES

Introduction

1. Ideocracies referred to in this work include the ancient empires of Babylon and Egypt, the empires of Incas and Aztecs, Sparta, Imperial China, Calvin's Geneva, Puritan Massachusetts, Fascist Italy, Salazar's Portugal, Peron's Argentina, Nazi Germany, Ba'thist Iraq and Syria, apartheid Republic of South Africa, Islamic fundamentalist Iran and Sudan, and communist countries: USSR, Albania, Bulgaria, Czechoslovakia, East Germany, Hungary, Poland, Romania, Cuba, China, Vietnam, and North Korea. At times, all of these have been ideocracies, as we define the term. In addition, we have studied a number of ideocratic movements and guerrilla and terrorist groups.

2. E. Adamson Hoebel and Thomas Weaver, *Anthropology and the Human Experience*, 1979.

3. On the ideocratic characteristics of these two empires, see Geoffrey W. Conrad and Arthur A. Demarest, *Religion and Empire: The Dynamics of Aztec and Inca Expansionism*, 1984; and, Rafael Karsten, *A Totalitarian State of the Past: The Civilization of the Inca Empire in Ancient Peru*, 1969.

4. "Dottrina . . .", *Encyclopedia Italiana*, 1932; American translation in *Political Quarterly* 4 (July 1933): 341-356. Benito Mussolini, 1883-1945; prime minister and dictator of Italy, 1922-1943.

5. Adolf Hitler, 1889-1945; dictator of Germany, 1933-1945.

6. Such as by Franz Borkenau, *The Totalitarian Enemy*, 1940; or William Ebenstein, *The Nazi State*, 1943.

7. The *Aryan* was a Nazi term for a superior human race—the supermen. In the twentieth century Europe these were people of Germanic origin: German, Dutch, Danish, Swedish, Norwegian, and Anglo-Saxon.

8. Among works in this period, the most interesting were Merle Fainsod, *Smolensk Under Soviet Rule*, 1958; and R. A. Bauer, A. Inkeles, and C. Kluckhohn, *How the Soviet System Works*, 1960.

9. Especially in *The Origins of Totalitarianism* first published in 1951 in New York.

10. Many other writers observed similar phenomena and tried to provide answers, e.g., Jose Ortega y Gasset, *The Revolt of the Masses*, 1985 ed.

11. It is instructive to observe that a similar feeling exists among some Israelis toward the Arabs and among many Arabs toward the Jews or "infidels" in general.

12. This is often referred to as *Social Darwinism*, understood as the application of Darwin's theory to humanity in which those stronger, more aggressive, and ruthless groups survive at the expense of weaker groups of humans.

13. The last argument is central to Ortega y Gasset, *The Revolt of the Masses*. The idea of the superman came from a French aristocrat, Arthur de Gobineau, *The Inequality of Human Races*, first published in 1853, and writings of German philosopher, Friedrich Nietzsche, 1844-1900.

14. Arendt, *The Origins of Totalitarianism*, 1973 ed., p. 469.

15. First published by Harvard University Press in 1956.

16. The main framework was developed by Friedrich already in late 1930s in an unpublished book-length manuscript: "Totalitarian Dictatorship," pp. vii and viii. In

1953 Friedrich edited a volume of proceedings for the American Academy of Arts and Sciences, in Chapter 1 of which he provided a general conception of totalitarianism (C. J. Friedrich, ed., *Totalitarianism*, 1954). Brzezinski was already an author of *The Permanent Purge: Politics in Soviet Totalitarianism*, 1956.

17. Among others, especially works by Aron, Bauer, Borgese, Borkenau, Bullock, Carr, Dallin, Deutscher, Fainsod, Finer, Germino, Gilbert, Inkeles, Kulski, Leites, Mehner, Barrington Moore, Franz Neumann, Sigmund Neumann, Pipes, Salvemini, Seton-Watson, Ulam, Veblen, and Bertram D. Wolfe.

18. In an insightful article on models, typological constructs, and other conceptual schemes in political science, Giovanni Sartori suggests that totalitarianism is more appropriately treated as a typological construct than as a model. We delve into this issue later in Chapter I. See Sartori, "Totalitarianism, Model Mania, and Learning from Error," *Journal of Theoretical Politics* 5, no. 1 (1993): 5-22.

19. John N. Hazard, *Soviet System of Government*, 1969.

20. Ludwig Bertalanffy, *General System Theory: A New Approach to the Unity of Science*, 1968 ed.

21. Friedrich and Brzezinski, *Totalitarian Dictatorship*, 1965 ed., p. 9.

22. Michael Weinstein, *Philosophy, Theory, and Method in Contemporary Political Thought*, 1971, p. 46.

23. Aiming at "scientific" precision, the "new" behavioral school preferred the less exacting term *paradigm* denoting a theoretical construct synthesizing aspects of empirical reality to the more exacting term *model* with its connotation of a structural isomorphism with the real world.

24. The configurative school assumed each political system to be strictly culturally bound, and hence unique, on

a country by country, or at least on a regional, basis. It stressed the importance of national or regional culture.

25. For example, H. Gordon Skilling and Franklin Griffiths, who were pioneers in application of interest group approach (*Interest Groups in Soviet Politics*, 1971) or in more general sense Jerry Hough, who used pluralistic theory (*The Soviet Union and Social Science Theory*, 1977).

26. Adam Przeworski and Henry Teune in their study of political attitudes in India, Poland, and the United States (*The Logic of Comparative Social Inquiry*, 1970).

27. Walt Whitman Rostow, *The Stages of Economic Growth*, 1971 ed. A. F. K. Organski, *Stages of Political Development*, 1967.

28. Zbigniew Brzezinski and Samuel P. Huntington, *Political Power: USA/USSR, Similarities and Contrasts, Convergence and Evolution*, 1964.

29. Claude Saint-Simon (1760-1825) was a French social philosopher and the author of *Social Organization, the Science of Man*, 1964 ed.; Thorstein Veblen, *The Engineers and the Price System*, 1936; James Burnham, *The Managerial Revolution*, 1941; Jacques Ellul, *The Technological Society*, 1964. Peter C. Ludz applied managerial theory to his study of German Democratic Republic (East Germany) in *The Changing Party Elite in East Germany*, 1972; and with some reservations the theory was utilized by Thomas A. Baylis in *The Technical Intelligentsia and the East German Elite*, 1974. It was tested empirically with mixed results by Randall D. Oestreicher, "Technocracy and Public Policy: Poland, 1950-1980," 1981.

30. Typical was a formulation by a scholar of Spanish, Portuguese, and Nazi regimes, Juan Linz, who suggested the following characteristics of totalitarianism:

1. A monistic but not monolithic center of power.
2. An exclusive, autonomous, and more or less intellectually elaborate ideology that serves to legitimize the leader's power.

3. Citizen participation and active mobilization for political and collective social tasks.

"Totalitarian and Authoritarian Regimes" in F. Greenstein and N. Polsby, eds., *Handbook of Political Science*, vol. 3, 1975, pp. 187-252. A more recent book on the subject is basically a restatement of syndromes of Friedrich and Brzezinski—Michael Curtis, *Totalitarianism*, 1979.

31. James A. Gregor, *Contemporary Radical Ideologies: Totalitarian Thought in the Twentieth Century*, 1968.

32. C. W. Cassinelli, *Total Revolution*, 1976.

33. Samuel P. Huntington and Clement H. Moore, eds., *Authoritarian Politics in Modern Society*, 1970.

34. Robert Tucker, "Towards a Comparative Politics of Movement Regimes," *American Political Science Review* (June 1961).

35. Such as Joseph Nyomarkay, *Charisma and Factionalism in the Nazi Party*, 1967; Dennis Mark Smith, *Mussolini's Roman Empire*, 1976; Merle Fainsod, *Smolensk Under Soviet Rule*, 1958.

36. The problem that the Soviet Union had in reforming its economy and in making it more productive was exactly the result of that ideological predilection in which the belief in superiority of state ownership and central planning for human needs, rather than for profit, stifled private initiatives. Even in the East-Central European countries, on which communism was imposed by the Soviets, indoctrination succeeded in convincing many people of the superiority of socialism (e.g., Jaroslaw A. Piekalkiewicz, *Public Opinion Polling in Czechoslovakia, 1968-69*, 1972, pp. 3-6 and 334-336).

37. The best example here was the government of Taiwan in 1970s-1980s, which although authoritarian politically, left relatively free of interference economic, religious, artistic, or other private aspirations of its subjects.

38. The Eastonian definition of politics as the authoritative allocation of values encourages this broad view of political authority in authoritarian systems (David Easton, *A Framework for Political Analysis*, 1965).

39. In strictly Islamic countries freedom of scientific pursuits is hard to maintain because Islam does not recognize the separation of religion and the state. The Quar'an (Koran) provides exact prescriptions for political and legal systems. A striking example of Nazi ideological control of science was the exclusion from scientific work of all individuals of Jewish origin (e.g., Hannah Arendt). Because many of these people were leaders in their disciplines, parts of German science and technology fell behind that of Great Britain and the United States. This became plainly obvious during the later stages of World War II and especially in the creation of the atomic bomb in the United States, on which some of these Jewish emigrate scientists from Europe worked.

40. Milton Rokeach, *The Open and Closed Mind*, 1960.

41. For example, Vaclav Havel in *Power of the Powerless*, 1985; Adam Michnic in *Letters from Prison and Other Essays*, 1987; or Krystyna Kersten in *The Establishment of Communist Rule in Poland, 1943-1948*, 1992.

42. For example Giovanni Sartori, "Totalitarianism, Model Mania and Learning from Error," *Journal of Theoretical Politics* 5, no. 1 (1993): 5-22.

43. See, for example, Ellen Frankel Paul, ed., *Totalitarianism at the Crossroads*, 1990.

44. Sartori, "Totalitarianism," p. 13.

45. Nicolas Berdyaev, *The Russian Idea*, 1947; *The Russian Revolution*, 1961; *The Origins of Russian Communism*, 1960.

46. Sidney and Beatrice Webb, *Soviet Communism: A New Civilization*, 2nd. ed., 1936, p. 450.

47. Waldemar Gurian, "Totalitarianism as Political Religion," in Friedrich, ed., *Totalitarianism*, 1964, p. 122.

48. Ibid., pp. 122-126.

49. One of the authors of this work employed this framework for his analysis of the dynamics of the Polish communist system in an article in 1977: Jaroslaw Piekalkiewicz, "Polish Politics Since the 1960's," in George W. Simmons, ed., *Nationalism in the USSR and Eastern Europe in the Era of Brezhnev and Kosygin*, 1977. The concept has also been used by Carl A. Linden, *The Soviet Party-State: The Politics of Ideocratic Despotism*, 1983, and in some other works; for example, Michael Urban, *The Ideology of Administration: American and Soviet Cases*, 1982. Most recently Andrzej Walicki writes about "ideocratic dimension of the totalitarian phenomenon" (Walicki in Frankel Paul, *Totalitarianism at the Crossroads*, p. 55).

50. Emile Durkheim recognized the critical importance of this phenomenon in his *The Division of Labor*, 1984. He did, however, believe that an extreme division of labor would ensure pluralism. We argue that an ideocratic movement may rise to power and override such pluralism.

51. In a very conceptually interesting work, Mark Juergensmeyer argues that all nationalism is similar to a tribal religion and that both secular nationalism and religion involve (1) identity with, and loyalty to, a large community and (2) an insistence on the moral legitimacy of authority vested in leadership in that community. In distinguishing political from religious authority, we rely upon Weber's distinction that political authority holds the legitimate monopoly over the use of physical coercion within its territory. We also distinguish pluralistic systems (whether secular or religious in their ideological basis) from ideocracies whose monistic ideology encompasses all of social life. This difference is, we assert, of fundamental importance in comparative political analysis. See Mark Juergensmeyer, *The New Cold War? Religious Nationalism Confronts the Secular State*, 1993.

52. Max Weber, *The Theory of Social and Economic Organization*, ed. Talcott Parsons, 1964.

53. For discussion of this, see Cassinelli, *Total Revolution*.

54. Weber's average type.

Chapter I. Ideocracy as a Distinctive Form of Politics

1. For other discussions of ideology, see William T. Bluhm, *Ideologies and Attitudes: Modern Political Culture*, 1974, pp. 1-10; and M. Rejai, ed., *Decline of Ideology*, 1971; Leon Baradat, *Political Ideologies*, 1988; Reo M. Christenson et. al., *Ideologies and Modern Politics*, 1975; Lewis Feuer, *Ideology and the Ideologists*, 1975; James Gould and Willis H. Truitt, *Political Ideologies*, 1973; Mark N. Hagopian, *Ideals and Ideologies of Modern Politics*, 1985; Roy C. Macridis, *Contemporary Political Ideologies*, 1985.

2. Wayne Penn, "Authority, Ideology, and Problem-Solving," *Political Science Review*, 11 (January-March 1972): 12-19.

3. Such other standards do enter into decision made in ideocracies (see later); however, the *public justification* for these decisions is purely ideological.

4. Juan J. Linz, "Totalitarian and Authoritarian Regimes," in Fred I. Greenstein and Nelson W. Polsby, eds., *Handbook of Political Science*, vol. 3, 1975, pp. 179-180.

5. Ibid., p. 264.

6. See, for example, William Shirer, *The Rise and Fall of the Third Reich*, *1962*; Eugen Kogon, *The Theory and Practice of Hell: The German Concentration Camps and the System Behind Them*, 1950; Kazimierz Smolen, ed., *Kl Auschwitz Seen by the SS*, 1972; Aleksandr I. Solzhenitsyn, *The Gulag Archipelago*, 1974, 1975; Jeffrey Richelson, *Sword and Shield: Soviet Intelligence and Security Apparatus*, 1986.

7. For example, see T. H. Breen, *Puritans and Adventures*, 1980; John Demos, *A Little Commonwealth*, 1970; Kai T. Erikson, *Wayward Puritans*, 1966; Benjamin W. Labaree, *Colonial Massachusetts*, 1979; Perry Miller, *Orthodoxy in Massachusetts, 1630-1650*, 1965; Morris Talpalar, *The Sociology of the Bay Colony*, 1976; Margo Todd, *Christian Humanism and the Puritan Social Order*, 1987; Richard Weisman, *Witchcraft, Magic, and Religion in the Seventeenth Century Massachusetts*, 1984; William C. Innes, *Social Concern in Calvin's Geneva*, 1983; E. William Monter, *Studies in Genevan Government, 1536-1605*, 1964.

8. See, for example, Alexander S. Cudsi and Ali E. Hillal Dessouki, *Islam and Power*, 1981; Ali E. Hillal Dessouki, *Islamic Resurgence in the Arab World*, 1982; John L. Esposito, *Islam: the Straight Path*, 1988; Fred Halliday and Hamza Alavi, eds., *State and Ideology in the Middle East and Pakistan*, 1988; Dilip Hiro, *Holy Wars*, 1989; Shireen T. Hunter, *The Politics of Islamic Revivalism*, 1988; Edward Mortimer, *Faith and Power*, 1982; Daniel Pipes, *In the Path of God*, 1983; James P. Piscatori, *Islam in the Political Process*, 1983; Robert C. Liebman and Robert Wuthnow, eds., *The New Christian Right*, 1983.

9. This view of Marxism is argued by Robert C. Tucker in *Philosophy and Myth in Karl Marx*, 1964, p. xx.

10. Adolf Hitler, *Mein Kampf*, 1962 ed.

11. Thus the element of political enforcement over a geographic territory separates ideocracy from religion proper. In this regard, see Max Weber, *The Theory of Social and Economic Organization*, ed. Talcott Parsons, 1964, pp. 154-157.

12. Gurian, "Totalitarianism as Political Religion," in Carl J. Friedrich, ed., *Totalitarianism*, 1964, p. 122.

13. Mark Juergensmeyer, *The New Cold War? Religious Nationalism Confronts the Secular State*, 1993, p. 41.

14. A. James Gregor, *Contemporary Radical Ideologies*, 1968, pp. 333-334.

15. In the consensual form, the whole group takes on this leadership whereas individuals, as individuals, remain followers.

16. Carl J. Friedrich and Zbigniew Brzezinski, *Totalitarian Dictatorship and Autocracy*, 1956 ed., pp. 10-11.

17. Daniel Lerner, *The Passing of Traditional Society*, 1958, pp. 43-65; Joel M. Halpern, *The Changing Village Community*, 1967; Alex Inkeles, *Exploring Individual Modernity*, 1983; Winberg Chai and Ch'u Chai, *The Changing Society of China*, 1962; Rupert Emerson, ed., *The Political Awakening of Africa*, 1965; C. Northcote Parkinson, *East and West*, 1963.

18. The most vivid case of this was in Iran prior to the 1979 Islamic fundamentalist revolution. Cassettes of the tape recorded speeches of the leader, Ayatollah Khomeini, were circulated in the country. At that time Khomeini was living in France.

19. This possibility contradicts Madison's belief that an "extended republic" would, by its size and diversity, prevent majority factions from gaining power. See James Madison, "The Federalist No. 10" in *The Federalist*, ed. Jacob E. Cooke, 1961, pp. 61-65. Madison might have been right in his time.

20. For example, Imperial China. See Joseph R. Levenson and Herbert Franz Schurmann, *China: An Interpretative History*, 1969, especially pp. 68, 71, 98, 103; P. Fitzgerald, *China, A Short Cultural History*, 1954, pp. 156, 312; John A. Harrison, *The Chinese Empire*, 1972, pp. 82, 85, 99, 120-121, 148, 210-211, 269, 330-331; Wolfgram Eberhard, *A History of China*, 1977, pp. 216-217; Karl Wittfogel, *Oriental Despotism*, 1957, p. 32.

21. Rann Singh Mann, *Tribal Culture and Change*, 1989; Akbar S. Ahmed and David M. Hart, eds., *Islam in Tribal Societies*, 1984.

22. Today, it is much more difficult to establish such ideocracies because of lack of territory for the settlement. The most recent attempt, in the United States, ended in tragedy in May 1993. Branch Davidians, a breakaway sect of the Seventh-Day Adventists, led by David Koresh (Vernon Wayne Howell), for five years were forging their independent religious community at Mount Carmel near Waco, Texas. In February 1993, the Bureau of Alcohol, Tobacco and Firearms, after a month of investigation, raided the compound to serve a warrant for alleged numerous firearms violation. They were fired upon, and in the ensuing battle four agents and a number of Davidians were killed. After months of siege and fruitless negotiations, the Federal Bureau of Investigation pumped tear gas to force out the cultists. A fire erupted, most likely started by the Davidians. Over 100 people, children, women, and men, were burned alive. Jim McGee and William Claiborne, "The Waco Messiah," *The Washington Post National Weekly Edition* (May 17-23, 1993), pp. 10-11.

23. See J. L. Talmon, *The Rise of Totalitarian Democracy*, 1952, and *The Origins of Totalitarian Democracy*, 1961.

24. Our use of the terms *organic* and *pragmatic* are as used by John Dewey in *Reconstruction in Philosophy*, 1920, pp. 187-193. This usage is at variance with that in many works of sociological theory, e.g., Walter Buckley, *Sociology and Modern Systems Theory*, 1967, pp. 8-17.

25. This view is expressed in pragmatic philosophy of John Dewey, in which he argues for casting aside all ways of thought and action that fail to meet perceived problems. Institutions, in this view, are limited, problem-solving devices. *Reconstruction in Philosophy* (enlarged edition, 1948), pp. 22-27, 206-207.

26. For example, in the Soviet Union Freudian psychoanalysis was regarded as incompatible with Marxist materialism. As the result Soviet psychology and psychiatry

suffered greatly. See Raymond A. Bauer, ed., *Some Views on Soviet Psychology*, 1962; Levy Rahmani, *Soviet Psychology*, 1973; Elizabeth O'Leary Carson, ed., *Psychiatry and Psychology in the USSR*, 1976. It goes without saying that study of politics, political science, is impossible in ideocratic countries. That also impedes any inquiry aimed at improving the efficiency of state and other organizations. See Jaroslaw Piekalkiewicz, "Political Science in Poland," in Antoni Kuklinski, ed., *Society, Science, Government*, 1992, pp. 106-115. In another example, Nazi ideology permitted medical experiments on "inferior" people in the concentration camps. See Robert J. Lifton, *The Nazi Doctors*, 1970.

27. Karl Wolfgan Deutsch, *The Nerves of Government*, 1963, pp. 165-166.

28. Nazi ideology claimed that the Aryans, a blond and blue-eyed race of physical fit supermen, had an innate understanding of nature. They were the only ones among humanity who had the ability to create something new. They were founders and rulers of all lasting human civilizations: Greek, Roman, Germanic. Thus, the purity of their blood had to be preserved at all cost. Civilizations have failed because the Aryans mixed with other inferior people and lost their special gift. Jews, who lived among Aryans and who endangered that purity had to be exterminated (Adolf Hitler, *Mein Kampf*, 1962 ed.; J. Lucien Radel, *Roots of Totalitarianism*, 1975, pp. 97-125).

The *Umma* means the distinctiveness and oneness of all Moslems. For Islamic fundamentalists that also signifies a superiority of Moslems over all other people (John L. Esposito, *Islam: the Straight Path*, 1988). Some extreme fundamentalists even argue that, because Moslems have lived a "pure" life for many generations, among other things not drinking alcohol or eating pork, a physical mutation transpired among them. They are physically as well as spiritually select (Hossein Manoochehri, "Toward an Explanation of the Islamic Ideal of Human Perfection," 1988).

29. For example, the difference between emigration from the United States and Cuba. There is no law forbidding emigration from the United States and no citizen of the United States settling in another country is automatically regarded as a traitor. Cuba permits emigration only in exceptional cases and regards any citizen leaving the country permanently as a traitor to the cause of socialism. To leave Cuba is to join the other ideological camp.

30. One point should be made clear in this regard. To the extent that a community pursues a mission perceived as unique and superior to other causes, the community thereby takes on characteristics associated with ideocracy. Thus, avowedly democratic leaders may encourage movement in this direction when they assert the unique quality of their nation's or their party's, moral importance; e.g., the assertion of the "white man's burden" under colonial imperialism.

31. Some tribes based on kinship ties move in this direction by creating elaborate means of "improvising" new kinship ties as relations with new groups develop.

32. The Chinese communists used so-called national bourgeoisie in their antiimperialist struggle against the West and Japan, see Mao Tse-Tung, "On the Correct Handling of Contradictions Among the People," in George P. Jan, ed., *Government of Communist China*, 1966, pp. 71-82.

33. To a substantial extent this classification is based on that of A. James Gregor (*Contemporary Radical Ideologies*, 1968, p. 327). Also, it should be noted that, in primitive systems, the "tribe" is the functional biological equivalent of the "race." Here we will simply consider it as a subtype of racial ideocracy. Ernst Cassirer, *The Myth of the State*, 1973, pp. 38-40. Also culture includes religion.

34. Herman Finer, *Mussolini's Italy*, 1935; James A. Gregor, *Italian Fascism and Development Dictatorship*, 1979; Ernst Nolte, *Three Faces of Fascism*, 1966, pp. 209-228; Stanley Payne, *Fascism: Comparison and Definition*, 1980.

35. Ashley Montagu, *Man's Most Dangerous Myth*, 1965, especially pp. 23-62.

36. This is of course based on Marx's economic theory of history in which change and progress comes about as the result of class struggle (Karl Marx, *Capital*, or for a short version, Marx and Engels, *The Communist Manifesto*).

37. Consider the myriad of definitions of culture contained in A. L. Kroeber and Clyde Kluckhohn, *Culture: A Critical Review of Concepts and Definitions*, 1952.

38. Farrokh Moshiri, *The State and Social Revolution in Iran*, 1985.

39. Brian Bunting, *The Rise of the South African Reich*, 1969; Robin Cohen, *Endgame in South Africa?*, 1986; Frank Cooney, Gordon Morton, and Barry White, *Studies in Race Relations: South Africa and USA*, 1986; Joseph Lelyveld, *Move Your Shadow: South Africa, Black and White*, 1985; David M. Smith, *Apartheid in South Africa*, 1987; Alfred W. Stadler, *The Political Economy of Modern South Africa*, 1987; Harold Wolpe, *Race, Class, and the Apartheid State*, 1988.

Chapter II. Psychological and Cultural Aspects of Ideocracy

1. It is more and more evident that living in an ideocratic system eventually leads to personality changes. Individuals develop specific personality traits to succeed, or simply to survive, in ideocracy. This was noted by Czeslaw Milosz in his *The Captive Mind*, 1955; and Arthur Koestler in his perceptive psychological novel, *Darkness at Noon*, 1941. Other studies confirmed this phenomenon, as for example, R. A. Bauer, A. Inkeles, and C. Kluckhorn, *How the Soviet System Works*, 1960; Jaroslaw Piekalkiewicz, *Public Opinion Polling in Czechoslovakia, 1968-1969*, 1972; William Welsh, ed., *Survey Research and Public Attitudes in Eastern Europe and the Soviet*

Union, 1981; Dan Baron, *Legacy of Silence: Encounters with Children of the Third Reich*, 1989; Vaclav Havel et al., *Power of the Powerless*, 1985; Tony Smith, *Thinking Like a Communist*, 1987; Gerald L. Posner, *Hitler's Children*, 1991. Those personality trends have persisted long after the demise of the ideocratic system, as in Germany after 1945 (see Richard Stoss, *Politics Against Democracy*, 1991), or today in the postcommunist Central Europe and the successor states of the USSR. They have been great impediment to democratization of the countries in question (see, for example, Timothy J. Colton, *The Dilemma of Reform in the Soviet Union*, 1986; Roy D. Laird, *The Soviet Legacy*, 1993; Jaroslaw Piekalkiewicz, "Habitual and Structural Impediments to Democratization and Economic Pluralization of Local Communities," a paper presented at the Rutgers University-Warsaw University Conference on Democratization and Privatization in Poland, May 1991.

2. An extended debate has surrounded studies of the "authoritarian personality" first conceived and analyzed by Theodore Adorno et al., in an assessment of the emotional appeal of fascism in *The Authoritarian Personality*. Discussion of this debate and other analyses linking ideology and particular psychological syndromes may be found in Michael Billig, *Ideology and Social Psychology: Extremism, Moderation, Contradiction*, 1982. A later, more adequate, development of the authoritarian syndrome may be found in Bob Allemeyer, *Enemies of Freedom*, 1988.

3. Robert J. Lifton, *Thought Reform and the Psychology of Totalism: A Study of "Brainwashing" in China*, 1961.

4. Some of the most dramatic examples of this process are provided in ibid., pp. 419-437.

5. Milton Rokeach, *The Open and Closed Mind*, 1960.

6. See Rokeach, ibid., pp. 16, 67-70.

7. Max Weber described charismatic authority as resting upon "an absolutely personal devotion and personal confidence in revelation, heroism, or other qualities of individual leadership." H. H. Gerth and C. Wright Mills, eds., *From Max Weber: Essays in Sociology*, 1946. The original Greek meaning of *charisma*, "the gift of grace," is attributed to such a leader by his followers. See the interesting discussion of James C. Davies, *Human Nature in Politics: The Dynamics of Political Behavior*, 1963, pp. 298-307, and Ann Ruth Willner, *The Spellbinders*, 1984.

8. Arthur Koestler describes how rapid changes in the party line produced in followers an ability to accept mutually contradictory ideas simultaneously. "To survive," he writes "we all had to become virtuosos of Wonderland eloquence." In Richard Crossman, *The God That Failed*, 1949, p. 48.

9. In an article on communist totalitarianism, Andrzej Walicki, discusses Milosz's *The Captive Mind* and notes that in the name of "historical necessity" the initiated understood that "lies could serve the cause of truth and that true freedom consisted in the scientific understanding of necessity." "The Captive Mind Revisited," in Ellen Frankel Paul, ed., *Totalitarianism at the Crossroads*, 1990.

10. See, for example, Lifton, *Thought Reform and the Psychology of Totalism*, pp. 253-273.

11. In primitive ideocracies, rituals of purification are set at fairly regular intervals and seem to be a more natural part of the social system. Still, the process of purification is as central in these as in modern ideocratic systems. In the religious context, confessions and communion serve the same purpose as well as Friday prayers at the Mosque. Andrzej Walicki describes private and organized group action to attack his deviant individualism and bring him back into the collectivity, in Paul, *Totalitarianism at the Crossroads*, pp. 74-78.

12. Processes of rehabilitation—in mental hospitals, in harsh work camps. or through ritual isolation in some primitive systems—provide intermediate sanctions that arouse much the same fear as full-scale excommunication.

13. Bahais are adherents of a religious movement originating among Shia Moslems in Iran in the nineteenth century and emphasizing the spiritual unity of humankind. They are brutally prosecuted under the fundamentalist Islamic government of Iran.

14. This projection of a sense of personal guilt is clearly recognized in the psychology of prejudice, Else Frenkel-Brunswik, "A Study of Prejudice in Children," *Human Relations* (1948): 295-306.

15. Most Germans, even those directly involved, genuinely felt no guilt over the extermination of millions of Jews and others by the Nazi regime, which they wholeheartedly supported. See, for example, in G. M. Gilbert, *Nuremberg Diary*, 1947; Kazimierz Smolen, ed., *Kl Auschwitz Seen by the SS*, 1972; Hannah Arendt, *Eichman in Jerusalem*, 1976; Jack Fishman, *The Seven Men of Spandau*, 1954; Gerald Reitlinger, *The SS—Alibi of a Nation*, 1968.

The most recent example of this is in Bosnia where yesterday's neighbor changes overnight into a rapist and killer feeling no guilt over his actions. This also explains callousness of contemporary terrorists engaged in indiscriminate bombing. Regis Debray, *Revolution in the Revolution*, 1967; Ivo Feierabend, Rosalind Feierabend, and Ted Robert Gurr, eds., *Anger, Violence, and Politics*, 1972; Carl Friedrich, ed., *The Pathology of Politics*, 1972; Kenneth Grundy and Michael Weinstein, *The Ideologies of Violence*, 1974; Irving L. Horowitz, *The Struggle is the Message*, 1970; Walter Laquer, *Terrorism*, 1977; Fawaz Turki, *Soul in Exile*, 1988.

16. Feierabend et al., ibid., pp. 49-50.

17. A high level of anxiety thus may lead to ritualistic action, use of stereotyped symbols and the resort to magical

interpretations of events. See Richard M. Merelman, "The Development of Political Ideology: A Framework for the Analysis of Political Socialization," *American Political Science Review* (September 1969): 761. See also Rokeach, *The Open and Closed Mind*, pp. 348-357.

18. Some insecure individuals are found in all societies, but specific cultures may be associated with a disproportionally high number of such people, who are good candidates for ideocratic recruitment.

19. The invasion of Western culture may greatly heighten the insecurity of individuals socialized in a traditional non-Western culture. See Rupert Wilkinson, *The Broken Rebel: A Study in Culture, Politics, and Authoritarian Character*, 1972, pp. 74-88. Consider also his discussion of interconnections between culture and disruptive economic change in pre-Nazi Germany, ibid., pp. 206-222.

20. David Krech, Richard Crutchfield, and Edgarton Ballachy, *Individual in Society*, 1962, pp. 505-506, 512-516, 525-538.

21. That was the case with many supporters of "imposed communism" in the countries of Central Europe. They felt that the Soviet Union would not permit any other system, so why not collaborate with it?

22. Dmitrii Nelidov, "Ideocratic Consciousness and Personality," in Michael Meerson-Aksenov and Boris Shragin, eds., *The Political, Social, and Religious Thought of Russian Samizdat*, 1977, pp. 256-290.

23. Milosz, *The Captive Mind*.

24. Walicki, in Paul, *Totalitarianism at the Crossroads*, pp. 73-74.

25. Niccolo Machiavelli (1469-1527), the first great theorist of power politics, argued that the justification for acquisition of power by the ruler is simply its use to obtain

still more power. Constant increase in the power of the ruler is necessary for the survival of the ruler. See *The Prince*.

26. To a significant degree, Edward Gierek was such a leader of communist Poland (1970-1980). See Adam Bromke and John W. Strong, eds., *Gierek's Poland*, 1973; Keith J. Lepak, *Prelude to Solidarity*, 1988; Jaroslaw Piekalkiewicz, "Polish Politics Since the 1960s," in George W. Simmons, ed., *Nationalism in the USSR and Eastern Europe in the Era of Brezhnev and Kosygin*, 1977, pp. 369-374. This was perhaps true of all the communist leaders in Central Europe of that time. They were commanding systems of "imposed communism," enforced by the Soviet Union under the "Brezhnev doctrine," and lacking ideological support among the population. The doctrine permitted Soviet intervention, even with its armed forces, to preserve Soviet-style communism in the countries of the Warsaw pact alliance. See Neal Ascherson, *The Polish August: The Self-Limiting Revolution*, 1982; E. J. Czerwinski and Jaroslaw Piekalkiewicz, eds., *The Soviet Invasion of Czechoslovakia: Its Effects on Eastern Europe*, 1972; Stephen Fisher-Galati, *Eastern Europe in the 1980s*, 1981; Lyman H. Legters, *Eastern Europe: Transformation and Revolution, 1945-1991*, 1992; Teresa Rakowska-Harmstone, ed., *Communism in Eastern Europe*, 1979; Robin A. Remington, *The Warsaw Pact*, 1971; Thomas W. Simons, Jr., *Eastern Europe in the Postwar World*, 1991; Jonathan Steele, *Inside East Germany*, 1977; Gale Stokes, ed., *From Stalinism to Pluralism: A Documentary History of Eastern Europe Since 1945*, 1991; Peter Summerscale, *The East European Predicament*, 1982; Ivan Volgyes, *Politics in Eastern Europe*, 1986.

27. Fred I. Greenstein, "Harold D. Lasswell's Concept of Democratic Character," in Greenstein and Michael Lerner, eds., *A Source Book for the Study of Personality and Politics*, 1971, pp. 527-537; Abraham Maslow, *Toward a Psychology of Being*, 1968; and Chris Argyris, *Personality and Organization: The Conflict Between System and the Individual*, 1957.

28. Penn, "Authority, Ideology and Problem-Solving." *Political Science Review* (September, 1972), 37-56.

29. This tolerance *may* be seen as a mixed trait, in that Machiavellian leaders may use such creative people in critical problem-solving areas, while isolating them from the masses, whom they might corrupt. For literary description of Stalin's use of such people, see Aleksandr I. Solzhenitsyn, *The First Circle*, 1969.

30. For example, Milosz, *The Captive Mind*; plays by Vaclav Havel, *Hry 1970-1976*, 1977, or in English, *Largo Desolato*, 1987; and a novel by Milan Kundera, *The Unbearable Lightness of Being*, 1991.

Chapter III. Ideocratic Framework of Politics

1. It could be argued that these less optimistic variants of ideocracy are not legitimate ideocracies. However, in each case, it holds to a monistic ideology and mobilizes all those defined as potential members within their designated communities. Although less expansive than the more optimistic form of ideocracy, it develops essentially the same *internal* dynamics of organization in relation to its defined membership group, (e.g., the Puritan colony in America, Calvinist Geneva).

2. In the current era, Islamic fundamentalism envisions creation of the economically just state on earth and subsequent salvation for the faithful.

3. For example, the Branch Davidians discussed in Chapter I.

4. Karl Wittfogel, *Oriental Despotism*, 1957; Joseph R. Levenson and Franz Schurmann, *China: An Interpretive History*, 1969, pp. 68-69; C. P. Fitzgerald, *China, A Short Cultural History*, 1954, p. 156; John A. Harrison, *The Chinese Empire*, 1972, p. 99.

5. A more extensive discussion of theory and doctrine is found in A. James Gregor, *Contemporary Radical Ideologies*, 1968, pp. 9-10.

6. For example, in the Soviet Union at its height, economic reforms based on the profit motive failed because of ideological reasons. It was considered ideologically unthinkable to limit central planning and the general control of prices. The abandonment of ideological commitment under Gorbachev led to disintegration of the Soviet Union because the system lost its legitimacy. Equally so, the Islamic leaders of Iran can go only so far in moderating the system after Khomeini's death lest they lose legitimacy. In this sense, southern U.S. politics until the passage of the Civil Rights Act, resembled this ideocratic pattern in its commitment to white rule and all the beliefs supporting this. In China, due to the populism of Chinese ideology, economic decentralization is more acceptable, because it is consistent with the "Mass Line," the general will of the people.

7. The term *movement* will be used broadly here to include any elect group in an ideocracy that is organized to provide for the central mobilization of political participation in that system. In a primitive tribe this may be a group of elders, whereas in a religious ideocracy it may be an elect group in the church (such as the Islamic clergy). Other terms in this chapter will be drawn from large-scale modern ideocracies: terms such as *administrative system, mass media,* and *secret police*. The reader should recognize that these institutions have their equivalents in premodern ideocratic systems.

8. For example, prior to the takeover by the Nazis in Germany in 1933, the National Socialist German Workers party grew to approximately 1 million members, because the movement needed a large following to compete in elections. After the takeover, and especially after the purge of the party's storm troopers wing (S.A.) in 1934, much of the real power passed to a much smaller group called the S.S.

(Schutzstaffeln), which originally was formed to protect the party leaders. See Carl J. Friedrich and Zbigniew K. Brzezinski, *Totalitarian Dictatorship and Autocracy*, 1965, pp. 38 and 136.

9. Very small populist ideocracies are an exception to this. A high level of conformity based upon integral group interaction allows for group-based ideological change. But even in such small ideocracies prophets usually arise.

10. For example, in the Soviet Union after Stalin's death in 1953, Georgi Malenkov emerged as the dominant leader. Malenkov argued for policies emphasizing attention to production of consumer goods rather than the previous focus on heavy industry. In 1955 he was replaced by a collective leadership of Nikita Khrushchev and Nikolai Bulganin, which originally denounced "revisionist" program of Malenkov. Eventually, in 1957 Nikita Khrushchev emerged victorious, stripped Bulganin of his post as the prime minister, and promoted many of Malenkov's policies as his own (Hugh Seton-Watson, *From Lenin to Khrushchev*, 1963, pp. 357-360; Basil Dmytryshyn, *USSR: A Concise History*, 1965, pp. 265-270).

11. We use masculine terms to refer to the top leader, because all ideocratic leaders in recent history have been men.

12. For an example, see Inoue Shuhachi, *Modern Korea and Kim Jong Il*, 1984, and especially his introduction pp. 1-5.

13. For the characteristics of the top leader in an ideocratic system, see, among others, Alan Bullock, *Hitler*, 1962; Robert Crassweller, *Peron and the Enigmas of Argentina*, 1987; Isaac Deutscher, *Stalin*, 1949; Herman Finer, *Mussolini's Italy*, 1935; Nikita Khrushchev, *Khrushchev Remembers*, 1976; Herbert L. Matthews, *Fidel Castro*, 1969; Zhores A. Medvedev, *Andropov*, 1984; Robert Payne, *The Life and Death of Adolf Hitler*, 1973; Saddam Hussein, *Iraqi*

Policies in Perspective, 1981; Judith Miller and Laurie Mylroie, *Saddam Hussein and the Crisis in the Gulf*, 1990. For the general model of public policy formulation on which our discussion is based here, see Jaroslaw Piekalkiewicz, "The Communist Administration in Poland Within the Frame-Work of Input-Output Analysis," *East European Quarterly* 4, no. 2 (June 1972): 230-256; and by the same author, *Communist Local Government*, 1975, Chapter IV and especially pp. 173-186 and Appendix 4, Diagram 2, p. 259.

14. For the Soviet Union, see Frederick C. Barghoorn, "Trends in Top Political Leadershiip in USSR," in R. Barry Farrell, ed., *Political Leadership in Eastern Europe and the Soviet Union*, 1970, pp. 61-87; for Iraq, Samir Al-Khalil, *Republic of Fear*, 1989, pp. 6, 25, 70-71, 295.

15. An excellent study of this relationsh between the top leader and his lieutenants is Joseph Nyomarkay, *Charisma and Factionalism in the Nazi Party*, 1967; also the memoirs of Albert Speer, *Inside the Third Reich*, 1970.

16. Merle Fainsod, *Smolensk Under Soviet Rule*, 1958; Philip D. Stewart, *Political Power in the Soviet Union: A Study of Decision-Making in Stalingrad*, 1968; Jaroslaw Piekalkiewicz, *Communist Local Government*, 1975; Daniel Nelson, ed., *Local Politics in Communist Countries*, 1980; Robert Kleinberg, "The Spirit of Chinese Socialist Bureaucracy," in Piekalkiewicz and Hamilton, eds., *Public Bureaucracies Between Reform and Resistance*, 1991; Majid Khadduri, *Socialist Iraq*, 1978.

17. The organizational structures of most of the modern secular ideocratic movements are fashioned on the model of the Communist party originally developed by Lenin. This is easily understood for communist movements. The originator of Fascism, Mussolini, was originally a socialist and adopted the same model for his own organization. Italian fascism inspired many other similar movements, including today Ba'thists in Iraq and Syria. Contemporary religious-based

movements differ structurally and organizationally as they are not so formally constructed. They do, however, follow the general hierarchical patterns that we describe.

18. Specific aspects of this domination by the movement will be discussed later in relation to mobilization and penetration.

19. Of course, such selective transmission of upward communication is a commonly recognized trait of hierarchical organizations, in general, see for example Nicos P. Mouzelis, *Organization and Bureaucracy*, 1974, especially pp. 130-133.

20. Gordon H. Skilling and Franklin Griffiths, eds., *Interest Group in Soviet Politics*, 1971; Speer, *Inside the Third Reich*.

21. For a specific case study of this, see J. Piekalkiewicz, *Communist Local Government*, 1975, pp. 179-186. See Chapter V for a fuller discussion of this phenomenon.

22. Frederick Axelgard, ed., *Iraq in Transition*, 1986; Hanna Batatu, *The Old Social Classes and the Revolutionary Movements of Iraq*, 1978; Milovan Djilas, *The New Class*, 1958, and *The Unperfect Society*, 1969; William Ebenstein, *Fascist Italy*, 1939; Herman Finer, *Mussolini's Italy*, 1935; David Forgacs, ed., *Rethinking Italian Fascism*, 1986; James A. Gregor, *Italian Fascism and Development Dictatorship*, 1979; John N. Hazard, *Soviet System of Government*, 1980; Samuel Hendel, *The Soviet Crucible*, 1980; Carl A. Linden, *The Soviet Party-State*, 1983; Franz Neumann, *Behemoth: The Structure and Practice of National Socialism*, 1944; Stanley Rothman and George W. Breslauer, *Soviet Politics and Society*, 1978; Tony Smith, *Thinking Like a Communist: State and Legitimacy in the Soviet Union, China, and Cuba*, 1987; Hansjakob Stehle, *The Independent Satellite: Society and Politics in Poland Since 1945*, 1965.

23. John A. Armstrong, *Ideology, Politics, and Government in the Soviet Union*, 1978; Donald D. Barry and

Carol Barner-Barry, *Contemporary Soviet Politics*, 1991; Thomas A. Baylis, *The Technical Intelligentsia and the East German Elite*, 1974; Gary K. Bertsch and Thomas W. Ganschow, *Comparative Communism: The Soviet, Chinese, and Yugoslav Models*, 1976; J. F. Brown, *Eastern Europe and Communist Rule*, 1988; Robert Conquest, *Russia After Khrushchev*, 1965; Richard Grunberger, *The 12-Year Reich*, 1971; John N. Hazard, *Communists and Their Law*, 1969; Leslie Holmes, *Politics in the Communist World*, 1986; Peter C. Ludz, *The Changing Party Elite in East Germany*, 1972; Randall D. Oestreicher, "Technocracy and Public Policy: Poland 1950-1980," 1981; Piekalkiewicz and Hamilton, eds., *Public Bureaucracies Between Reform and Resistance*; Jan B. Weydenthal, *The Communists of Poland*, 1986; Jane Shapiro Zacek, ed., *The Gorbachev Generation*, 1989.

24. The most famous was Stalin's purge of the Red Army, 1937-1938, in which three of the five marshals, all commanders of the military districts, and many of the generals and even colonels were executed. All corps commanders and almost all division commanders and brigade commanders were eliminated from the Armed Forces, and most of them were imprisoned. This was one of the reasons for devastating defeats initially suffered by the Soviet Army after the German attack in June 1941 (Harriet Fast Scott and William F. Scott, *The Armed Forces of the USSR*, 1979, pp. 18-19). Hitler consolidated his power with the "night of the long knifes," the June 30, 1934 bloody purge of the S.A. leadership and others who could have challenged him later or knew too many "secrets" of his ascension to power or his personal life. The S.A. were the street fighters who through violent intimidation of the opponents contributed significantly to Hitler's victory. It was established during a trial in 1957 that as many as over 1,000 people were murdered, although Hitler himself, in a speech to the Reichstag (the parliament) admitted to only 77. The German Army was reined in the same day president Hindenburg died, August 2, 1934. Its members were made to "swear by God

this sacred oath, that [they] will render unconditional obedience to Adolf Hitler, the Fuehrer of the German Reich and people, Supreme Commander of the Armed Forces" (Shirer, *The Rise and Fall of the Third Reich*, pp. 297-315). The German Army claimed that this very oath bound it to blindly obey all orders of Hitler, even to commit acts of utter barbarism. For other evidence of the ideocratic consolidation, see Zbigniew Brzezinski, *The Permanent Purge*, 1956; Edward H. Carr, *The Russian Revolution: From Lenin to Stalin*, 1979; Michael Curtis, *Totalitarianism*, 1979; Alexander Dallin and George W. Breslauer, *Political Terror in Communist Systems*, 1970; Thomas T. Hammond, ed., *The Anatomy of Communist Takeovers*, 1975; Krystyna Kersten, *The Establishment of Communist Rule in Poland*, 1992; Khadduri, *Socialist Iraq*; Robert J. Lifton, *Thought Reform and the Psychology of Totalism*, 1961; Czeslaw Milosz, *The Captive Mind*, 1955.

25. See, for example, Jaroslaw Piekalkiewicz, "Poland 1981-1984: White, Red, and Black," *Universities Field Staff International*, 1984, no. 30, Europe.

26. The bazaar is a traditional place in most of the Middle Eastern cities, either a maze of narrow streets or a large open space under one roof, in the middle of a city, where most of trade was once done. With modernization, the bazaar merchants, "bazaarniks," are being squeezed out by modern single and chain shops and contemporary wholesale distribution systems. The bazaarniks generally support Islamic fundamentalism, for they see it as preventing "Western ways," which destroy their traditional trade. However, they are less enthusiastic about the strict prescription of the Quar'an against "unjust" profits and usury (the Quar'an forbids charging interest on loans). In Iran the bazaarniks were one of the most enthusiastic supporters of the fundamentalist revolution and aided it financially.

27. For example, see Milton Lodge, "'Groupism' in the Post-Stalin Period"; H. Gordon Skilling, "Interest Groups

and Communist Politics"; Joel J. Schwarts and William R. Kech, "Group Influence and the Policy Process in the Soviet Union," all in Frederic J. Fleron, Jr., ed., *Communist Studies and the Social Sciences*, 1969, pp. 254-317; or H. Gordon Skilling and Franklin Griffiths, eds., *Interest Groups in Soviet Politics*, 1971.

28. On "official" interest groups, see William L. Morrow, *Public Administration*, 1975, pp. 52-54, 165-176.

29. See Friedrich and Brzezinski, *Totalitarian Dictatorship and Autocracy*, 1965, pp. 239-281.

30. For general works on political socialization, consult: Richard E. Dawson and Kenneth Prewitt, *Political Socialization*, 1969; Jack Dennis, *Comparative Political Socialization*, 1970.

31. See, for example, for Iraq, Al-Khalil, *Republic of Fear*, pp. 77-80, 82-88, 93-94, 103, 151, 155-158, 160-161, 165-166, 193, 196; for Nazi German, Dan Baron, *Legacy of Silence*, 1989; for Italian Fascism, Nazi Germany, and the Soviet Union, Carl J. Friedrich and Zbigniew K. Brzezinski, *Totalitarian Dictatorship and Autocracy*, pp. 61, 64, 148-160, 233, 323-325; Lucian W. Pye, *China*, 1978, pp. 264-268, 345-347; James R. Townsend, *Politics in China*, 1980, pp. 56, 131, 136-137, 151, 185, 191-199, 219-220, 222, 348, 354; Brian Bunting, *The Rise of the South African Reich*, 1969, pp. 188-189, Chapter II, 277, 280.

32. *Aryan* was the term used by Nazis to denote the master race. *Socialist realism* was the name of the official style of art condoned in the Soviet Union. Art had to be "with a social message in its content and realistic in its form."

33. The most revealing document on the control of the media is *The Black Book of Polish Censorship*, trans. and ed. Jane Leftwich Curry. These were rules and guidelines for Polish censors smuggled out of Poland by a censor who defected to the West in 1977.

34. See, for example, Piekalkiewicz, *Communist Local Government*, pp. 66, 83, 88-90, 92-95, 98, 100, 103-104, 112, 123, 126-128, 153, 155, 159, 161, 184-185, 187, 190-191, 212; Al-Khalil, *Republic of Fear*, Chapter III.

35. As for example, in the Great Proletarian Cultural Revolution in China. The best example of mass demonstrations of huge, fanatical crowds comes from Iran.

36. Krech, Crutchfield, and Ballachy, *Individual in Society*, p. 486; Arendt, *The Origins of Totalitarianism.*

37. Al-Khalil, *Republic of Fear;* Dallin and Breslauer, *Political Terror in Communist Systems;* Simon Wolin and Robert M. Slusser, eds., *The Soviet Secret Police,* 1957; Boris Levytsky, *The Use of Terror: The Soviet Secret Police, 1917-1970,* 1972; Brzezinski, *The Permanent Purge* and *The Soviet Bloc,* 1961; John A. Armstrong, *Ideology, Politics, and Government in the Soviet Union,* 1978, Chapter V; C. W. Cassinelli, *Total Revolution,* 1976; Lionel M. Chassin, *The Communist Conquest of China,* 1965; Theodore Draper, *Castro's Revolution,* 1962; Fainsod, *Smolensk Under Soviet Rule;* C. P. Fitzgerald, *The Birth of Communist China,* 1971; G. M. Gilbert, *Nuremberg Diary,* 1947; Grunberger, *The 12-Year Reich;* Kersten, *The Establishment of Communist Rule in Poland;* Eugen Kogon, *The Theory and Practice of Hell,* 1950; Lyman H. Legters, *Eastern Europe: Transformation and Revolution, 1945-1991,* 1992; Robert J. Lifton, *Thought Reform and the Psychology of Totalism,* and *Boundaries: Psychological Man in Revolution,* 1970; Adam Michnik, *Letters from Prison,* 1987; Gerald Reitlinger, *The S.S.,* 1968; Jeffrey T. Richelson, *Sword and Shield,* 1986; Eliot B. Wheaton, *The Nazi Revolution, 1933-1935,* 1969; Paul Zinner, *Communist Strategy and Tactics in Czechoslovakia,* 1963. A number of personal recollections of the ex-political police functionaries throw an interesting light on this subject. One systematic study stands out: Michael Checinski, *Terror and Politics in Communist Poland,* 1983. In dramatic form the subject is treated in a number of a semi-biograph-

ical novels, such as Koestler, *Darkness at Noon*; Petru Dumitriu, *Incognito*, 1964; and Kundera, *The Unbearable Lightness of Being*.

38. In addition to the literature mentioned previously, this discussion is based on personal observations of and stories related to one of the authors—J. Piekalkiewicz.

39. Hannah Arendt, *The Origins of Totalitarianism*, 1973, pp. 476-479.

40. An excellent example of using scapegoats was the aforementioned taking of American Embassy personnel as hostages in Teheran in 1979. They were freed when the attack by Iraq provided a much more adequate subject for generating hatred as a vehicle of mobilization.

41. Bruno Bettelheim, *The Informed Heart*, 1960.

Chapter IV. Causes of Ideocracy

1. Most of the contemporary theorists of revolutions, such as Charles Tilly, Theda Skocpol, and Jack Goldstone, argue that revolutions are the result of the breakdown of the state.

2. See Talcott Parsons, "An Outline of the Social System" in Parsons et al., *Theories of Society*, 1961, pp. 40-41.

3. Thomas Hobbes built his theory of politics upon this assumption. In *The Leviathan*, participants accept a common superior precisely because of the equally destructive character of their unregulated conflict.

4. Our use of *severe social disruption* is similar to terms used by others. Dysynchronization or disequilibrium is an important part of the conflict theories of Brinton, Johnson, and Gurr. See Clarence Crane Brinton, *The Anatomy of Revolution*, 1965; Chalmers Johnson, *Revolutionary Change*, 1966; and Ted Robert Gurr, *Why Men Rebel*, 1970.

5. See Charles Tilly, *From Mobilization to Revolution*, 1978; Theda Skocpol, *States and Social Revolutions*, 1979; and Jack A. Goldstone, *Revolution and Rebellion in the Early Modern World*, 1991. The most recent and extensive scrutiny of the state breakdown, based on number of case studies, is Jack A. Goldstone, Ted Robert Gurr, and Farrokh Moshiri, eds., *Revolutions of the Late Twentieth Century*, 1991.

6. This concept was introduced by Johnson, *Revolutionary Change*.

7. Few political scientists consider impact of the natural environment on society. Some of the ideas expressed here are based on writings of Barrington Moore in *Social Origins of Dictatorship and Democracy; Lord and Peasant in the Making of the Modern World*, 1967.

8. This argument was the crux of the theory of Thomas Malthus. He vividly illustrated the danger of population explosion, picturing a large table loaded with food. Initially, all the guests find plenty of free spaces and plenty to eat. But, as more and more arrive, eventually the space and food become scarce. Now they must struggle to obtain a bare minimum. Malthus failed to consider the capacity of the kitchen to supply more and more dishes—the technological advances in production a society can make. But in general terms he was undeniably right, especially that technology develops unevenly. Contemporary application of Malthusian theory to revolution led Jack A. Goldstone to conclude that population growth is one of its more important causes. He found the periods of rapid population growth in Europe, 1500-1650 and 1730-1850, to correlate perfectly with times of revolutionary upheaval (*Revolution and Rebellion*).

9. The explosion occurred in the eighteenth century, when Chinese population grew from 150 million to over 300 million. By 1850 there were 430 million people in China, and the first communist census, in 1953, counted 583 million (James R. Townsend, *Politics in China*, 1980, p. 52).

10. This was one of the reasons for the continuous anticommunist upheavals in Poland, especially in the 1970s and 1980s (Jaroslaw Piekalkiewicz, "Poland: Nonviolent Revolution in a Socialist State," in Goldstone et al., *Revolutions of the Late Twentieth Century*).

11. Here lies the tremendous contribution of Karl Marx, whose analysis opened our eyes to the importance of economics to human history.

12. The most influential in this are W. W. Rostow, an economist, and A. F. K. Organski, a political scientist. W. W. Rostow, *The Stages of Economic Growth: A Non-Communist Manifesto*, 1971; A. F. K. Organski, *The Stages of Political Development*, 1967.

13. Stephen E. Medvec, "Poland and Czechoslovakia: Can They Find That They Need Each Other?" *Polish Review* no. 4 (1991): 489.

14. This is an important part of the Brinton's theory of revolution (Brinton, *The Anatomy of Revolution*), but such group conflict is the focus of Tilly's polity model of revolution (Tilly, *From Mobilization to Revolution*). In Gurr's "relative deprivation" paradigm, violence is visited through group action (Ted Robert Gurr, *Why Men Rebel*).

15. See Louis Feuer, *The Conflict of Generations: The Character and Significance of Student Movement*, (1969) p. 8. He describes the coming together of student groups, with concerns regarding structural contradictions, and "carrier " movements, made up of peasants, workers, or others, who have categorically based problems.

16. Brinton, *The Anatomy of Revolution*.

17. Robert Dahl, *After the Revolution*, 1970.

18. Mobilization is crucial to Charles Tilly's polity model of revolution. But, he focuses more on groups' mobilization of their members rather than mobilization by the government. See Tilly, *From Mobilization to Revolution*.

19. In even the last stages of the Cuban revolution, Castro's military force did not exceed 3,000 men and women, whereas Batista's army stood at 40,000 strong (Theodore Draper, *Castro's Revolution: Myths and Realities,* 1962, pp. 13-14). A similar situation developed in Iran, where the initial student protest was met with severe repression resulting in several killings (William H. Forbis, *The Fall of the Peacock Throne,* 1980; Amin Saikal, *The Rise and Fall of the Shah,* 1980). Brutal suppression of student demonstration is often dangerous to the government, especially if it results in serious injuries or deaths. The parents of the victims could be members of the ruling elite. This could lead to a split in the elite, which is one of the causes of revolution.

20. On China, see Lionel Max Chassin, *The Communist Conquest of China,* 1965; on Vietnam, Bernard B. Fall, *The Two Viet-Nams,* 1965.

21. Our "multipliers" are similar to Chalmers Johnson's "accelerators" (see *Revolutionary Change*).

22. Historically and in contemporary times, most revolutions and resulting ideocracies have occurred when traditional rural societies have been evolving toward more technologically advanced and urban communities. Therefore our discussion here focuses primarily on the disruption of a society with patriarchal families and in which women are mostly employed at home or on the farm.

23. Drastic expression of these are street gangs in most Western urban centers. See, for example, Herbert C. Covey, Scott Menard, and Robert J. Franzese, *Juvenile Gangs,* 1992, or a novel by Jess Mowry, *Way Pass Cool,* 1992.

24. For example, large groups of Americans of Japanese origin were detained in camps during World War II. Surely an act impossible in peacetime, of extremely dubious constitutionality even in war, and since condemned by students of the period.

25. For more discussion, see John Keegan and Joseph Darracott, *The Nature of War*, 1981; Martin Shaw, *Dialectics of War: An Essay in the Social Theory of Total War and Peace*, 1988; and Howard Tolley, *Children and War; Political Socialization to International Conflict*, 1973.

26. For example, in Germany the unemployment figures were as follows: 1928, 8 percent; January 1930, 16 percent; January 1931, nearly 25 percent; January 1932, 30 percent; at the time when Hitler was appointed chancellor, January 1933, also 30 percent; and in October of that year already rapid decline to about 19 percent, mainly because of public works and government orders for armament industry (Fritz Stern et al., *The Path to Dictatorship 1918-1933: Ten Essays by German Scholars*, 1966, Appendix D, p. 210). One cannot wonder that many Germans were pessimistic about the system. That, however, does not totally explain their support for a movement like Nazism.

27. A classical case of depression's impact on society and the resulting ideocratic takeover was the 1929-1933 Germany, see Eliot Barculo Wheaton, *The Nazi Revolution 1933-1935: Prelude to Calamity*, 1969, and especially Chapter 5. On smaller scale this is evidenced in the inner cities. See, for example, David Robins, *Tarnished Vision: Crime and Conflict in the Inner City*, 1992.

28. Brinton, *The Anatomy of Revolution*, pp. 60-64. As Brinton suggests, a serious restriction on careers open to talent in a few particularly sensitive areas may contribute to instability. For example, in the Soviet Union, in the early 1950s 77 percent of all regular secondary school graduates were being admitted to higher education—a requirement for a professional or managerial career; 57 percent in the early 1960s, only 22 percent in the early 1970s, and a mere 20 percent in 1977. A lot of dissatisfied youth! See Colton, *The Dilemma of Reform in the Soviet Union*, p. 49.

29. For example, the middle class was heavily over-represented in the Nazi party. In 1933, the middle-class occupations (white collar employees, independents, and officials) composed 45.5 percent of the party membership, while their portion of the gainfully employed population was only 26.7 percent. Excluding officials, who by the end of the year were forced to join the party or resign and who might have been entering the Nazi ranks in expectation of such a ruling, the respective figures were 38.8 and 22.1 percent. This still shows a heavy middle-class involvement. By comparison manual workers were underrepresented, having 31.5 and 38.5 percent, respectively. Peasants were even less enthusiastic about the Nazis, showing only 12.6 percent of the Nazi membership out of their 28.9 percent portion of the gainfully employed. See Hans Gerth, "The Nazi Party: Its Leadership and Composition," *American Journal of Sociology*, 45 (January 1940): 527.

30. Brinton studied four revolutions: the English (1640), American (1776), French (1789), and Russian (1917). Prior to the revolution all four governments had serious financial difficulties (*The Anatomy of Revolution*, p. 24). For Goldstone resource crisis is not necessarily fatal for the state if the influential elites rally to its support (Goldstone et al., *Revolutions of the Late Twentieth Century*, p. 38; and Goldstone and Gurr, ibid., p. 325).

31. In 1979-1980 Germany, those with right-wing extremist views, about 13 percent of the population, were most likely to be less educated and unskilled or semiskilled workers—those who felt most threatened by the fast changing and prosperous West German economy (see Richard Stoss, *Politics Against Democracy*, 1991). This is also the case with the recent upsurge of the right-wing extremist violence against foreigners in the new united Germany (over 2,000 attacks resulting in 17 deaths in 1992 alone). Most of these took place in what used to be the German Democratic Republic. East Germans see their previous stable, even if at a lower economic level and oppressive, regime demolished

by the absorption into West German system. They have difficulty functioning under free market and democratic rule. The unemployment rate in that part of Germany has reached 30 percent (*New York Times* [March 8, 1993], p. C3).

32. James C. Davies, Jr., "Towards a Theory of Revolution," *Sociological Review* 27 (1952): pp. 5-19. A perfect example of the boom that lead to revolution was Iran prior to 1979 (see, for example, Farrokh Moshiri, *The State and Social Revolution in Iran: A Theoretical Perspective*, 1985).

33. Farrokh Moshiri, "Iran: Islamic Revolution Against Westernization," in Goldstone et al., *Revolutions of the Late Twentieth Century*, especially pp. 124-129.

34. As was the case with the English Revolution (1640) and the French Revolution (1789) (see, for example, Jack A. Goldstone, *Revolution and Rebellion in the Early Modern World*, 1991).

35. Mancur Olson, Jr., "Rapid Growth as a Destabilizing Force," *Journal of Economic History* 23, (1963): 529-552.

36. According to Karl Marx, increasing workers' class consciousness is one of the contradictions of capitalism. It eventually leads to revolution (Karl Marx, *Kapital* [English title: *Capital: A Critique of Political Economy*]). The importance of group alienation as a cause of revolution is stressed by Brinton, *The Anatomy of Revolution*; Tilly, *From Mobilization to Revolution*; and Ted Robert Gurr, *Why Men Rebel.*

37. For Brinton, ibid., leadership is essential to success of revolution.

38. Lin Piao, *Long Live the Victory of People's War!* reprinted in K. Fan, ed., *Mao Tse-tung and Lin Piao: Post Revolutionary Writings*, 1972, p. 377.

39. In the United States these tactics have been closely followed by the John Birch Society, the Unification Church (Moonies), and more recently by the religious Right. None of these organizations have aspired to capture total political power. Rather they have been trying to use the system to promote their own extreme views.

40. This distinction reflects the twin revolutionary themes of alliance and struggle, the one aimed at spreading the movement and the other aimed at destroying the opposition (Lin Piao, in Fan, ed., *Mao Tse-tung and Lin Piao*, pp. 366-373).

41. As pointed out previously, most of the contemporary communist and fascist, but not Islamic fundamentalist, movements follow the organizational patterns developed by the Bolshevik party under Lenin. The importance of mobilization to the success of revolution is well-understood by Brinton, Tilly, and Goldstone.

42. That explains the cooperation between leftist guerrilla movements and drag traffickers in some Latin American countries, e.g., Colombia. Apart from providing funds for guerrilla operation, drugs cartels undermine the established society. After its victory the leftist movement plans to suppress the drug lords.

Chapter V. Ideocracy in Dynamic Perspective: Inception and Stabilization

1. Such as *At Sea*, or *Policjanci* (Policemen).

2. Harry Eckstein, ed., *Internal War*, 1964; Feliks Gross, *The Seizure of Political Power in a Century of Revolutions*, 1958; Andrew C. Janos, *The Seizure of Power*, 1964; Nathan C. Leites and Charles Wolf, Jr., *Rebellion and Authority*, 1970; Barrington Moore, *Injustice: Social Bases of Obedience and Revolt*, 1978; H. L. Nieburg, *Political Violence*, 1969; Franklin M. Osanka, *Modern Guerrilla Warfare*, 1962;

Charles Tilly, *From Mobilization to Revolution*, 1978; Fawaz Turki, *Soul in Exile*, 1988; Bertram D. Wolfe, *Three Who Made a Revolution*, 1978.

3. Edward H. Carr, *The Bolshevik Revolution*, 1951; Lionel M. Chassin, *The Communist Conquest of China*, 1965; Jean Chesneaux, *Peasants Revolts in China*, 1973; Michael C. Conley, *The Communist Insurgent Infrastructure in South Vietnam*, 1967; Regis Debray, *Revolution in the Revolution*, 1967; C. P. Fitzgerald, *The Birth of Communist China*, 1971; Jack Goldstone, *Revolution and Rebellion in the Early Modern World*, 1991; Jack Goldstone et al., eds., *Revolutions in the Late Twentieth Century*, 1991; Thomas H. Greene, *Comparative Revolutionary Movements*, 1990; Samuel Griffith, *Peking and People's Wars*, 1966; Lawrence Kaplan, ed., *Revolutions*, 1973; Krystyna Kersten, *The Establishment of Communist Rule in Poland*, 1992; John Melby, *The Mandate of Heaven*, 1971; Allan Mitchell, *Revolution in Bavaria, 1918-1919*, 1965; Robert A. Scalapino, ed., *The Communist Revolutions in Asia*, 1965.

4. For liberation theology, see Gustavo Gutierrez, *A Theology of Liberation*, 1973.

5. For China, see Chassin, *The Communist Conquest of China*; for Vietnam, Conley, *The Communist Insurgent Infrastructure*.

6. See, for example, Paul Shoup, "The Yugoslav Revolution: The First of a New Type." The situation was similar in Albania, see Stephen Peters, "Ingredients of the Communist Takeover in Albania," both in Thomas T. Hammond, *The Anatomy of Communist Takeovers*, 1975, pp. 244-292. Even many Soviet partisans in World War II joined not because they supported Stalinist Soviet Union but because they hated Germans, see John A. Armstrong, ed., *Soviet Partisans in World War II*, 1964.

7. For a general discussion of this model, see Lin Piao, in Fan, ed., *Mao Tse-tung and Lin Paio*, 1972.

8. These tactics contained in the Mao's revolutionary theory, were applied to perfection in the Communist takeovers of countries in Central Europe after World War II, 1945-1948. See Samuel Griffith, *Peking and People's Wars*; Edward Benes, *Memoirs*, 1954 (Benes was the pre-WW II and post-WW II democratic president of Czechoslovakia); Paul E. Zinner, *Communist Strategy and Tactics in Czechoslovakia, 1918-1948*, 1963; and on Poland, Kersten, *Establishment of Communist Rule*; Hugh Seton-Watson, *The East European Revolution*, 1962. Earlier examples include the Fascist takeover in Italy in 1922 and the Nazi takeover in Germany in 1933. See Giuseppe A. Borgese, *Goliath: The March of Fascism*, 1938; Herman Finer, *Mussolini's Italy*, 1935; David Forgacs, ed., *Rethinking Italian Fascism*, 1986; James A. Gregor, *Italian Fascism and Development Dictatorship*, 1979; Gaetano Salvemini, *Under the Axe of Fascism*, 1936; Roland Sarti, *The Ax Within: Italian Fascism in Action*, 1974; Richard Grunberger, *The 12-Year Reich: A Social History of Nazi Germany, 1933-1945*, 1971; Andreas Hillgruber, *Germany and the Two World Wars*, 1981; David Shoenbaum, *Hitler's Social Revolution*, 1966; William L. Shirer, *The Rise and Fall of the Third Reich*, 1962; Fritz Stern et al., *The Path to Dictatorship, 1918-1933*, 1966; Eliot B. Wheaton, *The Nazi Revolution, 1933-1935*, 1969. More recent examples include Iraq and Iran, see Hanna Batatu, *The Old Classes and the Revolutionary Movement of Iraq*, 1978; Majid Khadduri, *Republican Iraq*, 1969, and *Socialist Iraq*, 1978; William H. Forbis, *The Fall of the Peacock Throne*, 1980; Farrokh Moshiri, *The State and Social Revolution in Iran*, 1985; Amih Saikal, *The Rise and Fall of the Shah*, 1980.

9. The masters of this use of violence were Nazis in Germany prior to their takeover in 1933. It has been employed in a similar fashion by both the Left and the Right political forces in Latin America, e.g., Salvador, Guatemala, Nicaragua, and Peru.

10. Votes for the Nazi party in the Reichstag (Parliament) elections increased from 2.6 percent in 1928 to

18.3 percent in 1930, 37.4 percent in July 1932, 31.1 percent in November 1932, and 43.9 in March 1933 (the last election after Hitler became the chancellor—prime minister—in January 1933).

11. Hannah Arendt, *The Origins of Totalitarianism* (1960), pp. 257 and 308.

12. For examples, see James A. Gregor, *The Ideology of Fascism*, 1969; Saikal, *The Rise and Fall of the Shah*.

13. *Mein Kampf* (My Struggle), written by Hitler between 1925 and 1927 when he was in prison, spelled out Hitler's program for Germany, Europe, and for the Jews, including a vision of their total extermination. The book was written in a convoluted, hysterical tone; and few people, including many Nazis, took it seriously at the time of its publication. It was read by few of those who voted for the Nazi party or those industrialists who lavishly financed Hitler's campaigns. Both groups brought Nazis to power. See Shirer, *Rise and Fall of the Third Reich*.

14. Ann R. Willner, *The Spellbinders*, 1984; Robert Crassweller, *Peron and the Enigmas of Argentine*, 1987; Finer, *Mussolini's Italy*; Joseph Goebbels (Hitler's minister of propaganda), *The Diaries*, 1978; Herbert L. Matthews, *Fidel Castro*, 1969; Joseph Nyomarkay, *Charisma and Factionalism in the Nazi Party*, 1967; Robert Payne, *The Life and Death of Adolf Hitler*, 1973; Stanley G. Payne, *The Franco Regime: 1936-1975*, 1987; Barry Rubin, *Modern Dictators, Third World Coup Makers, Strongmen and Populist Tyrants*, 1987; Albert Speer, *Inside the Third Reich: Memoirs*, 1970; Wolfe, *Three Who Made a Revolution*.

15. For example, Khomeini and his supporters in Iran, see Saikal, *The Rise and Fall of the Shah*. Hitler, as well as communists in Central Europe, was very aware of the necessity to subvert these institutions, see Shirer, ibid.; Benes, *Memoirs*; Kersten, *Establishment of Communist Rule*; and Zinner, *Communist Strategy and Tactics*.

16. The classical case was the coalition government in Czechoslovakia between 1945-48, resulting in the communist coup of 1948, see Zinner, ibid.

17. This was especially true of the Protestant churches in Germany, prior and during the Nazi period. In fact, many German Protestant denominations split on this issue, with the majority supporting the Nazis. The situation was the same with German Catholics. The pope signed a concordat with Hitler in 1933. Generally, frightened by the possibility of a communist revolution or later of the Soviet domination of Europe, the Catholic Church supported the Fascists in Italy and Spain, and at best stayed neutral in regard to Nazis; see Finer, *Mussolini's Italy*, and Shirer, *Rise and Fall of the Third Reich.*

18. Followers of the Reverend Jones, the People's Temple, a San Francisco-based sect, established a camp at Jonestown in Guyana. In November 1978, the whole settlement of several hundred people, men, women, and children, including the Reverend Jones, committed suicide by poison. Prior to that, U.S. Representative Leo J. Ryan and several of his aides were shot to death. Representative Ryan had gone to Guyana to investigate reports from his California constituents of forced labor and brutality at the camp. Sometimes a "territory" could be a settlement within the country to which all faithful move. There are a number of such settlements in the United States; e.g., Amish, Mennonites. Most recently the Branch Davidians attempted to separate themselves from the larger society by settling near Waco, Texas, discussed in Chapter I.

19. To some degree this is also true of Israel, but the Jewish case is different, as the foundation of their state was the result of the shock suffered by the survivors of the holocaust. The state mixes strong religious elements with a commitment to basic civil rights for minority groups. Only some of the extremely religious Jewish settlers and the ultranationalist (racist) groups seek an ideocratic solution.

20. This was exactly the relationship between David Keresh, the leader of the Branch Davidians, and his followers, even to the degree that he was the only one permitted to have sex with all the women of the sect. Many were wives, girlfriends, and daughters of the male followers.

21. For example, in the case of Islamic fundamentalism, the organization of mullahs (Muslims of a quasi-clerical class) provides leadership for this function.

22. Stalin's model of economic development in many ways followed the original Marxist theory. For a country to reach socialism it had to be industrialized. The Soviet Union could not borrow capital abroad because it was an international pariah. This had to be obtained internally by restricting consumption of peasants through collectivization and paying workers bare subsistence wages. In contrast, party and state managers were well rewarded materially as long as they did what they were told to do (see J. V. Stalin, "The Question of the Victory of Socialism in One Country," in Dan N. Jacobs, ed., *From Marx to Mao and Marchais*, 1979, pp. 106-119; Robert C. Tucker, *Political Culture and Leadership in Soviet Russia*, 1987, Chapter V). In Nazi Germany preparation for war dominated all endeavor. The economy was revived by massive orders for war material. The famous *Autobahn* (motorway) was built to facilitate rapid troop movement from one end of Germany to another, or from the Western to the Eastern Front. All this was done at the expense of consumption. Extermination of the Jews, the Final Solution, eventually was given priority by Hitler even over the war effort. Transportation of Jews to extermination camps had priority over transportation of supplies to the Eastern Front for the troops, who were short of everything—ammunition, equipment, food, and clothing. See Payne, *Life and Death of Adolf Hitler*, pp. 357-473; Speer, *Inside the Third Reich*, pp. 193-546; Shirer, *Rise and Fall of the Third Reich*.

23. And therefore Stalin eliminated Leon Trotsky, the founder of the Red Army and the most likely successor to

Lenin. Hitler murdered Ernst Roehm, his comrade in the struggle and the head of the S.A.—the Nazi storm troopers. In Nicaragua, after the Sandinistas victory, their leadership excluded Eden Pastora Gomez, the famous Commander Zero, the leader of spectacular 1978 attack and occupation of the National Palace in Managua.

24. See, for example, Joseph Nyomarkay, *Charisma and Factionalism in the Nazi Party.*

25. Samir Al-Khalil, *Republic of Fear*, 1989; Carl Beck et al., *Comparative Communist Political Leadership*, 1973; Isaac Deutscher, *Stalin*, 1949; Theodore Draper, *Castro's Revolution*, 1962; Barry R. Farrell, ed., *Political Leadership in Eastern Europe and the Soviet Union*, 1970; Finer, *Mussolini's Italy*; Goebbels, *The Diaries*; Nikita Khrushchev, *Khrushchev Remembers*, 1976; Zhores A. Medvedev, *Andropov*, 1984; Nyomarkay, ibid.; Speer, *Inside the Third Reich*; Tucker, *Political Culture and Leadership in Soviet Russia*; James Townsend, *Politics in China*, 1980; Jan B. Weydenthal, *The Communists of Poland*, 1986.

26. Michael H. Kater, *The Nazi Party*, 1983; Jan B. Weydenthal, ibid.; Shu-tse Peng, *The Chinese Communist Party in Power*, 1980; Ronald J. Hill and Peter J. Frank, *The Soviet Communist Party*, 1986; Amatzia Baram, *Culture, History, and Ideology in the Formation of Bathist Iraq*, 1991; Samir Al-Khalil, ibid., pp. 142-144, 222-225; Raymond A. Hinnebusch, *Authoritarian Power and State Formation in Ba'thist Syria*, 1990; Robert W. Olson, *The Bath and Syria*, 1982; David Roberts, *The Bath and the Creation of Modern Syria*, 1987.

27. The original model of this type of control was developed in Fascist Italy under the name of corporate state. All employees were organized into syndicates (trade unions), one for each type of production (e.g., steel manufacturing). The syndicates progressed from the local to the national federations. Equally so, employers were grouped into employers' associations. The national federation of a given

syndicate and the national federation of employers in the same type of production bargained with one another for a labor contract. The contract included wages and conditions of work, as well as all welfare provisions. Failing agreement, the case was referred to the labor court. The court's verdict could have been appealed to the minister of corporations, whose decision was final. The federations were bunched into twenty-two corporations representing different branches of the economy (e.g., agriculture, industry, trade). The corporations formulated an economic plan for their own economic sector. The plans of all the corporations constituted the national plan of economic development. Of course, all these organizations were controlled through the Fascist party members who were their officers (see, for example, Finer, *Mussolini's Italy*; or Gregor, *Italian Fascism and Development Dictatorship*). Today a similar arrangement exists in Ba'thist Syria and Iraq. For nonideocratic variants of corporatism, see Harmon Zeigler, *Pluralism, Corporatism, and Confucianism*, 1988.

28. Some authors confused them with interest groups (as, for example, Gordon H. Skilling and Franklin Griffiths, in *Interest Group in Soviet Politics*, 1971). As we have argued before, the fundamental characteristic of the true interest groups is that they are independent of the government. The mass organizations in ideocracies are not. They are only internal influence groups and lack autonomous political or economic resources that they can use to impel the government to adopt a new policy or to change the existing one.

29. We see today that even after seventy years of official atheism in the Soviet Union religion revived rapidly, especially the traditional orthodoxy of the Russians and Byelorussians, the Ukrainian Catholic Church, and the Islam of the Central Asian republics. This occurred despite occasional brutal persecution of the clergy and the members of different faiths and continuous antireligious propaganda of the Soviet state. For religion in communist ideocracy, see Bohdan R. Bociurkiw and John W. Strong, eds., *Religion*

and Atheism in the USSR and Eastern Europe, 1975; William
C. Fletcher, *Soviet Believers*, 1981; James H. Forest,
Religion in the New Russia, 1990; Michael Meerson-Aksenov
and Boris Shragin, eds., *The Political, Social, and Religious
Thought of Russian Samizdat*, 1977; Paul D. Steeves,
Keeping the Faith, 1989; Saleh M. F. Al-Khathllan, "Uzbeks
and Islam," 1993; Jaroslaw Piekalkiewicz, "Poland 1981-
1984: White, Red, and Black," *Universities Field Staff
International* no. 30, Europe (1984).

30. Carl J. Friedrich, ed., *The Pathology of Politics*,
1972; for an excellent discussion of terror in the Soviet
Union, see Zbigniew Brzezinski, *The Permanent Purge*, 1956;
for terror in communism, Alexander Dallin and George W.
Breslauer, *Political Terror in Communist Systems*, 1970; for
Poland, Michael Checinski, *Terror and Politics in Communist
Poland*, 1983; for Iraq, al-Khalil, *Republic of Fear*, and on
the impact of terror in Nazi Germany, Grunberger, *The 12-
Year Reich*. The phenomenon discussed here is perhaps
best expressed in fiction. Among others, by Milan Kundera
in *The Unbearable Lightness of Being*, 1991; by Petru
Dumitriu in *Incognito*, 1964; and Heinrich Boll in *Billiards at
Half-Past Nine*, 1962 and *Group Portrait with Lady*, 1973.

31. Fainsod, *Smolensk Under the Soviet Rule*; Jaroslaw
Piekalkiewicz, *Communist Local Government*, 1975.

Chapter VI. The Evolution of Ideocracy

1. In Argentina, the army, feeling more and more left
out of power, took the opportunity of Peron's conflict with
the Catholic Church to overthrow him in a bloodless coup.
Peron was permitted to leave for Spain (see Donald Hodges,
Argentina, 1943-1976, 1976; Jeane J. Kirkpatrick, *Leader
and Vanguard in Mass Society*, 1971). In Poland, one could
argue that communist ideocracy ended already in 1980,
when the government was forced to legalize an independent
trade union "Solidarity." The military coup in 1981 did not

really bring the communists back because it replaced them with the military. Under the military rule the system was deideologized and changed from ideocracy to authoritarianism. In 1989, in view of a dismal performance of the economy and the threat of strikes and widespread civil unrest, the military government decided to hold "round table talks" with the opposition. The resulting agreement on power sharing ended with the complete victory by the opposition. See George Sanford, ed., *Democratization in Poland: 1988-90*, 1992; Lech Walesa, *The Struggle and the Triumph*, 1992; Andre Gerrits, *The Failure of Authoritarian Change*, 1990; Bartolomiej Kaminski, *The Collapse of State Socialism*, 1991; Jaroslaw Piekalkiewicz, "Poland: Nonviolent Revolution in a Socialist State," in Jack A. Goldstone et al., eds., *Revolutions of the Late Twentieth Century*, 1991. In Romania, what started as a protest of parishioners against the removal of their pastor, ended with the execution of the dictator Ceausescu and his wife. After the "securitate" (the political police) fired on the protesters, killing several, the unrest spread to the whole country and expecially to the capital, Bucharest. The armed forces, as in Argentina very much out of power, joined the rebellion, eventually capturing Ceausescus, trying them in a military court and executing them on the spot. See Trond Gilberg, *Nationalism and Communism in Romania*, 1990; Mary E. Fisher, *Nicolae Ceausescu*, 1989; Martyn C. Rady, *Romania in Turmoil*, 1992; John Sweeney, *The Life and Evil Times of Nicolae Ceausescu*, 1991.

2. Jaroslaw Piekalkiewicz, "Poland 1981-84: White, Red and Black," *Universities Field Staff International* no. 30, Europe (1984); Dae-Kyu Lee, "A Causal Analysis of Military Intervention in Polish Politics," 1987.

3. All those ideocracies had party militias, but they proved ineffective against the united army. When the armed forces were divided, as for example, in Nazi Germany during an attempt on Hitler's life on June 20, 1944, the coup had little chance.

4. The earlier interventions were sanctioned by what the West called the *Brezhnev Doctrine*. The doctrine, pronounced at the time of Soviet invasion of Czechoslovakia in 1968, permitted or even obliged the Soviet Union to intervene militarily in any socialist (communist) country in which socialism (communism) was endangered. The doctrine was spelled out in detail, in Brezhnev's November 1968 speech to the V Congress of the Polish United Workers' Party. For the text, see Dan N. Jacobs, *From Marx to Mao and Marchais*, 1979, pp. 320-329. This doctrine drew the Soviets into a disastrous intervention in Afghanistan. In 1990, Gorbachev explicitly renounced the doctrine, especially in his speech in Prague. For discussion of the doctrine and Gorbachev's position, see David S. Mason, *Revolution in East-Central Europe*, 1992, p. 36; Leslie Holmes, *Politics in the Communist World*, 1990, p. 364; Nancy Bermeo, *Liberalization and Democratization*, 1992, pp. 2, 9, 34-36, 37-38, 43.

5. In Afghanistan, in April 1978, a communist coup overthrew the pro-Western president Muhammad Daoud Khan. Insurgency of the Islamic tribal people broke out and could not be suppressed by the communist government. In September 1979 the Soviet Union invaded the country and helped to install, in a bloody coup, a more radical leader, Hafizullah Amin. The previous president, Nur Muhammad Taraki, was killed either by the Amin supporters or by the Soviets. Around 1982-1983, the Reagan administration, pressed by public opinion in the United States and concerned about the growing commitment of the Soviet troops, began to provide aid to the anticommunist and anti-Soviet guerrillas. In Nicaragua, in 1979, the long years of guerrilla war against the Somoza dictatorial government ended with the victory of the Sandinista National Liberation Front. The United States recognized the Sandinista government and the Carter administration asked Congress to provide aid for reconstruction of Nicaragua. In 1981, the new Reagan administration branded Sandinista government totalitarian

and a source of left-wing subversion in neighboring coun-
tires. The American aid was cut off. Soon after, the
American government provided arms and finances to the
anti-Sandinista guerrillas, "Contras," a number of whom
were from the old Somoza's National Guard. The Kurds are
a distinct ethnic group of some 22 million people, scattered
across parts of Iran, Iraq, Turkey, Syria, and the area that
was the Soviet Union. For centuries they have fought for
their independence. In early 1991, following the crushing
defeat of Iraq in the Persian Gulf War, Iraqi Kurds (about 5
million) rose against the Ba'th regime of President Saddam
Hussein. No real support came from the UN coalition and
the rebellion was suppressed with considerable brutality.
The Kurdish guerrillas and the civilian refugees (together
about 2 million people) withdrew into the mountains, where
they have barely survived on some U.S. humanitarian aid
and where they have been nominally protected by the U.S.-
declared no-flight zone patrolled by U.S. aircraft.

6. John Bradley, *Allied Intervention in Russia: 1917-
1920*, 1968; George A. Brinkley, *The Volunteer Army and
Allied Intervention in South Russia*, 1966.

7. For Friedrich and Brzezinski this was the prereq-
uisite for totalitarianism (Carl J. Friedrich and Zbigniew
Brzezinski, *Totalitarian Dictatorship and Autocracy*, 1965).

8. Howard J. Wiarda, *Introduction to Comparative
Politics*, 1993, p. 108.

9. Thomas A. Baylis, *The Technical Intelligentsia and
the East German Elite: Legitimacy and Social Change in
Mature Communism*, 1974, especially pp. 261-277.

10. Robert Tucker, *Political Culture and Ledership in
Soviet Russia*, 1987.

11. Frederic J. Fleron, ed., *Technology and Communist
Culture*, 1977.

12. John Hazard, *Communists and Their Law*, 1969.

13. Tucker, *Political Culture and Leadership in Soviet Russia*, Chapter VI.

14. In fact, the lessened systemic role of terror leads to a reduction in the size of political police. Its functionaries are retired from the service and assume "civilian" employment. Eventually their stories demystify the secret police and diminish its fearful isolation from the society.

15. Jane Leftwich Curry, *Poland's Journalists*, 1990; Jim Riordan and Sue Bridger, eds., *Dear Comrade Editor*, 1992.

16. Slawomir Mrozek's *Tango, At Sea, Police*, and Vaclav Havel's *Largo Desolato* and many others.

17. First to notice this was Ted Robert Gurr in his *Why Men Rebel*, 1970.

18. Thomas W. Simons, Jr., *Eastern Europe in the Postwar World*, 1991; Bernard Gwertzman and Michael Kaufman, eds., *The Collapse of Communism*, 1991; Kaminski, *The Collapse of State Socialism*; Bermeo, *Liberalization and Democratization*; Holmes, *Politics in the Communist World*; Mason, *Revolution in East-Central Europe*; Gale Stokes, *From Stalinism to Pluralism*, 1991; Donald D. Barry and Carol Barner-Barry, *Contemporary Soviet Politics*, 1991; Timothy Garton Ash, *The Uses of Adversity*, 1990; Judy Batt, *East Central Europe from Reform to Transformation*, 1991; William E. Griffith, ed., *Central and Eastern Europe: The Opening Curtain*, 1989; Lyman H. Legters, *Eastern Europe: Transformation and Revolution, 1945-1991*, 1992; Michael G. Roskin, *The Rebirth of East Europe*, 1991; Joseph Rothschild, *Return to Diversity*, 1989; Jane Shapiro Zacek, ed., *The Gorbachev Generation*, 1989; Tucker, *Political Culture and Leadership in Soviet Russia*; Michael McFaul, *Post-Communist Politics*, 1993.

19. George C. Malcher, *Poland's Politicized Army*, 1984; Andrew A. Michta, *Red Eagle: The Army in Polish Politics, 1944-1988*, 1990.

Conclusion

1. Mark Juergensmeyer, *The New Cold War?* 1993, pp. 30-35.

2. L. Harmon Zeigler, and G. Wayne Peak, *Interest Groups in American Society*, 1972, pp. 96-100. Gradually, however, these marginal groups gain status and are included within a pluralistic political system.

3. Richard Hofstadter, *The Paranoid Style in American Politics*, 1965, pp. 29-40.

4. Howard J. Wiarda, *Introduction to Comparative Politics*, 1993, pp. 69-72 and 152-155; Harmon Zeigler, *Pluralism, Corporatism, and Confucianism*, 1988.

BIBLIOGRAPHY

Abcarian, Gilbert, ed. *American Political Radicalism.* Waltham, MA: Xerox College Publishing, 1971.

Adorno, Theodor W., et al. *The Authoritarian Personality.* New York: Harper Books, 1950.

Ahmed, Akbar S., and David M. Hart, eds. *Islam in Tribal Societies: From the Atlas to the Indus.* London: Routledge and Kegan, 1984.

Al-Khalil, Samir. *Republic of Fear: The Politics of Modern Iraq.* Berkeley: University of California Press, 1989.

Al-Kathllan, Saleh M. F. "Uzbeks and Islam: Their Contemporary Political Culture, An Empirical Study." Ph.D. dissertation, University of Kansas, 1993.

Ali, Tarig. *The Stalinist Legacy: Its Impact on Twentieth Century World Politics.* Harmondsworth, England: Penguin Books, 1984.

Allemeyer, Robert. *Enemies of Freedom.* San Francisco: Jossey Bass Publishers, 1988.

Almond, A. Gabriel, and Sidney Verba, eds. *The Civic Culture Revisited.* Boston: Little, Brown and Co., 1980.

Alton, Thad P., et al. *Research Project on National Income in East Central Europe.* New York: L. W. International Financial Research, Inc.; vols. 1986, 1987, 1988, 1989, and 1990.

Andrews, Nicholas. *Poland 1980-81: Solidarity Versus the Party.* Washington, DC: National Defense University Press, 1985.

Arendt, Hannah. *The Origins of Totalitarianism.* New York: Meridian Books, 1958, 1960; New York: Harcourt, Brace, Jovanovich, 1973.

————. *Eichman in Jerusalem: A Report on the Banality of Evil.* New York: Penguin Books, 1976.

Argyris, Chris. *Personality and Organization: The Conflict Between System and Individual.* New York: Harper Books, 1957.

Armstrong, John A. *Ideology, Politics, and Government in the Soviet Union.* New York: Praeger Publishers, 1978.

————, ed. *Soviet Partisans in World War II.* Madison: University of Wisconsin Press, 1964.

Aron, Raymond. *Democracy and Totalitarianism,* trans. by Valence Ionescu, London: Weidenfeld and Nicolson, 1968.

————. *The Industrial Society.* New York: Simon and Schuster, 1968.

Ascherson, Neal. *The Polish August: The Self-Limiting Revolution.* New York: Viking Press, 1982.

Ash, Timothy Garton. *The Uses of Adversity: Essays on the Fate of Central Europe.* New York: Vintage Books, 1990.

Ashkenasi, Abraham. *Modern German Nationalism.* New York: John Wiley and Sons, 1976.

Avishai, Bernard. *The Tragedy of Zionism: Revolution and Democracy in the Land of Israel.* New York: Farrar, Straus, Giroux, 1985.

Axelgard, Frederick W., ed. *Iraq in Transition: A Political, Economic and Strategic Perspective.* Boulder, CO: Westview Press, 1986.

Baradat, Leon P. *Political Ideologies: Their Origins and Impacts.* Englewood Cliffs, NJ: Prentice-Hall, 1988.

Barager, Joseph R., ed. *Why Peron Came to Power: The Background to Peronism in Argentina.* New York: Alfred A. Knopf, 1968.

Baram, Amatzia. *Culture, History, and Ideology in the Formation of Bathist Iraq, 1968-89.* New York: St. Martin's Press, 1991.

Baron, Dan. *Legacy of Silence: Encounters with Children of the Third Reich.* Cambridge, MA: Harvard University Press, 1989.

Barry, Donald D., and Carol Barner-Barry. *Contemporary Soviet Politics.* Englewood Cliffs, NJ: Prentice-Hall, 1991.

Batatu, Hanna. *The Old Social Classes and the Revolutionary Movements of Iraq.* Princeton, NJ: Princeton University Press, 1978.

Batt, Judy. *East Europe from Reform to Transformation.* New York: Council on Foreign Relations Press, 1991.

Bauer, Raymond Augustine, ed. *Some Views on Soviet Psychology.* Washington, DC: American Psychological Association, 1962.

———— , A. Inkeles, and C. Kluckhohn. *How the Soviet System Works.* New York: Vintage Books, 1960.

Baylis, Thomas A. *The Technical Intelligentsia and the East German Elite: Legitimacy and Social Change in Mature Communism.* Berkeley: University of California Press, 1974.

Beck, Carl, et al. *Comparative Communist Political Leadership.* New York: David McKay Co., 1973.

Bell, Daniel, ed. *The Radical Right.* Garden City, NY: Anchor Books, 1964.

Benes, Edward. *Memoirs: From Munich to New War and New Victory,* trans. Godfrey Lias. London: Allen and Unwin, 1954.

Berdyaev, Nicolas. *The Russian Idea*, trans. R. M. French. London: G. Bles, 1947.

────── . *The Origins of Russian Communism*, trans. R. M. French. Ann Arbor, Michigan: University of Michigan Press, 1960.

────── . *The Russian Revolution*. Ann Arbor: University of Michigan Press, 1961.

Bermeo, Nancy, ed. *Liberalization and Democratization: Change in the Soviet Union and Eastern Europe*. Baltimore: Johns Hopkins University Press, 1992.

Bertalanffy, Ludwig von. *General System Theory: Foundations, Development, Applications*, rev. ed. New York: G. Braziller, 1968.

Bertsch, Gary K., and Thomas W. Ganschow. *Comparative Communism: The Soviet, Chinese, and Yugoslav Models*. San Francisco: W. H. Freeman and Co., 1976.

Bettelheim, Bruno. *The Informed Heart*. Glencoe, IL: The Free Press of Glencoe, 1960.

Billing, Michael. *Ideology and Social Psychology: Extremism, Moderation, and Contradiction*. New York: St Martin's Press, 1982.

Bluhm, William T. *Ideologies and Attitudes: Modern Political Culture*. Englewood Cliffs, NJ: Prentice-Hall, 1974.

Bociurkiw, Bohdan R., and John W. Strong, eds. *Religion and Atheism in the USSR and Eastern Europe*. London: Macmillan, 1975.

Boll, Heinrich. *Billiards at Half-Past Nine*. New York: McGraw-Hill, 1962.

────── . *Group Portrait with Lady*. New York: McGraw-Hill, 1973.

Borgese, Giuseppe Antonio. *Goliath: The March of Fascism*. New York: Viking Press, 1938.

Borkenau, Franz. *The Totalitarian Enemy*. London: Faber and Faber, 1940.

Bradley, John. *Allied Intervention in Russia: 1917-1920*. London: Weidenfeld and Nicolson, 1968.

Breen, T. H. *Puritans and Adventures: Change and Persistence in Early America*. New York: Oxford University Press, 1980.

Brinkley, George A. *The Volunteer Army and Allied Intervention in South Russia, 1917-1921*. Notre Dame, IN: University of Notre Dame Press, 1966.

Brinton, Clarence Crane. *The Anatomy of Revolution*. New York: Vintage Books, 1965.

Brinton, William M. and Alan Rinzler. *Without Force or Lies: Voices From the Revolution of Central Europe in 1989-90*. San Francisco: Mercury House, 1990.

Bromke, Adam, and John W. Strong, eds. *Gierek's Poland*. New York: Praeger Publishers, 1973.

Brown, J. F. *Eastern Europe and Communist Rule*. Durham, NC: Duke University Press, 1988.

Brzezinski, Zbigniew. *The Permanent Purge: Politics in Soviet Totalitarianism*. Cambridge, MA: Harvard University Press, 1956.

———. *The Soviet Bloc: Unity and Conflict*. New York: Praeger Publishers, 1961.

———. *Ideology and Power in Soviet Politics*. New York: Praeger Publishers, 1962.

——— and Samuel P. Huntington. *Political Power: USA/USSR, Similarities and Contrasts, Convergence and Evolution*. New York: Viking Press, 1964.

Buckley, Walter. *Sociology and Modern Systems Theory*. Englewood Cliffs, NJ: Prentice-Hall, 1967.

Bullock, Alan. *Hitler, A Study in Tyranny.* New York: Harper and Row, 1962, rev. ed. 1964.

Bunting, Brian. *The Rise of the South African Reich.* Harmondsworth, England: Penguin Books, 1969.

Burnham, James. *The Managerial Revolution: What Is Happening in the World.* New York: John Day Company, 1941.

Carr, Edward Hallett. *The Bolshevik Revolution, 1917-1923.* New York: Macmillan, 1951.

———. *The Russian Revolution: From Lenin to Stalin, 1917-1929.* London: Macmillan, 1979.

Carson, Elizabeth O'Leary, ed. *Psychiatry and Psychology in the USSR.* New York: Plenum Press, 1976.

Cassinelli, C. W. *Total Revolution: A Comparative Study of Germany Under Hitler, the Soviet Union Under Stalin, and China Under Mao.* Santa Barbara, CA: Clio Books, 1976.

Cassirer, Ernst. *The Myth of the State.* New Haven, CT: Yale University Press, 1973.

Chai, Winberg, and Ch'u Chai. *The Changing Society of China.* New York: Mentor Books, 1962.

Chassin, Lionel Max. *The Communist Conquest of China: A History of the Civil War, 1945-1949.* Cambridge, MA: Harvard University Press, 1965.

Checinski, Michael. *Terror and Politics in Communist Poland.* Jerusalem: The Hebrew University, 1983.

Chesneaux, Jean. *Peasant Revolts in China, 1840-1949.* New York: W. W. Norton and Co., 1973.

Christenson, Reo M., et al. *Ideologies and Modern Politics.* New York: Dodd, Mead and Co., 1975.

Cohen, Robin. *Endgame in South Africa? The Changing Structure and Ideology of Apartheid.* London: J. Currey, 1986.

Colton, Timothy J. *The Dilemma of Reform in the Soviet Union.* New York: Council on Foreign Relations, 1986.

Conley, Michael Charles. *The Communist Insurgent Infrastructure in South Viet Nam.* Washington DC: Center For Research In Social Systems, The American University, 1967.

Conquest, Robert. *Russia After Khrushchev.* New York: Praeger Publishers, 1965.

Conrad, Geoffrey W., and Arthur A. Demarest. *Religion and Empire: The Dynamics of Aztec and Inca Expansionism.* Cambridge: Cambridge University Press, 1984.

Cooney, Frank, Gordon Morton, and Barry White. *Studies in Race Relations: South Africa and USA.* Glasgow: Pulse Publication, 1986.

Covey, Herbert C., Scott Menard, and Robert J. Franzese. *Juvenile Gangs.* Springfield, IL: Charles C. Thomas, 1992.

Crassweller, Robert. *Peron and the Enigmas of Argentina.* New York: W. W. Norton and Co., 1987.

Crossman, Richard, ed. *The God That Failed.* New York: Harper and Row, 1949.

Cudsi, Alexander S., and Ali E. Hillal Dessouki. *Islam and Power.* Baltimore and London: Johns Hopkins University Press, 1981.

Curry, Jane Leftwich. *Poland's Journalists: Professionalism and Politics.* New York: Cambridge University Press, 1990.

Curry, Janey, ed. and trans. *The Black Book of Polish Censorship.* New York: Vintage Books, 1984.

Curtis, Michael. *Totalitarianism.* New Brunswick, NJ: Transaction Books, 1979.

Czerwinski, E. J., and Jaroslaw Piekalkiewicz, eds. *The Soviet Invasion of Czechoslovakia: Its Effects on Eastern Europe.* New York: Praeger Publishers, 1972.

Dahl, Robert. *After the Revolution: Authority in a Good Society.* New Haven, CN: Yale University Press, 1970.

Dallin, Alexander, and George W. Breslauer. *Political Terror in Communist Systems.* Stanford, CA: Stanford University Press, 1970.

Davies, James C. *Human Nature in Politics: The Dynamics of Human Behavior.* New York: Wiley, 1963.

Dawson, Richard E., and Kenneth Prewitt. *Political Socialization.* Boston: Little, Brown and Co., 1969.

Debray, Regis. *Revolution in the Revolution.* New York: Grove Press, 1967.

De Felice, Renzo. *Interpretations of Fascism.* Cambridge, MA: Harvard University Press, 1977.

Del Boca, Angelo, and Mario Giovana. *Fascism Today.* New York: Random House, 1969.

Demos, John. *A Little Commonwealth: Family Life in Plymouth Colony.* London and New York: Oxford University Press, 1970.

Dennis, Jack. *Comparative Political Socialization.* Beverly Hills, CA: Sage Publications, 1970.

Dessouki, Ali E. Hillal. *Islamic Resurgence in the Arab World.* New York: Praeger Publishers, 1982.

Deutsch, Karl Wolfgang. *The Nerves of Government: Models of Political Communication and Control.* New York: Free Press of Glencoe, 1963.

Deutscher, Isaac. *Stalin, a Political Biography.* London, New York: Oxford University Press, 1949.

—————. *The Prophet Armed: Trotsky, 1879-1921.* New York: Oxford University Press, 1954.

Dewey, John. *Reconstruction in Philosophy.* New York: H. Holt and Co., 1920.

Djilas, Milovan. *The New Class: An Analysis of the Communist System.* London: Thames and Hudson, 1958.

———. *The Unperfect Society: Beyond the New Class,* trans. Dorian Cooke. New York: Harcourt, Brace and World, 1969.

Dmytryshyn, Basil. *USSR: A Concise History.* New York: Charles Scribner's Sons, 1965.

Draper, Theodore. *Castro's Revolution: Myths and Realities.* New York: Praeger Publishers, 1962.

Dumitriu, Petru. *Incognito.* New York: Macmillan, 1964.

Dun, J. Li. *The Ageless Chinese.* New York: Charles Scribner's Sons, 1965.

Durkheim, Emile. *The Division of Labor in Society.* London: Macmillan, 1984.

Dziewanowski, M. K. *The Communist Party of Poland: An Outline of History.* Cambridge, MA: Harvard University Press, 1976.

Easton, David. *A Framework for Political Analysis.* Englewood Cliffs, NJ: Prentice-Hall, 1965.

Ebenstein, William. *Fascist Italy.* New York and Chicago: American Book Co., 1939.

———. *The Nazi State.* New York and Toronto: Farrar and Rinehart, 1943.

Eberhard, Wolfram. *A History of China,* 4th ed. Berkeley: University of California Press, 1977.

Eckstein, Harry, ed. *Internal War.* New York: The Free Press of Glencoe, 1964.

Eisenstadt, S. N. *The Transformation of Israeli Society: An Essay in Interpretation.* London: Weidenfeld and Nicolson, 1985.

Ellul, Jacques. *The Technological Society*, trans. John Wilkinson. New York: Alfred A. Knopf, 1964.

——— . *Autopsy of Revolution*, trans. Patricia Wolf. New York: Alfred A. Knopf, 1971.

Emerson, Rupert, ed. *The Political Awakening of Africa*. Englewood Cliffs, NJ: Prentice-Hall, 1965.

Epstein, Benjamin, and Arnold Forster. *The Radical Right: Report on the John Birch Society and Its Allies*. New York: Vintage Books, 1967.

Erikson, Kai T. *Wayward Puritans: A Study in the Sociology of Deviance*. New York: John Wiley and Sons, 1966.

Esposito, John L. *Islam: The Straight Path*. New York: Oxford University Press, 1988.

Fainsod, Merle. *Smolensk Under Soviet Rule*. London: Macmillan, 1958, 1959.

Fall, Bernard B. *The Two Viet-Nams: A Political and Military Analysis*. New York: Praeger Publishers, 1965.

Fan, K., ed. *Mao Tse-tung and Lin Piao: Post Revolutionary Writings*. Garden City, NY: Anchor Books, 1972.

Farrell, R. Barry, ed. *Political Leadership in Eastern Europe and the Soviet Union*. Chicago: Aldine Publishing, 1970.

Feierabend, Ivo K., Rosalind L. Feierabend, and Ted Robert Gurr, eds. *Anger, Violence, and Politics: Theories and Research*. Englewood Cliffs, NJ: Prentice-Hall, 1972.

Feuer, Lewis. *The Conflict of Generations: The Character and Significance of Student Movement*. New York: Basic Books, 1969.

——— . *Ideology and the Ideologists*. Oxford: Basil Blackwell, 1975.

Feuerwerker, Albert, ed. *Modern China*. Englewood Cliffs, NJ: Prentice-Hall, 1965.

Finer, Herman. *Mussolini's Italy*. New York: H. Holt and Co., 1935.

Fischer, Mary Ellen. *Nicolae Ceausescu: A Study in Political Leadership*. Boulder, CO: L. Rienner Publishers, 1989.

Fisher-Galati, Stephen. *Eastern Europe in the 1980s*. Boulder, CO: Westview Press, 1981.

Fishman, Jack. *The Seven Men of Spandau*. New York: Rinehart, 1954.

Fitzgerald, C. P. *China, A Short Cultural History*. New York: Praeger Publishers, 1954.

————. *The Birth of Communist China*. Harmondsworth, England: Penguin Books, 1971.

Fleron, Frederic J., Jr., ed. *Communist Studies and the Social Sciences: Essays on Methodology and Empirical Theory*. Chicago: Rand McNally, 1969.

————, ed. *Technology and Communist Culture: The Socio-Cultural Impact of Technology Under Socialism*. New York: Praeger Publishers, 1977.

Fletcher, William C. *Soviet Believers: The Religious Sector of the Population*. Lawrence: Regents Press of Kansas, 1981.

Forbis, William H. *The Fall of the Peacock Throne*. New York: Harper and Row, 1980.

Forest, James H. *Religion in the New Russia: The Impact of Perestroika on the Varieties of Religious Life in the Soviet Union*. New York: Crossroad, 1990.

Forgacs, David, ed. *Rethinking Italian Fascism*. London: Lawrence and Wishart, 1986.

Friedrich, Carl J., ed. *Totalitarianism*. New York: Grosset and Dunlap, 1954, 1964.

————, ed. *The Pathology of Politics: Violence, Betrayal, Corruption, Secrecy, and Propaganda*. New York: Harper and Row, 1972.

———— and Zbigniew K. Brzezinski. *Totalitarian Dictatorship and Autocracy.* New York: Praeger Publishers, 1956, 1961, 1964, rev. ed. 1965.

Germani, Gino. *Authoritarianism, Fascism, and National Populist.* New Brunswick, NJ: Transaction Books, 1978.

Gerrits, Andre. *The Failure of Authoritarian Change: Reform, Opposition, and Geo-politics in Poland in the 1980s.* Aldershot; Brookfield USA: Dartmouth, 1990.

Gerth, H. H., and C. Wright Mills, eds. *From Max Weber: Essays in Sociology.* New York: Oxford University Press, 1946.

Gilberg, Trond. *Nationalism and Communism in Romania: The Rise and Fall of Ceausescu's Personal Dictatorship.* Boulder, CO: Westview Press, 1990.

Gilbert, G. M. *Nuremberg Diary.* New York: Farrar, Straus, 1947.

Gobineau, Arthur de. *The Inequality of Human Races*, trans. Adrian Collins. New York: H. Fertig, 1967.

Goebbels, Joseph. *The Goebbels Diaries, 1942-1943.* Westport, CT: Greenwood Press, 1970.

————. *The Diaries: Final Entries 1945*, trans. Richard Barry, ed. Hugh Trevor-Roper. New York: G. P. Putnam's Sons, 1978.

Goldstone, Jack A. *Revolution and Rebellion in the Early Modern World.* Berkeley: University of California Press, 1991.

————, Ted Robert Gurr, and Farrokh Moshiri, eds. *Revolutions In The Late Twentieth Century.* Boulder, CO: Westview Press, 1991.

Gould, James A., and Willis H. Truitt. *Political Ideologies.* New York: Macmillan, 1973.

Greene, Thomas H. *Comparative Revolutionary Movements: Search for Theory and Justice.* Englewood Cliffs, NJ: Prentice-Hall, 1990.

Greenstein, Fred I., and Michael Lerner, eds. *A Source Book for the Study of Personality and Politics.* Chicago: Markham Publishing, 1971.

―――― and Nelson W. Polsby, eds. *Handbook of Political Science.* Reading, MA, 1975.

Gregor, A. James. *Contemporary Radical Ideologies: Totalitarian Thought in the Twentieth Century.* New York: Random House, 1968.

―――― . *The Ideology of Fascism: The Rationale of Totalitarianism.* New York: The Free Press, 1969.

―――― . *Interpretations of Fascism.* Morristown, NJ: General Learning Press, 1974.

―――― . *Italian Fascism and Development Dictatorship.* Princeton, NJ: Princeton University Press, 1979.

Griffith, Samuel. *Peking and People's Wars: An Analysis of Statements by Official Spokesmen of the Chinese Communist Party on the Subject of Revolutionary Strategy.* New York: Praeger Publishers, 1966.

Griffith, William, ed. *Central and Eastern Europe: The Opening Curtain.* Boulder, CO: Westview Press, 1989.

Gross, Feliks. *The Seizure of Political Power in a Century of Revolutions.* New York: Philosophical Library, 1958.

Grunberger, Richard. *The 12-Year Reich: A Social History of Nazi Germany, 1933-1945.* New York: Ballantine Books, 1971.

Grundy, Kenneth, and Michael Weinstein. *The Ideologies of Violence.* Columbus, OH: Charles E. Merrill, 1974.

Gurian, Waldemar. "Totalitarianism as Political Religion," in Carl J. Friedrich, ed., *Totalitarianism.* New York: Grosset and Dunlap, 1964.

Gurr, Ted Robert. *Why Men Rebel.* Princeton, NJ: Princeton University Press, 1970.

Gutierrez, Gustavo. *A Theology of Liberation: History, Politics and Salvation,* trans. Caridad Inda and John Eagleson. Maryknoll, NY: Orbis Books, 1973.

Gwertzman, Bernard, and Michael Kaufman, eds. *The Collapse of Communism.* New York: Time Books, 1991.

Hagopian, Mark N. *Ideals and Ideologies of Modern Politics.* New York and London: Longman, 1985.

Halliday, Fred, and Hamza Alavi, eds. *State and Ideology in the Middle East and Pakistan.* New York: Monthly Review Press, 1988.

Halpern, Joel M. *The Changing Village Community.* Englewood Cliffs, NJ: Prentice-Hall, 1967.

Hamilton, Alastair. *The Appeal of Fascism.* New York: Avon Books, 1971.

Hammond, Thomas T., ed. *The Anatomy of Communist Takeovers.* New Haven, CT: Yale University Press, 1975.

Harrison, John A. *The Chinese Empire.* New York: Harcourt Brace Jovanovich, 1972.

Havel, Vaclav. *Hry 1970-1976 (Plays).* Toronto: Sixty-Eight Publishers, 1977.

—— et al. *The Power of the Powerless: Citizens Against the State in Central Eastern Europe,* ed. John Keane. Armonk, NY: M. E. Sharpe, 1985.

—— . *Largo Desolato: A Play in Seven Scenes,* English version by Tom Stoppard. London, Boston: Faber and Faber, 1987.

Hazard, John N. *Communists and Their Law: A Search for the Common Core of the Legal Systems of the Marxian Socialist States.* Chicago: University of Chicago Press, 1969.

——— . *Soviet System of Government*, 5th ed. Chicago: University of Chicago Press, 1980.

Hendel, Samuel. *The Soviet Crucible*. North Scituate, MA: Duxbury Press, 1980.

Hill, Ronald J., and Peter J. Frank. *The Soviet Communist Party*. Boston: Allen and Unwin, 1986.

Hillgruber, Andreas. *Germany and the Two World Wars*. Cambridge, MA: Harvard University Press, 1981.

Hinnebusch, Raymond A. *Authoritarian Power and State Formation in Ba'thist Syria: Army, Party, and Peasant*. Boulder, CO: Westview Press, 1990.

Hiro, Dilip. *Holy Wars: The Rise of Islamic Fundamentalism*. New York: Routledge, 1989.

Hitler, Adolf. *Mein Kampf*. Munich: Zentralverlag der NSDAP, F. Eher Nachf., 1938; English trans. by Ralph Manheim (Boston: Houghton Mifflin, 1962).

——— . *The Speeches of Adolf Hitler, April 1922-August 1939*. New York: H. Fertig, 1969.

——— . *Hitler's Secret Conversations, 1941-1944*. New York: Octagon Books, 1976.

Hobbes, Thomas. *The Leviathan*, ed. with an introduction by C. B. Macpherson. London: Penguin, 1985.

Hodges, Donald. *Argentina, 1943-1976: The National Revolution and Resistance*. Albuquerque: University of New Mexico Press, 1976.

Hoebel, E. Adamson, and Thomas Weaver. *Anthropology and the Human Experience*. New York: McGraw-Hill, 1979.

Hofstadter, Richard. *The Paranoid Style in American Politics*. New York: Alfred A. Knopf, 1965.

Holmes, Leslie. *Politics in the Communist World*. Oxford: Clarendon Press, 1990.

Horowitz, Irving Louis. *The Struggle Is the Message: The Organization and Ideology of the Anti-War Movement.* Berkeley, CA: The Glendessary Press, 1970.

Hough, Jerry. *The Soviet Union and Social Science Theory.* Cambridge, MA: Harvard University Press, 1977.

Hunter, Shireen T. *The Politics of Islamic Revivalism.* Bloomington: Indiana University Press, 1988.

Huntington, Samuel P., and Clement H. Moore, eds. *Authoritarian Politics in Modern Society: The Dynamics of Established One-Party Systems.* New York: Basic Books, 1970.

Hussein, Saddam. *Iraqi Policies in Perspective.* Baghdad: Translation and Foreign Languages Publishing House, 1981.

Inkeles, Alex. *Exploring Individual Modernity.* New York: Columbia University Press, 1983.

Innes, William C. *Social Concern in Calvin's Geneva.* Allison Park, PA: Pickwick Publications, 1983.

Jacobs, Dan N., ed. *From Marx to Mao and Marchais: Documents on the Development of Communist Variations.* New York and London: Longman, 1979.

Jan, George P., ed. *Government of Communist China.* San Francisco: Chandler Publishing Co., 1966.

Janos, Andrew C. *The Seizure of Power: A Study of Force and Popular Consent.* Princeton, NJ: Center of International Studies, Princeton University, 1964.

Joes, Anthony James. *Fascism in the Contemporary World: Ideology, Evolution, Resurgence.* Boulder, CO: Westview Press, 1978.

Johnson, Chalmers. *Revolutionary Change.* Stanford, CA: Stanford University Press, 1966.

Juergensmeyer, Mark. *The New Cold War? Religious Nationalism Confronts the Secular State.* Berkeley: University of California Press, 1993.

Kaminski, Bartlomiej. *The Collapse of State Socialism: The Case of Poland.* Princeton, NJ: Princeton University Press, 1991.

Kaplan, Lawrence, ed. *Revolutions: A Comparative Study.* New York: Vintage Books, 1973.

Karpovich, Michael. *Imperial Russia, 1801-1917.* New York: Holt, Rinehart and Winston, 1963.

Karsten, Rafael. *A Totalitarian State of the Past: The Civilization of the Inca Empire in Ancient Peru.* Port Washington, NY: Kennikat Press, 1969.

Kater, Michael H. *The Nazi Party: A Social Profile of Members and Leaders, 1919-1945.* Cambridge, MA: Harvard University Press, 1983.

Kaufman, Arnold. *The Radical Liberal, the New Politics: Theory and Practice.* New York: Simon and Schuster, 1970.

Keegan, John, and Joseph Darracott. *The Nature of War.* New York: Holt, Rinehart and Wilson, 1981.

Kersten, Krystyna. *The Establishment Of Communist Rule in Poland, 1943-1948*, trans. and annotated John Micgiel and Michael H. Bernhard, Forword by Jan T. Gross. Berkeley: University of California Press, 1992.

Khadduri, Majid. *Republican Iraq.* London: Oxford University Press, 1969.

——— . *Socialist Iraq.* Washington, DC: Middle East Institute, 1978.

Khrushchev, Nikita. *Khrushchev Remembers*, trans. Strobe Talbott. New York: Bantam Books, 1976.

Kingston, Robert, ed. *Perestroika Papers: An Exercise In Supplemental Diplomacy*. Dubuque, IA: Kendall/Hunt Co., 1988.

Kirkpatrick, Jeane J. *Leader and Vanguard in Mass Society: A Study of Peronist Argentina*. Cambridge: M.I.T. Press, 1971.

Koestler, Arthur. *Darkness at Noon*. New York: The New American Library, 1941.

Kolb, Eugene J. *A Framework for Political Analysis*. Englewood Cliffs, NJ: Prentice-Hall, 1978.

Kogon, Engen. *The Theory and Practice of Hell: The German Concentration Camps and the System Behind Them*. New York: Berkley Publishing Co., 1950.

Kohn, Hans and Wallace Sokolsky. *African Nationalism in the Twentieth Century*. Princeton, NJ: Princeton University Press, 1965.

Kornhauser, William, A. *The Politics of Mass Society*. Glencoe, IL: The Free Press of Glencoe, 1959.

Krech, David, Richard S. Crutchfield, and Egerton Ballachy. *Individual in Society: A Textbook of Social Psychology*. New York: McGraw-Hill, 1962.

Kroeber, A. L., and Clyde Kluckhohn. *Culture: A Critical Review of Concepts and Definitions*. Cambridge, MA: The Museum, 1952.

Kuklinski, Antoni, ed. *Society, Science, Government*. Warsaw: State Committee for Scientific Research, Republic of Poland, 1992.

Kundera, Milan. *The Unbearable Lightness of Being*. New York: Harper Perenial, 1991.

Labaree, Benjamin Woods. *Colonial Massachusetts: A History*. Millwood, NY: KTO Press, 1979.

Laird Roy D. *The Soviet Legacy*. New York: Praeger Publishers, 1993.

————— and Betty A. Laird. *Soviet Communism and Agrarian Revolution.* Harmondsworth, England: Penguin Books, 1970.

Laquer, Walter. *Terrorism: A Study of National and International Political Violence.* Boston: Little, Brown and Co., 1977.

Lasswell, Harold D. *Political Writings of Harold Lasswell.* Glencoe, IL: The Free Press of Glencoe, 1952.

————— and Daniel Lerner, eds. *World Revolutionary Elites; Studies in Coercive Ideological Movements.* Cambridge: M.I.T. Press, 1966.

Latham, Earl. *The Group Basis of Politics: A Study in Basing-Point Legislation.* Ithaca, New York: Cornell University Press, 1952.

Lee, Dae-Kyu. "A Causal Analysis of Military Intervention in Polish Politics." Ph.D. dissertation, University of Kansas, 1987.

Legters, Lyman H. *Eastern Europe: Transformation and Revolution, 1945-1991.* Lexington, MA: D. C. Heath and Co., 1992.

Leites, Nathan Constantin, and Charles Wolf, Jr. *Rebellion and Authority: An Analytic Essay on Insurgent Conflicts.* Chicago: Markham Publishing Co., 1970.

Lelyveld, Joseph. *Move Your Shadow: South Africa, Black and White.* New York: Time Books, 1985.

Lenin, V. I. *Imperialism: The Highest Stage of Capitalism.* New York: International Publishers, 1939.

Lepak, Keith John. *Prelude to Solidarity: Poland and the Politics of the Gierek Regime.* New York: Columbia University Press, 1988.

Lerner, Daniel. *The Passing of Traditional Society: Modernizing the Middle East.* Glencoe, IL: The Free Press of Glencoe, 1958.

Levenson, Joseph R., and Herbert Franz Schurmann. *China: An Interpretative History*. Berkeley: University of California Press, 1969.

Levytinski, Boris. *The Use of Terror: The Soviet Secret Police, 1917-1970*. New York: Coward, McCann and Geoghegan, 1972.

Liebman, Robert C., and Robert Wuthnow, eds. *The New Christian Right*. New York: Aloine Publishing Co., 1983.

Lifton, Robert J. *Thought Reform and the Psychology of Totalism: A Study of "Brainwashing" in China*. New York: W. W. Norton, 1961.

————. *Boundaries: Psychological Man in Revolution*. New York: Random House, 1970.

————. *The Nazi Doctors: Medical Killing and the Psychology of Genocide*. New York: Basic Books, 1986.

Linden, Carl A. *The Soviet Party-State: The Politics of Ideocratic Despotism*. New York: Praeger Publishers, 1983.

Linz, Juan. "Totalitarian and Authoritarian Regimes." In F. Greenstein and N. Polsby, eds., *Handbook of Political Science*, vol. 3. Reading, MA: Addison-Wesley, 1975.

Lucian W. Pye. *China: An Introduction*. Boston and Toronto: Little, Brown and Co., 1972.

Ludz, Peter C. *The Changing Party Elite in East Germany*. Cambridge, MA: MIT Press, 1972.

Machiavelli, Niccolo. *The Prince*, trans. Robert M. Adams. New York: W. W. Norton, 1977.

Macridis, Roy C. *Contemporary Political Ideologies: Movements and Regimes*. Glenview, IL: Scott, Foresman and Co., 1985.

Madison, James. "Federalist No. 10." In Jacob E. Cooke, ed., *The Federalist*. Middletown, CT: Wesleyan University Press, 1961.

Malcher, George C. *Poland's Politicized Army: Communists in Uniform*. New York: Praeger Publishers, 1984.

Mann, Rann Singh. *Tribal Culture and Change*. New Delhi, India: Mittal Publications, 1989.

Manoochehri, Hossein. "Toward an Explanation of the Islamic Ideal of Human Perfection: With Emphasis on the Doctrine of Jihad." Ph.D. dissertation, University of Kansas, 1988.

Marcuse, Herbert. *Reason and Revolution: Hegel and the Rise of Social Theory*. Boston: Beacon Press, 1960.

Marx, Karl. *Capital: A Critique of Political Economy*. Harmondsworth, England: Penquin Books, 1976-1981.

—— and Friedrich Engels. *The Communist Manifesto*. New York: Appleton-Century Crofts, 1955.

Maslow, Abraham. *Toward a Psychology of Being*. Princeton, NJ: Van Nostrand, 1968.

Mason, David S. *Revolution in East-Central Europe: The Rise and Fall of Communism and the Cold War*. Boulder, CO: Westview Press, 1992.

Matthews, Herbert L. *Fidel Castro*. New York: Simon and Schuster, 1969.

McFaul, Michael. *Post-Communist Politics: Democratic Prospects in Russia and Eastern Europe*. Washington, DC: The Center for Strategic and International Studies, 1993.

Medvedev, Zhores A. *Andropov: An Insider's Account of Power and Politics Within the Kremlin*. Harmondsworth, England: Penguin Book, 1984.

Meerson-Aksenov, Michael, and Boris Shragin, eds., *The Political, Social and Religious Thought of Russian Samizdat: An Anthology*. Belmont, MA: Norland Publishing Co., 1977.

Melby, John F. *The Mandate of Heaven: Record of a Civil War, 1945-49*. Garden City, NY: Doubleday and Co., 1971.

Michnik, Adam. *Letters from Prison and Other Essays*, trans. Maya Latynski. Berkeley: University of California Press, 1987.

Michta, Andrew A. *Red Eagle: The Army in Polish Politics, 1944-1988*. Stanford, CA: Hoover Institution Press, 1990.

Miliband, Ralph. *Marxism and Politics*. Oxford: Oxford University Press, 1977.

Miller, Judith, and Laurie Mylroie. *Saddam Hussein and the Crisis in the Gulf*. New York: Time Books, 1990.

Miller, Perry. *Orthodoxy in Massachusetts, 1630-1650*. Gloucester, MA: P. Smith, 1965.

Milosz, Czeslaw. *The Captive Mind*. New York: Vintage Books, 1955.

Mitchell, Allan. *Revolution in Bavaria, 1918-1919: The Eisner Regime and the Soviet Republic*. Princeton, NJ: Princeton University Press, 1965.

Montagu, Ashley. *Man's Most Dangerous Myth: The Fallacy of Race*. Cleveland and New York: World Publishing Co., 1965.

Monter, E. William. *Studies in Genevan Government (1536-1605)*. Geneva: Droz, 1964.

Moore, Barrington. *Soviet Politics: The Dilemma of Power; The Role of Ideas In Social Change*. Cambridge, MA: Harvard University Press, 1950.

——— . *Social Origins of Dictatorship and Democracy; Lord and Peasant in the Making of the Modern World*. Boston: Beacon Press, 1967.

——— . *Injustice: The Social Bases of Obedience and Revolt*. White Plains, NY: M. E. Sharpe, 1978.

Morrow, William. *Public Administration: Politics and the Political System*, New York: Random House, 1975.

Mortimer, Edward. *Faith and Power: The Politics of Islam*. New York: Vintage Books, 1982.

Moshiri, Farrokh. *The State and Social Revolution in Iran: A Theoretical Perspective*. New York: Peter Lang, 1985.

Mouzelis, Nicos P. *Organization and Bureaucracy: An Analysis of Modern Theories*. Chicago: Aldine Publishing, 1974.

Mowry, Jess. *Way Pass Cool*. New York: Farrar, Straus, Giroux, 1992.

Mrozek, Slawomir. *Utwory Sceniczne Nowe*. Krakow: Wydawnictwo Literackie, 1975.

Mussolini, Benito. *Talks with Mussolini*, by Emil Ludwig. London: G. Allen and Unwin, 1932.

Nelson, Daniel N., ed. *Local Politics in Communist Countries*. Lexington: University Presses of Kentucky, 1980.

Neumann, Franz. *Behemoth: The Structure and Practice of National Socialism, 1933-1944*. Toronto and New York: Oxford University Press, 1944.

Neumann, Sigmund. *Permanent Revolution: The Total State in a World at War*. New York and London: Harper and Brothers, 1942.

Niebuhr, Reinhold. *Moral Man and Immoral Society: A Study in Ethics and Politics*. New York: Charles Scribner's Sons, 1960.

Nieburg, H. L. *Political Violence: The Behavioral Process*. New York: St. Martin's Press, 1969.

Nietzsche, Friedrich Wilhelm. *Thus Spake, Zarathustra*. New York: Modern Library, 1950.

——— . *Twilight of the Idols*; and, *The Anti-Christ*. Harmondsworth, England: Penguin, 1968.

Nolte, Ernst. *Three Faces of Fascism*. New York: Holt, Rinehart and Winston, 1966.

Nyomarkay, Joseph. *Charisma and Factionalism in the Nazi Party*. Minneapolis: University of Minnesota Press, 1967.

Oestreicher, Randall Dwight. "Technocracy and Public Policy: Poland, 1950-1980." Ph.D. dissertation, University of Kansas, 1981.

Olson, Robert W. *The Bath and Syria, 1947 to 1982: The Evolution of Ideology, Party, and State, From the French Mandate to the Era of Hafiz al-Asad*. Princeton, NJ: Kingston Press, 1982.

Organski, A. F. K. *Stages of Political Development*. New York: Alfred A. Knopf, 1967.

Ortega y Gasset, Jose. *The Revolt of the Masses*, trans. Anthony Kerrigan. Notre Dame, IN: University of Notre Dame Press, 1985.

Osanka, Franklin Mark, ed. *Modern Guerrilla Warfare: Fighting Communist Guerrilla Movements, 1941-1961*. New York: The Free Press of Glencoe, 1962.

Ozinga, James R. *Communism: The Story of the Idea and Its Implementation*. Englewood Cliffs, NJ: Prentice Hall, 1991.

Parkinson, C. Northcote. *East and West*. New York: Houghton Miffin Co., 1963.

Parsons, Talcott, et al. *Theories of Society: Foundations of Modern Sociological Theory*. New York: The Free Press, 1961.

Paul, Ellen Frankel, ed. *Totalitarianism at the Crossroads*. New Brunswick, NJ: Transaction Books, 1990.

Payne, Robert. *The Life and Death of Adolf Hitler*. New York: Praeger Publishers, 1973.

Payne, Stanley G. *Fascism: Comparison and Definition*. Madison: University of Wisconsin Press, 1980.

———. *The Franco Regime: 1936-1975*. Madison: University of Wisconsin Press, 1987.

Peng, Shu-Tse. *The Chinese Communist Party in Power*. New York: Monad Press, 1980.

Piekalkiewicz, Jaroslaw A. *Public Opinion Polling in Czechoslovakia 1968-1969: Results and Analysis of Surveys Conducted During the Dubcek Era*. New York: Praeger Publishers, 1972.

———. *Communist Local Government: A Study of Poland*. Athens: Ohio University Press, 1975.

——— and Chris Hamilton, eds. *Public Bureaucracies Between Reform and Resistance: Legacies, Trends, and Effects in China, The Soviet Union, Poland, and Yugoslavia*. Oxford: Berg Publishers, 1991.

Pipes, Daniel. *In the Path of God: Islam and Political Power*. New York: Basic Books, 1983.

Pipes, Richard. *The Formation of the Soviet Union: Communism and Nationalism, 1917-1923*. Cambridge, MA: Harvard University Press, 1964.

Piscatori, James P. *Islam in the Political Process*. Cambridge: Cambridge University Press, 1983.

Plato. *The Republic*, trans. Desmond Lee. Harmondsworth, England: Penguin Books, 1987.

Posner, Gerald L. *Hitler's Children: Sons and Daughters of Leaders of the Third Reich*. New York: Random House, 1991.

Przeworski, Adam, and Henry Teune. *The Logic of Comparative Social Inquiry*. New York: Wiley-Interscience, 1970.

Pye, Lucian W. *China: An Introduction*. Boston: Little, Brown & Co., 1978.

Radel, Jouffroy-Lucien. *Roots of Totalitarianism: The Ideological Sources of Fascism, National Socialism, and Communism.* New York: Crane, Russak and Co., 1975.

————. *Demise and Regenesis of East-Central Europe* Appleton, WI: Lakesider Publishing Co., 1991.

Rady, Martyn C. *Romania in Turmoil: A Contemporary History.* London and New York: IB Tauris, 1992.

Rahmani, Levy. *Soviet Psychology: Philosophical, Theoretical, and Experimental Issues.* New York: International Press, 1973.

Rakowska-Harmstone, Teresa, ed. *Communism in Eastern Europe.* Bloomington: Indiana University Press, 1979.

Rauschning, Hermann. *Hitler Speaks; A Series of Political Conversations with Adolph Hitler on His Real Aims.* London: T. Butterworth, 1940 printing.

Reitlinger, Gerald. *The SS—Alibi of a Nation, 1922-1945.* New York: Viking Press, 1968.

Rejai, M., ed. *Decline of Ideology?* Chicago: Aldine Atherton, 1971.

Remington, Robin Alison. *The Warsaw Pact: Case Studies in Communist Conflict Resolution.* Cambridge, MA: MIT Press, 1971.

Revel, Jean-Francois. *The Totalitarian Temptation.* New York: Penguin Books, 1978.

Richelson, Jeffrey T. *Sword and Shield: Soviet Intelligence and Security Apparatus.* Cambridge, MA: Ballinger Publishing Co., 1986.

Riordan, Jim, and Sue Bridger, eds. *Dear Comrade Editor: Readers' Letters to the Soviet Press Under Perestroika.* Bloomington: Indiana University Press, 1992.

Robins, David. *Tarnished Vision: Crime and Conflict in the Inner City.* Oxford and New York: Oxford University Press, 1992.

Roberts, David. *The Bath and The Creation of Modern Syria.* London: Croom Helm, 1987.

Rokeach, Milton. *The Open and Closed Mind: Investigations into the Nature of Belief Systems and Personality Systems.* New York: Basic Books, 1960.

Roskin, Michael G. *The Rebirth of East Europe.* Englewood Cliffs, NJ: Prentice-Hall, 1991.

Rostow, W. W. *The Stages of Economic Growth: A Non-Communist Manifesto,* 2d ed. Cambridge: Cambridge University Press, 1971.

Rothman, Stanley, and George W. Breslauer. *Soviet Politics and Society.* St. Paul, MN: West Publishing Co., 1978.

Rothschild, Joseph. *Return to Diversity: A Political History of East Central Europe Since World War II.* New York: Oxford University Press, 1989.

Rubin, Barry. *Modern Dictators, Third World Coup Makers, Strongmen, and Populist Tyrants.* New York: Meridian Books, 1987.

Saikal, Amin. *The Rise and Fall of the Shah.* Princeton, NJ: Princeton University Press, 1980.

Saint-Simon, Claude. *Social Organization, the Science of Man,* trans. Felix Markham. New York: Harper and Row, 1964.

Salvemini, Gaetano. *Under the Axe of Fascism.* London: V. Gollancz, 1936.

Sanford, George, ed. *Democratization in Poland: 1988-90: Polish Voices.* New York: St. Martin's Press, 1992.

Sarti, Roland. *The Ax Within: Italian Fascism in Action.* New York: New Viewpoints, 1974.

Scalapino, Robert A., ed. *The Communist Revolutions in Asia: Tactics, Goals and Achievements.* Englewood Cliffs, NJ: Prentice-Hall, 1965.

Schapiro, Leonard. *Totalitarianism.* New York: Praeger Publishers, 1972.

Schoenbaum, David. *Hitler's Social Revolution: Class and Status in Nazi Germany, 1933-1939.* Garden City, NY: Doubleday and Co., 1966.

Scott, Harriet Fast, and William F. Scott. *The Armed Forces of the USSR.* Boulder, CO: Westview Press, 1979.

Seton-Watson, Hugh. *The East European Revolution.* New York: Praeger Publishers, 1962.

————. *From Lenin to Khrushchev: The History of World Communism.* New York: Praeger Publishers, 1963.

Shaw, Martin. *Dialectics of War: An Essay in the Social Theory of Total War and Peace.* London: Pluto Press, 1988.

Shirer, William L. *The Rise and Fall of the Third Reich: A History of Nazi Germany.* Greenwich, CT: Fawcett Publications, 1962.

Shuhachi, Inoue. *Modern Korea and Kim Jong Il.* Tokyo: Yuzankaku, 1984.

Simmons, George W., ed. *Nationalism in the USSR and Eastern Europe in the Era of Brezhnev and Kosygin.* Detroit: University of Detroit Press, 1977.

Simons, Thomas W., Jr. *Eastern Europe in the Postwar World.* New York: St. Martin's Press, 1991.

Skilling, H. Gordon, and Franklin Griffiths, eds. *Interest Groups in Soviet Politics.* Princeton, NJ: Princeton University Press, 1971.

Skocpol, Theda. *States and Social Revolutions: A Comparative Analysis of France, Russia, and China.* Cambridge and New York: Cambridge University Press, 1979.

Smith, David Marshall. *Apartheid in South Africa.* New York: Cambridge University Press, 1987.

Smith, Denis Mark. *Mussolini's Roman Empire.* New York: Viking Press, 1976.

Smith, Tony. *Thinking Like a Communist: State and Legitimacy in the Soviet Union, China, and Cuba.* New York: W. W. Norton, 1987.

Smolen, Kazimierz, ed. *Kl Auschwitz Seen by the SS. Hoss, Broad, Kremer.* Oswiecim, Poland: Panstwowe Muzeum Publication, 1972.

Solzhenitsyn, Aleksandr I. *The First Circle.* New York: Bantam Books, 1969.

——— . *The Gulag Archipelago: 1918-1956,* vols. I and II. New York: Harper and Row, 1974.

——— . *The Gulag Archipelago: 1918-1956,* vols. III & IV. New York: Harper and Row, 1975.

Speer, Albert. *Inside the Third Reich: Memoirs,* trans. Richard Winston and Clara Winston. New York: Macmillan, 1970.

Stadler, Alfred William. *The Political Economy of Modern South Africa.* London: Croom Helm, 1987.

Steele, Jonathan. *Inside East Germany: The State That Came in from the Cold.* New York: Urizen Books, 1977.

Steeves, Paul D. *Keeping the Faiths: Religion and Ideology in the Soviet Union.* New York: Holmes and Meier, 1989.

Stehle, Hansjakob. *The Independent Satellite: Society and Politics in Poland Since 1945.* New York: Praeger Publishers, 1965.

Stern, Fritz, et al. *The Path to Dictatorship, 1918-1933: Ten Essays by German Scholars.* Garden City, NY: Doubleday and Co., 1966.

Stewart, Philip D. *Political Power in the Soviet Union: A Study of Decision-Making in Stalingrad.* Indianapolis: Bobbs-Merrill Co., 1968.

Stokes, Gale, ed. *From Stalinism to Pluralism: A Documentary History of Eastern Europe Since 1945.* Oxford: Oxford University Press, 1991.

Stoss, Richard. *Politics Against Democracy: Right-Wing Extremism in West Germany.* Oxford: Berg Publishers, 1991.

Summerscale, Peter. *The East European Predicament: Changing Patterns in Poland, Czechoslovakia and Romania.* Aldershot, England: Gower Publishing Co., 1982.

Sweeney, John. *The Life and Evil Times of Nicolae Ceausescu.* London: Hutchinson, 1991.

Talmon, J. L. *The Rise of Totalitarian Democracy.* Boston: Beacon Press, 1952.

————. *The Origins of Totalitarian Democracy.* New York: Praeger Publishers, 1961.

Talpalar, Morris. *The Sociology of the Bay Colony.* New York: Philosophical Library, 1976.

Thornton, Richard C. *China: The Struggle for Power 1917-1972.* Bloomington: Indiana University Press, 1973.

Tilly, Charles. *From Mobilization to Revolution.* New York: Newberry Award Records, 1978.

Todd, Margo. *Christian Humanism and the Puritan Social Order.* Cambridge and New York: Cambridge University Press, 1987.

Tolley, Howard. *Children and War; Political Socialization to International Conflict.* New York: Teachers College Press, 1973.

Townsend, James R. *Politics in China.* Boston: Little, Brown and Co., 1980.

Trevor-Roper, H. R. *The Last Days of Hitler.* London: Macmillan; New York: St. Martin's Press, 1956.

Tucker, Robert C. *Philosophy and Myth in Karl Marx.* Cambridge: Cambridge University Press, 1964.

——— . *The Soviet Political Mind: Stalinism and Post-Stalin Change.* New York: W. W. Norton, 1971.

——— . *Political Culture and Leadership in Soviet Russia: From Lenin to Gorbachev.* Brighton, England: Wheatsheaf, 1987.

Turki, Fawaz. *Soul in Exile, Lives of a Palestinian Revolutionary.* New York: Monthly Review Press, 1988.

Ulam, Adam. *The New Face of Soviet Totalitarianism.* Cambridge: Harvard University Press, 1963.

——— . *Dangerous Relations: The Soviet Union in World Politics, 1970-1982.* New York: Oxford University Press, 1984.

Urban, Michael. *The Ideology of Administration: American and Soviet Cases.* Albany: State University of New York Press, 1982.

Veblen, Thorstein. *The Engineers and the Price System.* New York: Viking Press, 1936.

Volgyes, Ivan. *Politics in Eastern Europe.* Chicago: Dorsey Press, 1986.

Walesa, Lech. *The Struggle and the Triumph: An Autobiography.* New York: Arcade, 1992.

Webb, Sidney, and Beatrice Webb. *Soviet Communism: A New Civilization,* vol. I. New York: Charles Scribner's Sons, 1936.

Weber, Max. *The Theory of Social and Economic Organization,* ed. Talcott Parsons. New York: The Free Press, 1964.

Weinstein, Michael. *Philosophy, Theory, and Method in Contemporary Political Thought.* Glenview, IL, and London: Scott, Foresman and Co., 1971.

Weisman, Richard. *Witchcraft, Magic, and Religion in the Seventeenth Century Massachusetts.* Amherst: University of Massachusetts Press, 1984.

Welsh, William, ed. *Survey Research and Public Attitudes in Eastern Europe and the Soviet Union.* New York: Pergamon Press, 1981.

Weydenthal, Jan B. *The Communists of Poland: An Historical Outline.* Stanford, CA: Hoover Institution Press, 1986.

Wheaton, Eliot Barculo. *The Nazi Revolution, 1933-1935: Prelude to Calamity.* Garden City, NY: Doubleday and Co., 1969.

Wiarda, Howard. *Introduction to Comparative Politics.* Belmont, CA: Wadsworth Publishing Co., 1993.

Wilkinson, Rupert. *The Broken Rebel: A Study in Culture, Politics, and Authoritarian Character.* New York: Harper and Row, 1972.

Willner, Ann Ruth. *The Spellbinders: Charismatic Political Leadership.* New Haven, CT: Yale University Press, 1984.

Wittfogel, Karl. *Oriental Despotism: A Comparative Study of Total Power.* New Haven, CN: Yale University Press, 1957.

Wolfe, Bertram D. *Communist Totalitarianism: Keys to the Soviet System.* Boston: Beacon Press, 1961.

——— . *An Ideology in Power: Reflection on the Russian Revolution.* New York: Stein and Day, 1969.

——— . *Three Who Made a Revolution, A Biographical History.* New York: Dell Publication Co., 1978.

Wolin, Simon, and Robert M. Slusser, eds. *Soviet Secret Police.* New York: Praeger Publishers, 1957.

Wolpe, Harold. *Race, Class, and the Apartheid State.* London: J. Currey, 1988.

Woolf, S. J., ed. *The Nature of Fascism.* New York: Random House, 1968; Vintage Books, 1969.

———— , ed. *European Fascism.* New York: Vintage books, 1969.

Zacek, Jane Shapiro, ed. *The Gorbachev Generation: Issues in Soviet Domestic Policy.* New York: Paragon House, 1989.

Zeigler, Harmon. *Pluralism, Corporatism, and Confucianism: Political Association in the United States, Europe, and Taiwan.* Philadelphia: Temple University Press, 1988.

———— and G. Wayne Peak. *Interest Groups in American Society.* Englewood Cliffs, NJ: Prentice-Hall, 1972.

Zinner, Paul E. *Communist Strategy and Tactics in Czechoslovakia, 1918-48.* New York: Praeger Publishers, 1963.

INDEX

35 /3 /536 .